The Origins of the
Second World War
Reconsidered

The Origins of the
Second World War
Reconsidered

The A. J. P. Taylor debate
after twenty-five years

Edited by
Gordon Martel
Royal Roads Military College,
Victoria, British Columbia

Boston
ALLEN & UNWIN
London   Sydney

Allen & Unwin, Inc.,
8 Winchester Place, Winchester, Mass. 01890, USA

Allen & Unwin (Publishers) Ltd,
40 Museum Street, London WC1A 1LU, UK

Allen & Unwin (Publishers) Ltd,
Park Lane, Hemel Hempstead, Herts HP2 4TE, UK

Allen & Unwin (Australia) Ltd,
8 Napier Street, North Sydney, NSW 2060, Australia

First published in 1986
Second impression 1986

Library of Congress Cataloging in Publication Data

The Origins of the Second World War
reconsidered
Bibliography: p.
Includes index.
1. Taylor, A. J. P. (Alan John Percivale), 1906–
Origins of the Second World War – Addresses,
essays, lectures. 2. World War, 1939–1945 – Causes
– Addresses, essays, lectures. I. Martel, Gordon.
D741.745   1986   940.53'11   85–20097
ISBN 0–04–940084–3 (alk. paper)
ISBN 0–04–940085–1 (pbk. : alk. paper)

British Library Cataloguing in Publication Data

The Origins of the Second World War
reconsidered:
the A. J. P. Taylor debate after twenty-five years.
1. World War, 1939–1945 – Causes
I. Martel, Gordon
940.53'11   D741
ISBN 0–04–940084–3
ISBN 0–04–940085–1 Pbk

Set in 10 on 11 point Baskerville by
Phoenix Photosetting, Chatham
and printed in Great Britain by
Billing & Sons Ltd,
London and Worcester

Contents

Introduction:

The Revisionist as Moralist –
A. J. P. Taylor and the Lessons
of European History

GORDON MARTEL

Historians a hundred years hence may be puzzled to discover that much of the rhetoric in which the political debates of the 1980s are conducted is firmly lodged in the events of the previous half-century. Images of the 1930s continue to flash past us: Hitler's moustache and Chamberlain's umbrella are still instantly recognizable; Nazi war criminals still make the front pages; novels and films warning of a new menace emanating from Brazil or Bavaria can be virtually assured of popular success. The Second World War, its symbols and personalities continue to grip the modern imagination. Thus the war – and its origins – functions today as a mental and moral shorthand; anyone wishing to evoke an image of wickedness personified need only mention "Hitler": for stupidity, blundering or cowardice substitute "Chamberlain". But political rhetoric extends the boundary beyond personality. The systems we condemn are "totalitarian" or "dictatorships" (frequently both), and we must never be guilty of "appeasement" in our relations with their leaders. Politicians find these words useful because ordinary citizens agree that the Second World War was caused by Hitler and his totalitarian dictatorship, and that it might have been prevented had it not been for the policy of appeasement that served only to whet his appetite.

Anyone who doubts that these simple assumptions are widely, almost universally, subscribed to is invited to witness the effect of setting loose a class of university undergraduates on A. J. P. Taylor's *The Origins of the Second World War*. There the effect is electrical; they are shocked to read that Hitler neither planned nor caused the war, that appeasement was not necessarily a bad thing, that new ideologies such as fascism and communism were much less significant than the traditional aims and ambitions of statesmen. If the student is converted to the Taylor view, war is almost certain to break out on the home front; the young may be prepared to embrace new ideas, even if only as a temporary fashion, but their parents are more likely to regard them as treasonable. Twenty-five years after its publication *Origins* has not lost its power to provoke.

When the book first appeared in 1961 it created a storm. Professional historians attacked Taylor for almost every imaginable sin; his evidence was scanty and unreliable, he distorted documents by means of selective citation and dismissed ones he disliked by claiming they did not count; his logic was faulty, he contradicted himself repeatedly and drew conclusions at variance with his own evidence. Nor was the storm confined to the citadels of academia – to scholarly journals, college corridors, senior common rooms and faculty clubs. The debate was carried on in public – in newspapers, on television and radio. Questions were asked in parliament. Lifelong friendships were dissolved. Careers were made and unmade. Taylor was soon the best-known historian in Britain and, it might be argued, still is. His recent autobiography was a best-seller, an entire issue of *The Journal of Modern History* was devoted to him, he has been honoured with two *festschriften*, and any book with his name on it has been assured of popular success. One eminent historian, when asked to contribute an essay to this book, declined on the ground that Taylor had no right to hold a first-mortgage on the subject of the origins of the Second World War. He may not have the right, but hold the mortgage he does. What other 25-year-old book on the war's origins continues not only to be available in paperback, but can be seen to be stacked high in university bookstores throughout the English-speaking world? Teachers wishing to shake students out of their lethargy do well to introduce them to A. J. P. Taylor.

Why did the book cause such a storm? Becaust Taylor challenged an interpretation of the war's origins that had previously satisfied almost everyone in the postwar world, and because he conducted his challenge in flamboyant prose and with a scathing wit. Before Taylor launched his attack, the only point being debated was whether the appeasers were stupid cowards who allowed themselves to be duped by Hitler, or cunning capitalists who hoped to use Hitler to crush communism in the Soviet Union. Blaming the war on Hitler certainly suited the Germans; with the Nazis either dead or in hiding, they could claim to be blameless and to take a respectable role in the new democratic alliance. This was equally satisfactory in the West, where one might have expected Orwellian uneasiness to emerge when the enemy was transformed into ally and the ally into enemy – but the West now claimed to be united against "totalitarianism" rather than against a state or nation. The Second World War had been fought for a great and noble principle, and this principle endured into the era of the Cold War. The enemy had merely changed location: his ambitions and tactics remained the same.

Taylor would have none of this. The war had not been fought over great principles, nor had Hitler planned its outbreak from the start. Taylor thereby challenged two of the most confident assumptions of the 1950s. Where others saw in Hitler a demonic genius who was able to pull the strings of European politics so masterfully because he had mapped out a plan in advance, Taylor saw only an ordinary politician who responded to events as they occurred, asking only how he might benefit from them. Where others saw a blueprint laid down in *Mein Kampf*, Taylor saw only a confused muddle of beer-hall chatter. Where others saw a timetable for war laid down in such documents as the "Hossbach Memorandum", Taylor saw the petty intrigue and political machinations typical of the Nazi system of government. If Taylor was right, if Hitler had not carefully plotted his route to world dominion well in advance and then followed the route "step-by-step", this could only raise new – and possibly awkward – questions. Some believed that Taylor was whitewashing Hitler, absolving him of guilt.

But Taylor did not stop with Hitler. He took a contrary view of almost every significant figure of the interwar period. Chamberlain was neither a bungler nor a coward, but a highly skilled politician who enjoyed the overwhelming support of his party and his nation. Stresemann, the "good German" but for whose death Germany might have followed a peaceful path, turns out to have shared Hitler's dreams of dominating eastern Europe. Roosevelt's economic policies were difficult to distinguish from Hitler's. Stalin, instead of the monstrous ideologue plotting world revolution, turns out to have been Europe's most conservative statesman, proposing to uphold the peace settlement of 1919 and wishing the League of Nations to be an effective international institution. If a reader was not offended by Taylor's revisionist sketch of Hitler, he was almost certain to find offense elsewhere.

If readers discovered heroes and villains being turned upside-down in *Origins*, they also found states being turned inside-out. Anyone who believed in a wicked Russia, a noble Poland, a beleaguered France, an efficient Italy or a nationalistic Czechoslovakia would have their assumptions rudely challenged. Russia never did more than ask to be accepted as a legitimate, sovereign state; Poland was not a state that one could be proud of having fought to save – as corrupt and elitist as it was; France had consistently aimed to draw in the new states of central and eastern Europe to fight on its behalf – while never intending to assist them in any way; Italy was not the powerful representative of a dynamic new political system, but the foolish plaything of a blustering and blundering egomaniac; Czechoslovakia, even though democratic, "had a canker at her heart", as the large German minority was alienated from the centralized state that was dominated by Czechs.[1]

Throughout *Origins* Taylor demonstrated an uncanny ability to see parallels and ironies that were certain to make readers squirm in their chairs, even if they did not believe them. The intervention of the League of Nations in the Abyssinian crisis resulted in Haile Selassie losing all of his country instead of half. Was Ramsay MacDonald not fittingly described as a "renegade socialist"? Was it better to be an abandoned Czech or a saved Pole? Did Munich not represent much that was best in British public life? There is hardly a page in the book that fails to unsettle complacent beliefs or challenge conventional wisdom – and this is always done crisply, with verve and frequently with biting sarcasm. Taylor's wit could cut deep. Sir Samuel Hoare, he said, was "as able intellectually as any British foreign secretary of the twentieth century – perhaps not a very high standard".[2] What was the response of the Slovaks to Hitler's destruction of their independence? They were to provide him with a steady, reliable satellite throughout the war.[3] When Britain and France declared war on Germany in September 1939, they went to war "for that part of the peace settlement which they had long regarded as least defensible".[4]

This embittered, ironic approach to the subject was certain to arouse an impassioned response because Taylor approached the subject in an old-fashioned way. Instead of treating statesmen and their policies as the excrescence of deeper, underlying, impersonal forces, he placed them at the center of the story. Readers always respond more enthusiastically to history that concentrates on people, and those who read *Origins* when it appeared still had vivid impressions of, and strong feelings toward, the people Taylor was writing about. Those who had fought Hitler's Germany, seen the newsreels of Chamberlain's triumphant return from Munich, argued over Franco's crusade in Spain were, when the book appeared, only in their forties and fifties. This proximity would have counted for less had Taylor been more concerned with impersonal forces – if he had, for instance, treated the diplomatic crises of the 1930s as reverberations of the economic collapse of 1929 – but this he steadfastly refused to do. "There was no reason why it should cause international tension. In most countries the Depression led to a turning-away from international affairs."[5] He put the actions of the interwar years back on the stage, and shone the spotlight on ambitions, schemes and characteristics that many preferred to forget. It was depressing to be reminded that Churchill had remained neutral or favored Franco during the civil war in Spain; that Chamberlain's desire to avoid intervention in Europe followed the traditions established by Cobden and Bright and revered by the Labour Party; that most British generals admired Mussolini; that the Labour Party's solution to the grievances aired by Hitler and Mussolini was economic appeasement.

Taylor struck a blow against the complacency of the 1950s. In his account the origins of the war ceased to be a simple morality play in which one or two weak-kneed men failed to face up to evil personified. His account really was old-fashioned. The interests of states and the ambitions of statesmen were treated as if there had been no break with the nineteenth century, as if ideology and technology were of trivial importance compared with the basic principles of modern statecraft that had first been enunciated by Machiavelli four centuries ago. The lines of continuity to be found in Germany's ambitious designs to dominate central and eastern Europe, in Russia's fears of invasion from the west, in Italy's dream of a neo-Roman Mediterranean and in the traditions of British foreign policy were, in Taylor's treatment, of vastly greater significance than swastikas and fasces, than Marx and Nietzsche. It is ironic that this traditionalism was, in the world of 1961, a form of rebellion.

Eschewing forces and philosophies, Taylor re-invigorated the drama of events. He told his story in the narrative form, strictly following the chain of events that led to September 1939. But the reader who followed this chain would not find himself, in the Churchillian phrase, being led "step-by-step" into the abyss. No – the events were not neat and simple but complicated, ragged, contradictory and ironic. Few things were what they seemed: the Reichstag fire should not be attributed to clever Nazi plotting but to a Dutch arsonist (and the Nazis genuinely believed it to be the communist intrigue they proclaimed it to be); the result of the Treaty of Locarno, "odd and unforeseen", was to prevent military co-operation between Britain and France; the *Anschluss* between Germany and Austria was not the result of a carefully planned invasion – 70 per cent of German vehicles broke down on their journey to the frontier, while 99 per cent of the people of united Germany and Austria voted in favour of the union, "a genuine reflection of German feeling"; when the war itself broke out it was not to be regarded as a conflict between totalitarian dictatorship and democracy but as "the war between the three Western Powers over the settlement of Versailles".[6]

The events leading to war were neither what they appeared to be, nor were they caused or controlled by those who had been led to believe as directing them. Instead of Hitler and Mussolini cleverly pulling all the strings that made events move, Taylor offered a picture of the weak, the second-rate and the forgotten as the ones who caused things to happen. It was Papen and Hindenburg who "thrust" power on Hitler by imploring him to become chancellor; he did not have to "seize" control.[7] It was Schuschnigg who caused the collapse of Austria when his police raided the headquarters of the Austrian Nazis; there was no "planned aggression only hasty improvisation" – Hitler was taken by surprise and it was Papen who "started the ball rolling".[8] It was Blum and Baldwin, not Hitler and Mussolini, who decided the outcome of the Spanish civil war: French radicals "objected to aiding an allegedly Communist cause abroad".[9] It was Benes who chose "to screw up the tension" in Czechoslovakia: negotiating with the Sudeten Germans in order to force them openly into demanding Czechoslovakia's dissolution and thereby compelling the Western powers to assert themselves against such an extreme and unfavourable solution.[10] Throughout *Origins* the reader is left with a distinct impression that no one was in control, that Hitler and Mussolini did no more than respond to the movements of others, to the agitations of Sudeten Germans, to the outbreak of civil war in Spain, to the Slovakian demands for autonomy. Meanwhile, "the statesmen of western Europe moved in a moral and intellectual fog".[11]

Finally, when men do act, seize the initiative, attempt to control events, the results they get are seldom what they bargain for. The Lytton commission, which condemned Japan for resorting to force in Manchuria and provoked it into withdrawing from the League of Nations, had actually been set up on the initiative of Japan. Franco rewarded the assistance of Germany and Italy by declaring his neutrality during the Munich crisis and remaining neutral throughout the Second World War. When Hitler, following Munich, denounced the "warmongers", Churchill, Eden and Duff Cooper, "in the belief that this would lead to an explosion against them", he produced the opposite effect. When Chamberlain signed the alliance with Poland in 1939 he had, "without design", made Danzig the decisive question and thereby took a stand "on peculiarly weak ground".[12] Even when men know what they want and believe they see their way clear to getting it, the consequences are rarely foreseen and often turn out to be the opposite of what was intended.

The reason why *The Origins of the Second World War* was so explosive is that Taylor's revisionism went far beyond the usual boundaries erected by the historical profession. Had he been content to create a more "balanced" view of Hitler by pointing out those occasions on which Hitler followed no timetable, contradicted himself or was pushed along by others, he might have caused a stir – but this would likely have been restricted to a few specialists arguing the merits of the case in scholarly journals. Instead, Taylor turned the interwar world upside down – and shook it hard. Leaders turned out to be followers; ideologues became realists; the weak were strong. Events followed no pattern. Accidents ruined plans. Readers who pick up *Origins* for the first time twenty-five years after it was written are still likely to find it exciting and entertaining: there is hardly a page that fails to provoke, that neglects to challenge someone's comfortable assumptions about something. The reverberations caused by Taylor's shaking are still being felt.

The most surprising feature of the controversy surrounding A. J. P. Taylor is that anyone familiar with his work could have been surprised by the approach he took when he turned to this new subject. All of the principal features of *Origins* – the crisp prose, the jokes, the biting sarcasm, the ironies, the narrative structure – were evident in his earlier works. So too were the basic lines of interpretation: statesmen everywhere schemed for advantage; accidents always destroyed plans; interests invariably took precedence over ideas; and, most significantly, the story of modern international history was mainly the story of Germany's attempt to dominate Europe and the efforts of others to prevent it from succeeding. The style, philosophy and interpretation were clearly evident in *The Italian Problem in European Diplomacy, 1847–1849* (1934), *Germany's First Bid for Colonies, 1884–1885* (1938), *The Habsburg Monarchy, 1809–1918* (1941), *The Course of German History* (1945), *Rumours of Wars* (1952), *The Struggle for Mastery in Europe, 1848–1918* (1954), *Bismarck, the Man and the Statesman* (1955), *The Troublemakers* (1957) and in numerous essays and reviews. As the titles of these works suggest, three subjects formed the core of Taylor's interests: central Europe, diplomacy and modern history. Of particular concern was the way in which states were made and unmade, and how nationalism and imperialism – the two driving forces of the modern era – were connected with the onset of total war in the modern world.

It would be astonishing if someone who reached maturity in the 1920s were not interested in war, nationalism and revolution. The consequences of 1914–18 were readily apparent: the physical destruction, the disabled veterans, the long lists of war dead inscribed on memorials; the Habsburg, the Ottoman and the Russian empires had disappeared to be replaced by new "national" states and the Soviet Union. The greatest historical controversy of the decade raged over the question of responsibility for the outbreak of war in 1914; and Taylor later explained how he was struck by the contrast between his stormy debate and the quiet complacency that surrounded the origins of the Second World War. Even historians whose training and work had been in other fields and earlier periods turned to recent diplomatic history following 1919. One of them, the Austrian A. F. Pribram, had turned from Cromwell and the Puritan revolution of the seventeenth century to recent Anglo-Austrian relations. Thus, in one of the many "accidents" that transformed his "personal history", Taylor – who had gone to Vienna to work on Cromwell with Pribram – was diverted from English domestic history to European diplomacy. His personal and professional life exemplified the connection between profound forces of the age and the effect of chance and circumstance.

Taylor also explained that he followed the fashion of the 1920s in assuming that Germany had been unfairly burdened with the guilt of having caused the First World War. But, as he set about investigating various aspects of modern European history, he discovered that he and the "revisionists" were wrong, that the peacemakers of Versailles were right: the responsibility for the war lay with Germany. By the time he came to write *Origins*, he regarded Germany as the dynamic element in European politics over the past century; it was Germany which was growing, expanding, looking forward to a future when it would be dominant in Europe and able to take up the position of a full-fledged world power.

One of the distinctive features of *Origins* is the connections that are constantly made between the interwar years and the nineteenth century; while most historians concentrated on Hitlerism and ideology – usually treating these as aberrations in statecraft – Taylor was keen to show the links between William II and Hitler, the parallels between Chamberlain and Gladstone, the continuity of Russian fears from the Romanovs to the Soviets. The great powers hoped the Spanish civil war would burn itself out, he insisted, "as Metternich had hoped would happen with the Greek revolt in the 1820s".[13] Schuschnigg suffered from the perpetual illusion, peculiar to the Austrians, that exposing nationalistic intrigue would stir the conscience of Europe into action – just as it had "seemed to them axiomatic in 1859 that Cavour would be deserted by Napoleon III".[14] Stresemann shared Bismarck's belief that peace was in Germany's interest, although he was "no more inclined to peace from moral principle than Bismarck had been".[15] These allusions to European politics of the nineteenth century warn the reader not to trust those who would treat the 1930s as if they had existed in a vacuum.

Taylor admires few statesmen. His favourite book, *The Troublemakers*, extolls the virtues of the dissenting tradition; his heroes are the critics and outsiders of English history – the Cobbetts and Cobdens, the Lloyd Georges and Beaverbrooks. And he shows how unreliable are the public utterances of men in power. While Lamartine, the foreign minister and romantic poet, was boldly announcing a revolutionary French foreign policy in his manifesto of 1848, he was also apologizing for it in private, pleading with the Duke of Wellington to "understand its real sense" – that it was a gesture in public relations.[16] When Taylor treated Hitler's speeches and *Mein Kampf* as meaningless or untrustworthy pieces of self-advertisement, readers recoiled from the shock. But Taylor treated all statesmen in this way. "Great men in public life love power," he explained, "they fight to get it and they use it ruthlessly when it is in their hands."[17] They make speeches, write books and strike poses in order to dupe an unsuspecting public; it is the job of the historian not to be duped, to look for the reality behind the façade.

The principal reality discovered by Taylor is that statesmen seek to maintain or extend the interests of their state. Those who take their own rhetoric and ideals too seriously are likely to land themselves in trouble. Palmerston's greatness resided in his ability to recognize that, although he trumpeted liberal–Whig ideas, the interest of peace sometimes meant co-operating with Austria in spite of the ideological incompatibility. Palmerston would do the right thing when opportunity and interest combined (as they did during the unification of Italy), but he would do nothing for Poland or Hungary as "the one was beyond his reach, the liberation of the other he supposed would have been against British interests".[18] Crispi, the prime minister who wished to turn his country into a great colonial power, "lived in a world of illusions and was leading Italy to disaster".[19] In all of Taylor's work a motif is created within which it is the dreamers, the speculators and the ambitious who allow their grand designs to overpower their appreciation of what is possible. Napoleon III, who attempted to destroy the balance of power, "substitute his own hegemony" and replace the Holy Alliance with the "revolutionary association" of his dreams, led the Second Empire to destruction.[20]

Dreamers who act out their dreams are not the only dangerous men in Taylor's world; there are also those reactionaries whose nightmare visions of the future lead them to oppose all change – and often end with them flinging themselves headlong into disaster in an act of national suicide. Such was Metternich, who "dreaded action, sought always to postpone decisions and cared only for repose"; when he fell from power he "brought down old Austria with him".[21] Conservatives are especially likely to fall prey to the temptation of believing that one dramatic act – against liberals, radicals, nationalists or revolutionaries – will destroy the enemy, restore the balance and remove uncertainty. When Austria–Hungary went to war in 1914, war was an end in itself: "the countless problems which had dragged on so long could all be crossed off the agenda". Instead Austria–Hungary disappeared from the map.[22] This is a complicated world that Taylor describes, one in which it is as dangerous to try to stop the movement of the world as it is to speed it up; and, whether one chooses to act or stand still, the consequences can rarely be foreseen with any accuracy. In this the world of Europe between the wars was little different than Europe of the nineteenth century. Men continued to dance "the perpetual quadrille of the Balance of Power" as much as some of them might wish the music to stop, "and that they could sit out a dance without maintaining the ceaseless watch on one another".[23]

Although the faces were different after 1919, the problem confronting European diplomacy remained the same: how to deal with the fact that Germany, still the greatest of the European powers, was more convinced than ever that the international system had been designed just to thwart her. In fact, ringing it with small states, and forcing the Soviet Union out of the European equation meant that when it recovered its cohesion and efficiency it would be stronger than ever. Taylor had certainly become convinced, long before writing *The Origins of the Second World War*, that Germany had decided to exploit its potential for establishing hegemony in Europe. This was signified most dramatically when William II dismissed Bismarck and replaced him with advisers who favoured "world policy", who imagined that Germany was capable of realizing this ambition "before she had secured the mastery of Europe".[24] The differences between Bismarck, Bethmann-Hollweg and Hitler were matters of temperament and tactics; when the heirs of Bismarck rose up in 1944 it was "Hitler's *failure*, not his *policy*" that drove them to resist.[25] In the 1930s the Germans sought to reduce Hungary to its true national size while incorporating the rest of the Habsburg monarchy into the German Reich; but before 1914 they had been restrained from this only by "dynastic scruples" and "twinges of Bismarck's caution".[26] The First World War sprang from Germany's world policy, from its decisions to challenge both Russia and Great Britain as world powers.[27] By the 1950s Taylor was repeatedly referring to the war of 1939–45 as "the second German war".

It must have seemed bizarre to Taylor when *Origins* was criticized by some as an apologia for Hitler, because the essence of his interpretation was the continuous line of development in modern European history whereby Germany sought to establish its domination of Europe by controlling the center and the east. Although he dismissed the notion that Hitler was a careful and meticulous planner, he clearly and unequivocally explained that Hitler "intended Germany to become the dominant power in

Europe". But he also insisted that in this Hitler was "like every other German statesman".[28] These were the two arguments that distinguished Taylor most clearly from other historians: Hitler ceased to be the mad genius who pulled all the strings and had the whole play worked out in advance; and he became just another German, struggling for mastery in Europe. Even Hitler's anti-Semitism had been "the Socialism of fools" for years: "everything which Hitler did against the Jews followed logically from the racial doctrines in which most Germans vaguely believed".[29] If Taylor was right, Hitler could not be expunged from the historical map as if he were unique; he must be seen as a part of German and even European history.

This simple revisionist perspective enabled Taylor to go far beyond a condemnation of Hitler and Nazism. If Hitler had had a simple "blueprint for aggression" it ought to have been the task of Western statesmen – and a fairly simple one at that – to divine the plan and to wreck it; the "Hitler blueprint" interpretation made Chamberlain and the other "appeasers" culpable, and let everyone else off the hook. But if Hitler had no plan, just vague wishes and daydreams, it meant that the range of responsibility extended far beyond a few individuals; it would include, in various ways and at different stages, those who believed in collective security, in self-determination, in disarmament, in anti-communism. And responsibility was different than guilt; those who believed in alternatives to war and the balance of power were not necessarily weak or evil – most of them genuinely believed that new ways for reconciling differences and righting wrongs had to be found if the world was to avoid a repeat performance of the catastrophe of 1914–18. Taylor attempted to show, against the background of the German drive to domination, how the whole complex of ideas and interests in interwar Europe helped to propel the Great Powers along the path to war. And it is this complexity – the contingencies, the accidents, the ironies and the paradoxes – that enriches *The Origins of the Second World War* and elevate it to the reputation it now enjoys as an historical classic. A work that merely turned Hitler on his head, while it might have enjoyed a brief sensation, would never have inspired the continuing controversy achieved by *Origins*.

Almost overlooked in the furor that its appearance provoked was Taylor's wider condemnation of the very nature of international politics; but his embittered, disillusioned treatment of politics and statesmanship must surely be one of the clues to his continuing popularity, as disillusionment with the simplicity of

Cold War rhetoric grew throughout the 1960s and 1970s. When reduced to its simplest elements, *Origins* stands as a monumental attack on the way in which the international system works; and here Taylor discovered, in Hitler, an ingenious medium through which to convey this attack. All those Taylorian references to affairs before 1919 are intended to demonstrate that affairs changed little with the advent of fascism: "Hitler and Mussolini glorified war and the warlike virtues. They used the threat of war to promote their aims. But this was not new. Statesmen had always done it."[30] The balance of power was an endless quadrille; states always sought to extend their power and statesmen everywhere grabbed every opportunity to aggrandize themselves. The only difference between the fascist dictators and other statesmen was "that their appetite was greater; and they fed it by more unscrupulous".[31]

Hitler, as Taylor sketches him, was about as evil a man as may be imagined. Even though he acted as a sounding-board for the German nation, he bore the responsibility for the destruction of German democracy, for the concentration camps and for the extermination of peoples during the Second World War. "He gave orders, which Germans executed, of a wickedness without parallel in civilized history."[32] But in foreign policy Hitler was not unusual; he aimed to make Germany dominant in Europe and, perhaps, in the world. "Other Powers have pursued similar aims and still do. Other Powers treat smaller countries as their satellites. Other Powers seek to defend their vital interests by force of arms."[33] What does it say about the way in which international affairs are conducted that this personification of wickedness, when regarded from the perspective of traditional European diplomacy, was simply an ordinary statesman going about his business in a time-honored fashion? "In international affairs there was nothing wrong with Hitler except that he was a German."

So, in the final analysis, Taylor too has chosen to make a morality play of the interwar years. But unlike his predecessors, the play he has written bears the signs of genius: few things are as they appear to the naked eye; honorable intentions lead to tragic conclusions: his work will surely endure if only because he rescued this vital part of the human story from the vapid simplicities of good versus evil and returned it to its proper place of complexity and paradox. "Human blunders . . . usually do more to shape history than human wickedness."[34]

In the past twenty-five years, much has been made of Taylor's "philosophy of history" – much too much. Taylor himself has consistently denied having a philosophy or even a systematic approach. These denials have the ring of truth. In all his work he has tried to tell stories, to explain how one thing leads to another, to answer the child's question, "what happened next?" But good stories have something to tell us, just as good jokes tell the truth. Such philosophy as may be found in *Origins* is the warning to distrust historical truths and parallels. Men do learn from their mistakes, he says – they learn to make new ones. The attempt to extract simple policies from the lessons of the 1930s is one of the enemies of clear thinking in our time: Munich and the argument over appeasement "still supplies superficial parallels and superficial terms of abuse for the present day".[35] A conciliatory policy towards Russia "would not be rejected so firmly now were it not for the recollection of the appeasement towards Germany that failed a decade ago".[36] This warning against the historical clichés offered up by historians and statesmen is as valuable a message today as it was when first uttered.

These new essays on the origins of the Second World War are designed neither to honor A. J. P. Taylor nor to replace him. They undoubtedly testify to his continuing influence; if anyone is to hold a first-mortgage on the subject, it is fortunate that it should be held by someone who is able to write vigorous prose and to stimulate debate – even among those not yet born when the book was written. But Taylor has claimed that in writing *Origins* he wished to examine events in detail, and the details of what happened behind the scenes are available to us today in a way that was almost unimaginable when it was written. Not surprisingly, the specialists writing here, having had the opportunity to examine these events in great detail, have found much in the book that requires revision or reconsideration. They have found that some of the charges levelled at Taylor twenty-five years ago, especially those of contradiction and overstatement, were justified. They have also found that he made mistakes and overlooked material available to him, that he sometimes guessed wrong or allowed prejudice to blind him.

Nevertheless, one is left with the distinct impression that Taylor will continue to be read and re-read with interest and profit for decades to come. These essays have been collected with that premise in mind: to contribute to the ongoing debate by clarifying vital aspects of Taylor's interpretation, by synthesizing the work that has been done over the past quarter century,

and by offering fresh evaluations of major themes connected
with the origins of the Second World War. This book is intended
not to signal the end of the debate, but to show where it stands
today, and where new discoveries are being made.

NOTES

1   A. J. P. Taylor, *The Origins of the Second World War* (Harmondsworth,
     1964), p. 190. All references in this essay are to the Penguin
     paperback edition, which includes the 1963 Foreword, "Second
     Thoughts".
2   ibid., p. 122.
3   ibid., p. 240.
4   ibid., p. 335.
5   ibid., p. 89.
6   ibid., p. 336.
7   ibid., p. 101.
8   ibid., p. 181.
9   ibid., pp. 157–8.
10   ibid., pp. 192–3.
11   ibid., p. 141.
12   ibid., pp. 264–5.
13   ibid., p. 158.
14   ibid., p. 178.
15   ibid., p. 79.
16   A. J. P. Taylor, *The Struggle for Mastery in Europe* (Oxford, 1954), p. 5.
17   A. J. P. Taylor, *Rumours of Wars* (London, 1952), p. 25.
18   A. J. P. Taylor, *The Italian Problem in European Diplomacy 1847–1849*
     (Manchester, 1934), pp. 236–42.
19   Taylor, *Struggle for Mastery*, p. 324.
20   ibid., p. 61.
21   A. J. P. Taylor, *The Habsburg Monarchy 1809–1918* (London, 2nd edn,
     1948), pp. 34, 56.
22   ibid., p. 232.
23   Taylor, *Struggle for Mastery*, p. xix.
24   ibid., p. 294.
25   A. J. P. Taylor, *Bismarck* (London, 1955), p. 272.
26   Taylor, *Habsburg Monarchy*, p. 230.
27   Taylor, *Bismarck*, p. 268.
28   Taylor, *Origins*, p. 171.
29   ibid., p. 100.
30   ibid., p. 136.
31   ibid., p. 140.
32   ibid., p. 27.
33   ibid., p. 27.

34   ibid., pp. 265–6.
35   Taylor, *Rumours of Wars*, p. 76.
36   ibid., p. 80.

1

1918 and After: The Postwar Era

SALLY MARKS

The controversy over A. J. P. Taylor's *The Origins of the Second World War* has, not surprisingly, centered on the immediate prewar years and the outbreak of war. Taylor's dissent from the prevailing assumption that Adolf Hitler was the primary cause and his views on appeasement angered many, leading to an intense debate focused on certain issues. Were Taylor's critics blinded by a settled conviction that Hitler caused the Second World War? As to other leaders of the 1930s, did Taylor equate ineptitude or error with evil? Above all, did Hitler "plan" the Second World War? On another level, Taylor had been charged with abuse and misuse of documentary evidence, dismissal of evidence, contradiction, overstatement, a narrow focus on diplomatic factors and ignoring fundamental causes.[1]

In the uproar, another question bearing directly on the issue of fundamental causes was ignored: how sound are his early chapters addressing the pre-Hitlerian period? Taylor would argue, and few historians would now disagree, that the origins of the Second World War did not suddenly emerge in 1935 or 1936. After all, Hitler gained power in the Weimar Republic because many of its citizens though he was the answer to their discontents. Strikingly, his first major political success came in 1930 during an era of recession but in an electoral campaign dominated by foreign policy issues, though many German grievances about the Versailles treaty had been partially or fully resolved. Thus one must ask why his foreign policy had such popular appeal. Taylor dismisses this problem by maintaining that Hitler's policy was that of his predecessors,[2] but he also argues that the entire interwar period forms a unit and that what happened at the end of the first war was a vital factor in causing the second. Certainly, what happened in 1918–19 affected what came after, especially in forming the attitudes of most Germans. In these circumstances, Taylor's early chapters, devoted to the failure to solve what he calls the German problem, warrant close examination.

Characteristically, Taylor starts with the balance of power. The unification of Germany had created a great nation in the center of the European continent but one soon balanced by a Russo-French alliance. Even so, Germany nearly won the First World War. In early 1918, it was triumphant in the east and undefeated in the west where an impasse existed on French soil. Yet by November, Germany had lost the war on the Western Front. None the less, the armistice and the peace treaty permitted the defeated nation to continue as a major entity only somewhat diminished in power in a Europe providing fewer neighboring checks upon it. This implied, after a period of recovery and of breaking treaty restrictions, a potential for renewed German continental dominance. Some, including many Britons, soon found this acceptable if domination were economic, not military. For these, German recovery was desirable, if peaceful, and the concern was German grievances, not fear of German aggression.[3]

The Versailles treaty produced the German grievances and confirmed the continuation of Germany as a great power. Taylor argues that, apart from some territorial clauses, the treaty focused on providing security against Germany. He says that it "lacked moral validity from the start",[4] meaning that Germans did not accept it as fair, that many others, especially in the English-speaking world, came to agree with them, and that Germans were united in hatred of the *Diktat* of Versailles, in determination to break it and to revert to continental domination. Without German co-operation, enforcement became ever more difficult and the German problem continued unabated.[5]

Taylor notes that Germans might have come to accept the treaty had not one portion of it remained unsettled. Owing to disagreement among the victors and British prime minister David Lloyd George's hope for cooler heads with the passage of time, the peace treaty deferred decision about reparations, the amount Germany was to pay for economic damages to the victors. Taylor states that the question remained open throughout the 1920s, exacerbating all sore points, generating heated emotions, and becoming a chronic grievance. In his view, Germans blamed all woes on reparations, whether related or not, and soon transferred their grievances on this score to the treaty as a whole. The British, despite initial avidity, had second thoughts, turned against the reparations clauses, and then projected these feelings onto the treaty in general excepting the clauses directly to British benefit.[6]

British attitudes were a key factor in the other problem Taylor cites, the lack of Allied unity. The close-run victory on the Western Front in 1918 derived from a major Russian contribution in 1914 and then a coalition of France, Britain, Italy and America. After the war, communist Russia was self-absorbed and widely distrusted. American withdrawal was less than complete but soon substantial. Italy was not really interested in the German problem. That left Britain and France, who disagreed regularly about Germany. France was consumed by fear of future German aggression despite alliances with Poland and Czechoslovakia in place of the old Russian tie. According to Taylor, Britain thought French fears foolish, was confident there would not be another war, and wished to revive Germany in a peaceful Europe. In one short-lived pretense at compromise after another, the two powers tended to cancel each other out. Then Britain hit upon giving a meaningless paper guarantee to France, confident it would never have to be honored, provided France gave up all else: great power status, treaty enforcement, and at least in part its eastern Allies. Though France initially balked at the price and struggled to enforce the Versailles treaty, Taylor argues that the French learned the futility of this. Thus the paper guarantee emerged as the Locarno treaty of 1925. Taylor claims it ended the First World War and brought peace to Europe whereas its repudiation in 1936 "marked the prelude to the second war".[7]

In examining Taylor's analysis of the period after the first war, which he argues largely caused the second, one discovers that most of the questions which have been so prominent in the debate about the book are irrelevant, for they focus on the Nazi era. The frequent charge of misuse of documentary evidence is also extraneous, for Taylor cites no documentary evidence before 1932. Of the usual charges, there remain dismissal of evidence, contradiction and overstatement, a narrow focus on diplomatic factors, and ignoring of fundamental causes. In addition, one should ask whether he spotted the key pieces in the puzzle and put them together properly. In regard to this last

most difficult problem, Taylor was perceptive about many of the
pieces but not always about the links between them.

To be fair to him, one must always bear in mind what evidence
was available when he wrote. In 1960–1, the material concerning
the Nazi years far exceeded that available on the earlier period.
Taylor said he "attempted to tell the story as it may appear to
some future historian, working from the records".[8] For the postwar era, most archives are now open, the future historians have
arrived, and the records have produced some surprises. Though
Taylor cannot fairly be charged with failure to read closed files,
he did not explore much of what was at hand. His bibliography for
the pre-Nazi years is skimpy. One could list many documentary
materials then available but not consulted, starting with Parliamentary Command Papers, *Documents diplomatiques*, and *Papers
relating to the Foreign Relations of the United States*. Taylor's list of
memoirs and monographs is also scant. Another problem in
assessing his use of the evidence available is that he fails to refer
to the works cited in his bibliography. Therefore, while his
interpretation of the postwar era often conflicts with some of the
opinions that prevailed in 1961, it is difficult to determine
whether his views were brilliant, perverse, derived from
research, or based on the work of other historians.

The charges of contradiction and overstatement are often
valid for the first chapters. The early exegesis glitters but is
marred by instability of viewpoint, contradiction, carelessness, a
fatal cleverness, and illogic. Examples abound. Taylor says both
that the Rapallo treaty afforded "little chance of active co-
operation between the two signatories"[9] and that, once it lapsed,
Germans regretted its "vanished intimacy".[10] He misdates the
treaty of Brest-Litovsk as January 1918[11] and then claims
"Russia disappeared from view – her revolutionary government,
her very existence ignored by the victorious Powers".[12] Though
Russia was rarely a major factor in the postwar equation, Taylor
has characteristically overstated his case.

He rightly says the interwar era centered on the German
problem but illogically adds, "if this were settled, everything
would be settled"[13] and argues that if Germany were treated as
an equal, there would be no basis for reparations,[14] though
inequality was never a justification for German payments. The
rationale was reconstruction of the civil damage done by German invasion, destruction, and seizures in France and elsewhere. Here Taylor is confusing matters and resting on the
German view which indeed sought equality. In German eyes,

this meant removal of their defeat and all its consequences and reversion not to early 1918 but to early 1914.

Taylor's analysis of the postwar balance of power is often penetrating, but he fails to differentiate between what it was and how it was viewed in the 1920s. In justice, it must be said that archival evidence now available clarifies the picture considerably. He does well in distinguishing between the short-term power balance and what it was likely to be in the longer range, particularly if the treaty was not enforced. He sees clearly that in this event Germany would revert to continental predominance, but, again, does not explore the distinction between reality and perception of it, notably in Britain. Though Taylor dwells on postwar diplomacy in a reasonably broad sense, his focus is more military than diplomatic in the early chapters. Despite attention to reparations, he scants economic factors and the emotional issues which can be important in democratic states. Public opinion played a greater role in the 1920s than he admits in setting the outer limits of policy.

Finally, there is the matter of fundamental causes. This issue warrants analysis of Taylor's opening chapters for it is here that he addresses underlying causes, as far as he does so at all. Naturally, most reviewers focused on later portions of the book, some praising the first section in passing.[15] Here Taylor informs us variously that the Second World War was caused by the First World War, the armistice, or the Versailles treaty.[16] Not only is this overstatement, contradiction and simplification, but it comes close to preaching historical inevitability. Taylor begins his account in 1918–19 because he believes that it was the Allies' failure to solve the German problem in the armistice and at the peace conference that laid the foundations for the Second World War. He is right to say that the German problem was not solved,[17] but to attribute the history of the next twenty years so exclusively to the events of those nine months is too categoric and omits many other factors which require exploration. Not least among them are his assumptions about the nature of the German problem.

Taylor never defines the German problem but seems to assume that if Germany remained united, it would automatically be both dominant and disruptive. Indeed, in the preface to the second edition of *Origins*, he asks why Britain and France did not resist German reversion to great power status.[18] His question ignores Allied assumptions, which he indicates elsewhere, about what had been accomplished by the military verdict of

1918 and overlooks the fact that the question was not whether Germany would be a great power but on what terms. It disregards as well the nature of German nationalism, the self-delusions of the citizenry and the reasons for both. Taylor is right that Weimar Germany was both resentful and revisionist, although his exploration of the reasons why is inadequate. He asserts that both Hitler and his predecessors wished to revert to the situation of March 1918, which hardly explains why Hitler's foreign policy was initially so much more popular than that of his predecessors. He assumes that, given a united Germany, there automatically would be a successful drive toward an equality tantamount to continental predominance, that it would take military forms, that little or anything could have been done to deter it, and that Germany was bound to revert to its natural place as "the greatest power in Europe from her natural weight".[19] His conclusion that a war between Germany and Britain and France over the Versailles settlement "had been implicit since the moment when the first war ended"[20] ignores not only how little of the 1919 settlement remained in September 1939 but also both the underlying reasons for German resentment, revisionism, and later larger aims and what the victors in the first war could have done in 1918–19 and in the 1920s to deflect what he considers the inevitable course of history. Here as elsewhere, Taylor often perceives many pieces of the puzzle but does not address their connections and implications.

In his approach to fundamental causes, Taylor deals in absolutes from the outset. In tackling the root of the problem, he posits an either-or situation. In November 1918, he argues, the Allies had a choice between breaking up Germany or accepting its continental predominance and reverting to the situation early in 1918 when Germany was triumphant in the east and undefeated in the west. Because they did neither, the German problem continued.[21] In fact, both options were unrealistic. This was clear at the time, and neither was seriously considered. Accepting German predominance after a long, bitter war was politically out of the question, amounting to acknowledging defeat on the day of victory. Breaking up Germany was no solution, given the relative modesty of Allied territorial aims in Europe, Wilson's opposition to dismemberment, and Anglo-American eagerness to retire militarily except for token contingents. Enforcement of disunification would have required a long-term, large-scale British and American military commitment politically impossible to both. Taylor says that in the armistice, the Allies committed themselves "almost without realizing it" to continued German unity.[22] Elsewhere and more accurately, he notes that the Allies had no desire to dismember Germany but rather to prove to it that aggression "could not succeed", and this they thought they had done.[23]

Thus Taylor's alternative solutions to the German problem, supremacy or destruction, were not viable in 1918. Were there other possibilities which neither the Allies then nor Taylor later considered? As he mentions in passing, in 1918 and 1919 there was a gap between reality and German popular perception of it. He says Germany was thoroughly defeated and its leaders knew it when the fighting ended;[24] a few pages on, he reports without comment that "no German accepted the treaty as a fair settlement between equals 'without victors or vanquished'".[25] Here Taylor brushes a key factor, the popular German perception that the First World War was a draw and that Wilson's "just peace" should mean the *status quo ante bellum* with rather more rectifications in Germany's favor than otherwise.[26] However, Taylor fails to explain how this situation arose, who was responsible for it, and what could have prevented it.

Some of the answers are obvious. The war was fought on the soil of the victors; they lay in ruins, not Germany. Clearly, German self-delusion was an important factor, but the victors let that happen. Perhaps this was their greatest single mistake. In November 1918 the victors had a choice between ending the war or fighting on. In retrospect, they probably should have fought on into Germany, but they did not know how quickly the end would have come. Further, as Taylor notes, beyond thinking their goal of German defeat was accomplished, Britain and France were exhausted and feared American domination if the war continued.[27] None the less, the document ending hostilities should have been called a surrender instead of an armistice, a misleading term which fostered German illusions about the war's outcome. Taylor ignores this possibility and also another, not considered either by the victors – that the surrender terms could have provided for a modest Allied occupation of Berlin and other key cities for a year. There was nothing to risk except German refusal, after which the Allies could decide to give way or fight on. Hindsight suggests that Germany would probably have accepted as the alternative was military collapse.

Playing the "if" game is usually futile, but German perceptions were so important that we may linger briefly. A durable peace must rest on what a defeated major power will accept, but what it will accept is affected by its perception of its circumstances. In 1814, Russia's army and tsar were in Paris. In 1871, the German empire was proclaimed at Versailles. In 1918, the Allies occupied only the Rhineland. Had they paraded troops in Berlin and Munich, reality would have intruded on the German people. Chancellor Friedrich Ebert would not have hailed German troops at the Brandenburg Tor in December 1918 with "As you return unconquered from the field of battle, I salute you"[28] if he had known Allied armies would march there the next week. Taylor repeatedly asserts that no German could accept the Versailles treaty, but he attributes this simply to the continued existence of a united Germany. Had symbols of defeat been visible in German cities, probably the average German's perception of his nation's circumstances would have been different and hence also perhaps his view of the treaty.

Ebert's statement both contributed to German self-delusion about the war's outcome and endorsed the *Dolchstoss* myth already circulating in the German army. To escape the onus of defeat, the army claimed it had not lost in battle but had been stabbed in the back by those perennial scapegoats at home, the pacifists, Jews, and socialists. As a Social Democrat, Ebert resented this myth but he needed army support and so he did nothing to counter it. Nor did the Allies. From belief that the army had not been defeated to belief that Germany had not lost was a short step. In the months between the armistice and arrival of the peace treaty, the German people, by and large, took that step unhindered except in the Rhineland by the Allies who were preoccupied in Paris with devising the treaty. The victors proceeded on the premise of German defeat but, meanwhile, Germany rejected the defeat. In these circumstances, any treaty the victors were likely to produce was bound to be viewed as unjust by most Germans. Clearly the first mistake of the Allies in late 1918 and early 1919 was their failure to bring defeat home to the German people. Thus the treaty terms, largely predictable in advance, came as a shock and generated bitterness.

Taylor argues that the peace treaty itself helped to perpetuate the German problem. In this, he is perhaps right for the wrong reasons. The victors assumed the continuation of a united Germany, but they also assumed it would accept its defeat and hence also accept a treaty based approximately on the Fourteen Points providing for a somewhat reduced but still united Germany in a redesigned Europe. Not only did they fail to make defeat visible, but they themselves overlooked the fact that the continental power balance was being arranged in a risky way, for the end result was a strong Germany largely surrounded by weak neighbors. The debates in Paris over Germany's future were long and earnest, if sometimes haphazard, but increasingly the French, together with other neighbors of Germany who also feared for the future, wanted German power reduced more than Britain and America did. As Taylor notes, the English-speaking nations thought the war had produced a final verdict, and they wished to go home.[29] The clash of views led to an array of compromises resulting in a treaty severe enough to generate intense German resentment, but not sufficiently draconian to constrain Germany for long, particularly without effective enforcement. This situation created an underlying instability that soon surfaced. Thus both the German problem and German self-delusion about the outcome of the war continued.

The overriding difficulty with the Versailles treaty, however, was not so much its terms but rather German hostility to it because it represented the defeat which Germans did not wish to face. Many historians, including Taylor, dwell on German hatred of the Polish Corridor[30] and some argue the boundary should have been drawn to include fewer Germans. Since most Germans rejected any transfer of territory to Poland as unjust, the exact line hardly mattered. The same could be said of other clauses. Owing to the structure of the peace conference and the original intention of negotiating with the foe, the treaty was more severe than intended, but how much difference this made is uncertain, given German reluctance to face decisions implicit in the Fourteen Points, which the imperial government had accepted as the basis for ending hostilities. Since opinion in Germany was so hostile to the treaty terms, its new leaders responded by telling the voters what they wished to hear, as most politicians do, thereby reinforcing the misperception of the war's outcome and the determination to undo the treaty.[31]

To the extent that Germans acknowledged defeat at all, they argued they were not defeated by continental powers nor by European powers alone. In this they were correct. The Versailles treaty was predicated on continuing active British and American participation in its enforcement, which did not occur. Both withdrew in varying but substantial degrees, leaving a battered France to impose enforcement upon Germany, a task beyond its capacity, particularly against Anglo-American resistance. Taylor notes the withdrawal but underestimates the resistance and its significance. The key point, however, is that the Anglo-American withdrawal meant that the Versailles treaty soon ceased to represent the true continental balance of power. This fact only heightened French fears and German demands for treaty revision.

There is another factor in the equation which Taylor does not address directly. As he notes, the kaiser was gone, Germany had a democratic republic, and the Allies expected it to settle down and live in peace with its democratic neighbors.[32] Perhaps the Allies were naive in assuming that democracies are peaceful but they, like Taylor, overlooked the tragedy of the birth of German democracy. Alas, the Weimar Republic was born of defeat; further, the Social Democrats, more democratic than most other parties, were saddled with the military verdict and the armistice, neither their doing, as well as the treaty and what followed. No wonder democracy was unpopular and deemed "unGerman" by so many Germans. The politics of the situation required Weimar coalitions to resist treaty enforcement constantly to prove their patriotism until this policy became axiomatic because it usually succeeded. The fragility of the republic and its concentration on foreign policy were major factors in both Germany's refusal to accept the treaty and its rapid fraying.

Taylor wonders why the Allies thought it possible to impose upon Germany a treaty that it would accept.[33] The Allies thought Germany knew it was defeated, and they assumed that, as other defeated great powers had honored peace treaties in the past, Germany would do so as well. As Taylor notes, they believed, at least at first, in the sanctity of contracts.[34] The Allies did not recognize the lack of political roots of the infant republic; they failed to see that German nationalism was adolescent and thus both assertive and a constant threat to governments in an unpopular democratic republic.

Taylor also suggests that the treaty was unenforceable because the Germans themselves were given the responsibility for carrying out its provisions.[35] Again, other powers had done so; the French never ceased to make analogies to 1871. The Allies, assuming acceptance of defeat and hence of the treaty by a sturdier republic than existed, expected German co-operation. For this reason and because Britain and America opposed lengthy continental involvement, the treaty lacked sufficient enforcement clauses, especially automatic ones not requiring prolonged Allied negotiation. Taylor has a point when he says the Allied assumption that Germany would carry out the settlement gave German governments a weapon against the treaty,[36] but he oversimplifies. Any treaty requires co-operation to be effective, but more important in the aftermath of the First World War was the rapid evaporation of the will to enforce it in Britain, the United States, and for the most part in Italy.

Of course Allied unity collapsed soon after the last shot was fired. It generally does. Also, the unforeseen American withdrawal from treaty implementation, erratic but rapid, threw both the peace structure and the power balance awry, exacerbating the situation in several senses, not least the German perception of injustice. But there is more to the matter than this. The reversal of British policy began in March 1919.[37] To assess the continuing German problem, one must investigate both the reasons for and the effects of British policy after the First World War, for it was British (and American) support to German resistance which made it effective. This Taylor does not do. Again, the documents clarify the picture but the basic outlines can be found in books he lists. And one must note that, while the extent and speed of Anglo-American reversal were not evident in 1918 and 1919 when the key treaty decisions were made, the French were slow thereafter to face the situation because they were no more eager to accept solitude than Germany was to accept defeat.

Taylor came close to the motive force behind British policy when he cited a remark by Ramsay MacDonald in 1932 about Britain needing to say that it supported both sides,[38] but he does not see the implications, nor that it predated 1924, the year to which he applies it. In fact, Britain began in 1919 to edge back towards its traditional role as the fulcrum in the power balance. It never abandoned France entirely, encouraging false hopes here,[39] and it never supported Germany completely, causing bitterness there.[40] But in general, it supported concessions to Germany at the expense of France. This policy, largely instinctive, was pursued by all British leaders in the postwar era, though Austen Chamberlain was less committed than most. It derived from isolationism and imperial crises, reaction against the cost in blood and money of the First World War, tradition and economic concerns, reluctance to do the job of treaty enforcement, and from fear of France. Here Taylor's crystal ball clouded. There is now ample evidence that the British fixed on the immediate situation and misjudged the long-term power balance. The momentary superiority of the French army and air force, along with France's submarine building program, alarmed Britain's leaders who seriously thought the next war might be against France.[41]

Thus Britain swung to the temporarily weaker power, inadvertently facilitating Germany's return to the continental predominance which Taylor identifies. This gradual move had profound implications for the Western Entente and its enforcement of the peace treaties. Taylor says that Britain and France blocked each other's policies[42] but fails to add that Britain did a better job of it, having more allies. He notes that Allied threats were progressively less effective,[43] but not that Britain increasingly refused to threaten, which is the chief reason why threats by continental victors lost force. Taylor adds that America constituted world opinion; here he is wrong. America could be useful and each state wanted its support, but Britain was the key power for the continental players, above all Germany,[44] who never defied the Entente when it was united, only when Britain stood aloof or gave Germany some support. As Britain steadily moved from its allies toward the middle ground, treaty enforcement quickly dissolved.

Taylor sees that America was more involved in postwar Europe than was generally recognized, but should add that the involvement was sporadic, financial, and often indirect and unofficial. In general, America supported Britain out of distaste for European embroilment, reluctance to bother, susceptibility to Anglo-German propaganda, and a hope that the continent would "settle down". It was much easier not to enforce the treaty; like the British, the Americans failed to see that a united front rendered enforcement unnecessary.[45]

Despite his strident denunciation of Italian fascism as illegal, "corrupting" and dishonest, and of Mussolini as "fraudulent" and "a vain blundering boaster without either ideas or aims",[46] Taylor's treatment of Italy's revisionism, its lack of genuine power status, and its general absence from involvement in the German problem is sound. Italy preferred words to action and enjoyed German nationalism provided it was at French expense. On the whole, both before and after 1922, Italy skittered around among the great powers, trying to sell itself to all sides at once. This effectively left France alone with Germany's other immediate neighbors, all weak, to face the German problem.

As Taylor sees, French policy stemmed from fear of German renascence. France read the long-term power balance correctly and saw a disparity even more severe than the one Taylor perceives. He cites Germany's population advantage, but its younger population and higher birth rate would, as the French foresaw, guarantee an ever greater advantage in the future. While he notes that Britain wished to reintegrate Germany in European trade, he does not see the effect this produced on France, who knew that time was on Germany's side. France was dependent on reparations coal; in addition, if it did not get a trade treaty with Germany (which Britain hindered) before economic clauses of the peace treaty expired in 1925, France's iron and steel industry would be at Germany's mercy. And effective transfer of the reparations bill from the losers to the winners only added to Germany's advantage, as did its success in wiping out its war and other debts during the 1923 inflation.

Though Taylor rightly says that France saw its eastern allies more as assets against Germany than as potential liabilities, he errs in thinking they dominated French foreign policy.[47] The overriding goal was always a British alliance, as the French assumed the next war would resemble the last, when the British navy, empire, and ties to Wall Street had saved France. Every French premier, including Raymond Poincaré, wished to revive the wartime alliance, but the British price proved prohibitive, higher than Taylor notes. None the less, a frightened France continued to seek British protection. Britain, alarmed at the prospect of being drawn into another continental bloodbath and wanting to turn away from Europe to other matters, pressed France to make still more concessions to Germany.

Germany wanted to break the treaty and to revert to the *status quo ante bellum*. This amounted to undoing the military verdict of 1918; thus the postwar became the continuation of war by other means.[48] Germany fought the battle with unceasing determination on many grounds and in many ways, including using John Maynard Keynes effectively as an unofficial German adviser and propagandist.[49] The key battlefield in the early years was that of reparations. Though the archives have proved him wrong on some points, Taylor must be commended for facing this topic at a time when most historians avoided it.[50] His assessment shows more comprehension of France's dilemma than many early accounts, although at times he comes close to hinting that if France had only thrown away its costly wartime victory without a murmur of protest, all would have been well.[51] To say that Britain was not ready "to underwrite every French claim against Germany"[52] misses the point that Britain was increasingly opposed to all French claims, however well-grounded, particularly if Germany was likely to refuse. Taylor perhaps oversimplifies in saying the Germans "deliberately kept their economic affairs in confusion" to escape reparations; however, he deserves credit for not blaming German fiscal and monetary chaos on French vindictiveness and reparations which, on the whole, were not being paid.[53]

The long reparations struggle was complicated by its link to war debts disputes between Anglo-American creditors and continental debtors, a subject on which the literature remains as unsatisfactory as it was twenty-five years ago. When Taylor says that reparations were perpetually unsettled, he forgets they were settled in 1921 by the London Schedule of Payments, then promptly came unsettled, as they did after each settlement in the future. The resultant uncertainty derived from Germany's resistance and the support it received from Britain and the United States. German threats of an export drive impressed the British, as did Keynes's pronouncements, which influenced opinion where it mattered. Taylor properly notes that German impoverishment derived from the war, not reparations, but should add that it was modest compared to that of the continental victors, especially France.

The key battle in the test of wills over reparations came with the "occupation" of the Ruhr in January 1923. Poincaré had tried to avoid military action and had hoped through 1922 for British co-operation in limited economic sanctions.[54] But as that year closed, he faced an adamant Anglo-American-German front opposing application of the peace treaty,[55] and he saw coal essential to French steel production, funds for reconstruction of France's devastated industrial areas, the treaty and victory in the war draining away; caught between Germany, Britain and the powerful French right, which pressed him for forceful measures,[56] he had no maneuvering room left, and so he acted reluctantly, cautiously and within sharply circumscribed limits. The Ruhr encirclement was profitable[57] and caused neither the German hyperinflation, which began in 1922 and ballooned as a result of German responses to the Ruhr occupation, nor the collapse of the French franc in 1924,[58] which arose from French financial practices and the steady evaporation of reparations since 1920. Poincaré won the battle and forced Germany to acknowledge its treaty obligations but lost the war, partly because legalism, procrastination and timidity kept him from capitalizing on his victory while he had the upper hand, partly because everyone else promptly swung to the other side.[59]

Poincaré also lost the 1924 election, more from collapse of the franc and ensuing taxation than from diplomatic isolation, so it was the inexperienced Edouard Herriot who led France to the first of two decisive defeats. Herriot made many mistakes before and during the July–August 1924 London reparations conference but, given the Anglo-American-German front against France, it is questionable whether another premier could have salvaged much more.[60] Taylor correctly gives MacDonald much credit for the 1924 reparations settlement though others prepared the way. MacDonald's policy did not differ from his predecessors' (and he gave France no more, except blither) but his style and tone did, and that mattered. Equally important, France was now at the mercy of American bankers who dictated much of the settlement.[61] When the conference ended in mid-August, reparations payments had been sharply reduced to German benefit with a scheme for a gradual increase to a substantial amount – at which point Germany would seek further revision. France had lost preponderance on the reparation commission, the right of sanctions against future German default and hope of a Franco-German trade treaty before 1925.[62] Taylor rightly notes that the peace treaty provided artificial compensations to France for Germany's inherently greater power but fails to add that many of these were temporary at best and that in 1924 France lost several advantages vital both to its economic future and to treaty enforcement. That, too, affected the power balance.

Taylor says that France had learned "the folly of coercion".[63] More accurately, it had learned the futility of attempting to enforce the Versailles treaty without at least token British co-operation and a modicum of American consent. Taylor tends to assume that because treaty enforcement largely collapsed in 1924–5 (while contradictorily also assuming that most of the Versailles treaty remained intact in 1939), it was inevitable that it do so. In actuality, the treaty could have been enforced – but that would have required an entirely different set of British and perhaps American assumptions and policies. Taylor is aware that Britain and the United States both thought the war had ended in 1918 and saw no cause for alarm in the prospect of German resurgence, but he does not explore the implications of their short-sightedness. In fact, between them, the English-speaking nations arranged a crushing defeat of France and a considerable victory for Germany, unappreciated by the latter because it was not total, at London in August 1924. Thereafter, France's will sagged.

France's second defeat, against which it did not struggle as it had in 1923, came when Britain rejected the Geneva Protocol and a pact with France in favor of the Locarno treaties, which formalized Britain's temporary return to the center of the power equation. When Chamberlain stated in March 1925 that Britain would reject the Protocol and urged France to pursue Germany's offer of a Rhineland pact, Herriot was visibly distraught, French foreign ministry officials were equally unhappy about the proposal but decided that rejection would end all hope of a British guarantee in any form. When Aristide Briand returned to the Quai d'Orsay soon thereafter, he reached the same conclusion and energetically pursued the Rhineland scheme, not daring to fail again in his quest for the British guarantee essential to French security, even if the pact gave parity to Germany.[64]

Taylor's discourse on Locarno is sometimes confused, but he correctly concludes that the military guarantee was inoperable.[65] He errs in thinking any leader other than Chamberlain and Stresemann liked the settlement.[66] The other men of Locarno knew defeat when they saw it. Well before the treaties were completed, they were interpreted as giving Germany a green light in the east.[67] When Stresemann refused to confirm in writing his verbal assurance that he would not try to revise the Polish frontier by force,[68] the final treaties reinforced this view. The Polish foreign minister, Alexandre Skyrzński, teetered on the brink of hysteria; his Czech counterpart, Eduard Benes, was more philosophical. In addition, Stresemann argued, with technical accuracy, that the Locarno treaties did not rule out peaceful territorial change in the west,[69] and a few days after the final ceremony at Locarno, he sought the retrocession of Eupen-Malmédy from Belgium.[70] He also told Germans that once circumstances had changed treaties were no longer valid; thus, when Germany had rearmed, the reconquest of Alsace–Lorraine could not be excluded.[71]

Taylor tells us Locarno ended the First World War;[72] about French military policy, he says France "had renounced the fruits of victory before the dispute over these fruits began"[73] and claims that in 1929 the Versailles security system against Germany was still complete. He is right about the first but not the other two points.[74] Locarno ended the First World War with the defeat of France and the return of Germany to diplomatic equality and potential superiority. France had deployed all weapons short of war, not always wisely or well, in an attempt to enforce the treaty and maintain its security, but it had been defeated by the combination of its former allies with the enemy and, perhaps, a certain relaxing of its own will. By 1925, much of the Versailles system was gone and more followed the Locarno and London meetings; what ensued in the next five years (the depression aside) was largely implicit in the settlement.

Accordingly to Taylor, "Locarno gave to Europe a period of peace and hope".[75] In fact, it failed to provide a real peace and offered only a respite of civility as Gustav Stresemann, the German foreign minister, and Briand circled warily, seeking interim solutions politically acceptable to both, with Chamberlain serving as refereee. In the mid and late 1920s, the question was not whether the peace settlement would be revised by war or peace, as Taylor argues,[76] but rather how soon revision would occur peacefully and when Germany would return to predominance. Both the principal players saw what lay ahead; Stresemann tried to accelerate its advent, Briand to postpone the evil day. When Stresemann complained, influential British and American voices supported him.[77] Scarred by France's renewed financial crisis in 1926 and trying to salvage something, Poincaré and Briand accepted an early evacuation of the Rhineland in exchange for a "final" reparations plan which, in fact, dissolved in eighteen months.[78] In desperation, Briand pursued the web of European union,[79] hoping to enmesh Germany in as many types of European integration as possible and to freeze the political status quo, because he knew the old weapons were gone.

Taylor's assessment of Briand and Stresemann is perceptive, though both were less sincere and Stresemann more skillful than he suggests. Much recent work by historians has focused on these two dominant figures of the late 1920s, along with British leaders, and has gone through several phases. No consensus has emerged, but rather a tendency to view both as less noble and more hardheaded than before. In general, Stresemann is now viewed by most not as a "good European" but rather as a great German nationalist, while a few regard Briand as craven and as the first French appeaser. Taylor rightly notes that Stresemann's task was more difficult than Bismarck's but he oversimplifies in saying Stresemann chose the path of peace over that of war.[80] Despite rapid improvement, Germany's position remained weak, and treaty revision by military means was not feasible. However, Stresemann substituted conciliation for confrontation as a more effective and less costly means to goals which had not changed.

The reassessment of British policy, which displayed similarly consistent goals through the 1920s despite variations in technique and tone, tends to downgrade it from far-seeing virtuous wisdom to blindness and ruthlessness encased in elevated rhetoric. With the advantage of hindsight it appears that, owing to a misreading of the power balance, Britain did all in its power to restore Europe's potentially strongest nation to continental predominance, a state of affairs which had never been deemed in Britain's interest. Lloyd George's historical reputation has not improved, though MacDonald has gained a few admirers; Chamberlain emerges as an exceptionally nice man of limited stature. On the other hand, Mussolini is now taken more seriously than Taylor regards him. Few would argue that he had much moral standing, but even Briand of the ennobling rhetoric falsified his report of the Thoiry meeting, and behind Mussolini's posturing, some historians discern considerable ability.

Most of the new work derives from opening of the major archives. The result has been a quantity of books and articles, good, bad, and mediocre. In addition to many works on the Paris peace conference,[81] the international history of the 1920s has enjoyed a considerable vogue, as the second postwar now does. The popularity of both periods seems to have derived chiefly from the availability of new evidence. For the first postwar period, nobody appears to have tested Taylor's ideas, for the debate about his book centered on the 1930s, not the 1920s. Such traumatic contemporary experiences as the Cold War and the Vietnamese War seem to have had little effect on historical interpretation of this era, presumably because analogies were difficult to draw. Certainly, those Americans most influenced by the war in Vietnam have tended to focus on other topics. More than anything else, shifts in interpretation have occurred as a result of which archives opened when.

The German files were accessible first. Hence a batch of books reflected the views of Weimar officials.[82] There was a chorus of regret for "poor old Weimar", destroyed by the Versailles treaty, the depression and the wicked French. For many years, it was almost axiomatic that these factors alone caused the advent of Hitler although a few lonely voices suggested otherwise;[83] the old view lingers, but one can now suggest that some responsibility fell to the citizenry. The Weimar records are valuable, but Western scholars using them wrote much nonsense about the need for German "reconstruction" when it was the victors who faced that problem, argued that the Maginot line threatened Germany – as if it could get up and move across the frontier – and made the false assumption that, since the Reischsverband der deutschen Industrie representing the German iron–steel–coal complex was so dominant, the Comité des Forges of the French steel companies must have been as well.

Next came the American and British archives, both tending to reinforce the German view of the postwar era. Of the two, the American files are less important for many European problems unless papers of the bankers are added. The massive, minuted British records are invaluable – and easily misleading since few British officials writing the minutes questioned their own assumptions or the policy they conducted. As Taylor notes, "morality" mattered to the British;[84] others call it self-righteousness; whichever it was, it played well to the historical galleries. Though one can infer from British files that Poincaré did not want to enter the Ruhr, few researchers did. Again, scholars took on the viewpoint of what they read, and for some years existing assumptions about British far-sightedness and generosity were reinforced,[85] despite evidence to the contrary. British Cabinet records, for example, indicate clearly that the purpose of the Balfour note of 1 August 1922, saying that Britain would collect from its continental debtors and Germany only what it must pay to America, was to embarrass the United States into sharp debt reduction, not to be generous to anybody, but the evidence has been remarkably slow to emerge in the literature.

Finally, the French, Italian, and Belgian archives opened (and those of the League of Nations), providing much new information and a corrective to previously one-sided evidence. The massive Belgian records compensate in part for the paucity of internal memoranda in the French files and for loss of some French dossiers in the Second World War, at least on matters of concern to Belgium, including the German problem. The surviving French files, often confirmed by Belgian records, reveal disorganization, disarray, and confusion in French policy planning, not only among government departments but also in their dealings with elements such as the Comité des Forges and the Comité des Houillères of the French coal mines; the contrast with German method and comparative cohesiveness is startling. One concludes that adminstratively and in policy planning, France had not yet reached the twentieth century, a factor which influenced not only the conduct of policy but also the power equation.[86] Further, Poincaré-la-guerre emerges as a timid procrastinator, fearful of decisions and ignorant of monetary matters in the early 1920s. The Italian archives have added to the pool of evidence, and not only about Italy; during the Cannes conference, for example, Sir Maurice Hankey, the British Cabinet secretary, was absent in Washington, and records of Lloyd George's meetings were not always kept by his staff, but Italian files plug some gaps. Books based on these archives, as well as those open earlier, are now appearing, some providing a more balanced analysis.[87] Others improve on the evidence or suppress it to French benefit, as still happens with German records to enhance the reputation of Weimar, for the craft imposes few external controls on the practitioner.

The international historians now have most of the evidence they can anticipate in the foreseeable future. Though some private papers remain closed and some government files, including key ones, are stubbornly withheld, most German, West European and American records are now available. To the east, the situation is less happy.[88] But for what one early author called *Great Britain, France and the German Problem*,[89] evidence is now plentiful and the international historians need only to master it. As D. C. Watt has remarked,[90] the sheer quantity of material renders the task daunting, but some scholars have the necessary fortitude.[91] And do these historians confirm or deny Taylor's arguments? Despite the lack of clear consensus, one can say in general terms that they do a bit of both.

The records have confirmed some of Taylor's judgments, and he was among the leaders in certain insights into the postwar era. He asserted that relaxing the Versailles treaty would render Germany "as strong, or almost as strong" as before;[92] others since have seen that, in relative terms, it was fundamentally stronger.[93] Taylor's approach to the Polish settlement of 1919 was calmer than others at the time. He pointed as well to rapid German resurgence and the internal pressures for German rearmament, since confirmed by archival research;[94] some still echo him in less measured tones about Germany's innate right to rearm, failing to ask the question: rearmament to what end? Taylor's focus on reparations was sound, if not always accurate in the particulars, and more judicious than some early literature. He was right in saying that Germans blamed all woes on reparations and then transferred these feelings to the treaty in general.[95] He also saw that Germans convinced British leaders that reparations were unjust (and harmful to Britain's economy), leading the British to apply this view of some clauses to all,[96] though he does not note the parallel development or its significance. The absence of the vital connection here is one of the more crucial instances of Taylor's failure to put the pieces together to discover why the interwar era went so far awry.

Since many key clashes in the continuing Franco-German struggle came over reparations, with implications for treaty enforcement and thus the underlying power equation, the present generation of historians has tackled this abstruse topic.[97] Much of what they have found could have been ascertained earlier, had their elders consulted published documents instead of journalistic accounts. It is interesting to learn that the British Treasury, which was doing its utmost to arrange Germany's release from the financial burden, took it for granted in late 1922 that Germany had destroyed its currency to escape reparations, and important to know that the British government then concluded that since Germany had succeeded in rendering the mark worthless, there was no alternative to a long moratorium.[98] But this sheds more light on British policy than on reparations. Historians have now returned to the texts, and to studies of economic theory, and have come to a degree of consensus. Most would now argue that the bill presented in the London Schedule of Payments probably lay within Germany's capacity to pay, had it shown any willingness to make the effort, and that it amounted to 50 milliard gold marks in nominal value, the present value being less. The rest of the ostensible figure of 132 milliard gold marks (nominal value) represented camouflage to bridge the gap between a feasible figure and popular expectations in receiver countries and also, if possible, to provide some worthless paper to exchange for war debt cancellation.[99] Most would also accept that the transfer problem, allegedly the barrier to substantial payments, was greatly exaggerated. Certainly, there is no dispute about the importance of the issue.[100]

Most historians now agree with Taylor about the speed of Germany's return to effective predominance. Instead of ascribing this phenomenon to Germany's natural place and an inevitable process, however, they ask why it happened so fast. Instead of declaring the Versailles treaty devoid of "moral validity",[101] they asked why Germany and others rejected it and why it broke down so quickly, noting that, because of the former, the answer to the latter in large part is the development of a formidable anti-French coalition with powerful economic, financial and propaganda weapons at its disposal.[102]

These historians deem the German problem to be more complex than Taylor does, and have examined aspects in Taylor's beloved power balance which he himself largely ignored. Rather than criticizing his concern with the power equation, as some did earlier, they have cast their net wider, focusing on German determination and self-delusion, the assertive nature of German nationalism and British blindness in helping Germany to undo the military verdict of 1918. In addition they point to French disorganization and exhaustion, Belgium's ambivalence as it tried to balance between Britain and France, and the considerable pressure exerted by American bankers toward "appeasement" of Germany. Instead of attacking Taylor's pre-occupation with the balance of power, these historians now examine economic, financial, and domestic political and emotional aspects of the situation to which Taylor gives scant attention. In particular, they have stressed the dependence of France's heavy industry upon Germany for coal, coke and outlets, along with Britain's obstruction of any Franco-German economic arrangement favorable to France, as important factors in what eventuated. On the whole they have judged the situation to be more complex and the possibilities more diverse than Taylor did. Although they agree that Germany had greater power potential than France in more senses than Taylor mentions, few view the postwar era with Taylor's determinism as merely an inevitable German drive "to restore the natural order of things".[103]

When *The Origins of the Second World War* appeared, some reviewers faulted Taylor for a narrow focus on diplomacy. In fact, his power balance for the postwar years operates largely in military terms even though no major wars were in sight. He talks of men available for armies and of whether the 1919 settlement would be revised peacefully or by war, but not of heavy industry, American financial power, diplomatic support of German revisionism by a Britain lacking an army to put into Europe, or other equally important pieces of the puzzle and of the power balance. This narrow military approach does not provide an adequate framework for analysis in an era when no power of consequence had aims in Europe achievable by war. Despite British fears of France, French fears of Germany, and perhaps Russian fears of the capitalist West, nobody seriously contemplated fighting. Stresemann talked privately of reconquest of Alsace–Lorraine when Germany was rearmed, but did he mean it? At best, this was at the bottom of his long agenda. Germany could not fight; the victors had no thought of doing so. Mussolini's oratory was bellicose but his escapades were minor; nobody else even talked of going to war. Taylor notes that it was easier to continue war in 1918 than to threaten to renew it in June 1919, and that threats of renewed war became less viable as time passed.[104] In fact, there was no mention of renewed war after June 1919. All actions debated or taken by the victors were carefully limited sanctions for enforcement purposes. In the largest action, in the Ruhr, Poincaré did not anticipate passive resistance. Though aware he was playing France's last trump in a decisive contest and critically short of troops and coal, he never considered barring food shipments to force the Ruhr miners back to work. Despite the recent precedent of Germany's refusal to feed civilians in territories it conquered in the First World War, he was neither so foolish nor so brutal.

Taylor's focus on the military aspect of the power equation obscures other factors. This is why he dismisses Russia, though Rapallo improved Germany's power position and impeded treaty enforcement, why he says "the only economic effect of reparations was to give employment to a large number of bookkeepers",[105] when in fact other economic, financial and power factors abounded. This is why he scants British fear of continental involvement and nostalgia for an earlier economy and power balance, ignores constraints imposed by public opinion on French and German leaders, and deems the Ruhr occupation a failure instead of looking at the array against France after passive resistance ended. This is why he concludes that France threw away its victory by a defensive military stance and cuts in the term of service, both largely after the victory had been lost owing to domestic and foreign pressures of other, non-military kinds, and why he essentially faults France for not being militarily aggressive in a period when it, like most countries, was searching for a stable peace.

This is also why Taylor barely mentions the Rhineland evacuation.[106] Frence forces there in 1929 and 1930 were negligible militarily but important not only as a bargaining counter and a theoretical deterrent to German military action in the east but as a symbol of German defeat in the late war; since recognition of that defeat had long since been dismissed from the German collective consciousness, the Rhineland occupation constituted a major grievance. When it ended, Hindenburg and his cabinet issued a fervently nationalistic proclamation pointedly invoking Germany's obligation to its war dead.[107] The French evacuation in June 1930 released the brake from pent-up German nationalism which exploded in the 1930 electoral campaign, in turn dominated by foreign policy issues. However, the Nazis aside, the focus was on reversion to the *status quo ante bellum.*[108] Taylor neither mentions these facts nor contemplates their significance, although Hitler bragged that he never accepted anything under the Versailles treaty and took his first long stride toward power in that election.

This brings us to Hitler in comparison to his Weimar predecessors. True, some of his early foreign policy moves polished off items on Stresemann's list. But Weimar politicians were preoccupied with the Polish Corridor, while Hitler was not. Although the war Taylor is concerned with, the European war of 1939, started there, Poland did not loom large in Hitler's thinking.[109] Some Weimar leaders hoped to regain Alsace–Lorraine but their wider aims did not extend far beyond the boundaries of 1914, *Anschluss* aside. They shrank from confrontation with Britain and would have swooned at the idea of attacking Russia. Granted, the opportunity was not yet there but many Weimar notables were horrified when it happened, and Hitler had laid this out as a primary goal long before it was possible.[110] Without becoming embroiled in continuity theory, one can say that Hitler's aims were more vast, his ideology different and his preferred methods more drastic than those of his predecessors. Weimar politicians wanted revisions of the Versailles treaty; even in the 1920s, Hitler deemed that a mistake and posited much more vast goals.[111] Germany did not fight "specifically in the second war to reverse the verdict of the first and to destroy the settlement which followed it".[112] Much of that had been destroyed before Hitler took office and much more by 1939. Despite Taylor's assertion that Hitler's "foreign policy was that of his predecessors",[113] his world view was far more grandiose.[114] Whether one looks back on the Weimar years from the perspective of the late 1930s or forward from the 1920s toward the Nazi era, the idea that the Second World War had been "implicit since the moment when the first war ended"[115] is simplistic and the concept of Hitler as one more Weimar politician struggling manfully against the shackles of Versailles contradicts the evidence from both eras.

NOTES

1   Most of the major essays in this debate are conveniently collected in: Esmonde M. Robertson (ed.), *The Origins of the Second World War*

(London, 1971); W. Roger Louis (ed.), *The Origins of the Second World War: A. J. P. Taylor and His Critics* (New York, 1972); and *Journal of Modern History*, vol. 49, no. 1 (March 1977). See also Keith L. Nelson and Spencer C. Olin, Jr., *Why War? Ideology, Theory, and History* (Berkeley, 1979), and W. H. Dray, "Concepts of causation in A. J. P. Taylor's account of the origins of the Second World War", *History and Theory*, vol. 18, no. 2 (May 1978).

2   A. J. P. Taylor, *The Origins of the Second World War* (New York, 1963 edn), p. 70. All citations are to this edition unless otherwise noted.

3   ibid., pp. 24–30.

4   ibid., p. 32.

5   ibid., p. 30–3.

6   ibid., pp. 46–52.

7   ibid., pp. 34–9, 44–58, quotation from p. 57.

8   ibid., p. 22.

9   ibid., pp. 52–3.

10   ibid., p. 249.

11   ibid., p. 25 and again on p. 71. This has been corrected in the second edition. He also misdates the writing of *Mein Kampf* in both editions.

12   ibid., pp. 25–6.

13   ibid., p. 44.

14   ibid., p. 61.

15   For example, Gordon A. Craig terms the early chapters "masterly", in his essay. "Provocative, perverse view of pre-1939", in Louis, *Origins*, p. 110. They are also praised in Robertson, *Origins*, by T. W. Mason, "Some origins of the Second World War" (pp. 105–6) and in E. M. Robertson's "Introduction" (p. 15).

16   For example, Taylor, *Origins*, pp. 23–6, 28, 43, 71, 267.

17   ibid., pp. 16, 28, 44.

18   ibid., 2nd edn, p. xiv.

19   ibid., 1st edn, p. 70.

20   ibid., p. 267.

21   ibid., p. 26.

22   ibid., p. 27.

23   ibid., p. 26.

24   ibid., p. 26.

25   ibid., p. 32.

26   On 10 March 1919, the American government officially but privately reminded German authorities that the Allies had won the war and explicitly rejected the German interpretation that the war was without victors. Weimar Republic, Akten der Reichskanzlei, *Das Kabinett Scheidemann* (Boppard-am-Rhein, 1971), p. 28.

27   Taylor, *Origins*, p. 26.

28   Robert G. L. Waite, *Vanguard of Nazism* (New York, 1969 edn), p. 7.

29 Taylor, *Origins*, pp. 34–5.

30 ibid., p. 51.

31 In two long debates on 21 and 22 March 1919, several members of the German cabinet privately acknowledged German impropriety and guilt in events at the outbreak of war in 1914, noting that the present leaders had not been involved in these decisions and thus bore no responsibility for the action of their predecessors. The cabinet, however, did not pursue this path. *Das Kabinett Scheidemann*, pp. 78–88.

32 Taylor, *Origins*, pp. 26–7.

33 ibid., p. 51.

34 ibid., p. 34.

35 ibid., pp. 28, 31.

36 ibid., pp. 31, 33.

37 In retrospect, Lloyd George's manufactured evidence about starving German children and his famous Fontainebleau memorandum, both in March 1919, signal the start of a trend. On the former, see Baron Riddell, *Lord Riddell's Intimate Diary of the Peace Conference and After, 1919–1923* (London, 1933), p. 210, and United States, Department of State, *Papers Relating to the Foreign Relations of the United States: The Paris Peace Conference, 1919*, 13 vols (Washington, 1942–7) [hereafter *FRUS PPC*], Vol. 2, pp. 139–43; for the latter, David Lloyd George, *Memoirs of the Peace Conference*, 2 vols (New Haven, 1939), Vol. 1, pp. 265–73. Shortly before, the British had informed the German government that German war guilt was "undeniably established" (*Das Kabinett Scheidemann*, p. 85).

38 Taylor, *Origins*, p. 56.

39 Comte de Saint-Aulaire, *Confession d'un vieux diplomate* (Paris, 1953), p. 644.

40 Weimar Republic, Akten der Reichskanzlei, *Die Kabinette Wirth I und II*, 2 vols. (Boppard am Rhein, 1973), Vol. 2, pp. 1059–60.

41 Italy, Ministero degli affari esteri, *I documenti diplomatici italiani*, settima serie (Rome, 1953–), Vol. 3, p. 320; Great Britain, Foreign Office, *Documents on British Foreign Policy, 1919–1939* (London, 1958–) (hereafter *DBFP*], First Series, Vol. 16, p. 862; Belgium, Académie Royale de Belgique, *Documents diplomatiques belges, 1920–1940*, 5 vols (Brussels, 1964–6) [hereafter *DDB*], Vol. 1, pp. 360–1, 385–6, 412–14. There is also much archival evidence, particularly in the records of the Committee of Imperial Defence and its subcommittees. The War Office alone favored alliance with France.

42 Taylor, *Origins*, p. 38.

43 ibid., p. 32.

44 See, for instance, Weimar Republic, Akten der Reichskanzlei, *Das Kabinett Cuno* (Boppard am Rhein, 1968), pp. 49–50.

45 Melvyn P. Leffler, *The Elusive Quest* (Chapel Hill, NC, 1979) indicates the reluctance of the American government to be involved

and also the inadequacy of much American diplomatic reporting
from the continent.

46   Taylor, *Origins*, p. 59.

47   ibid., p. 42.

48   *Das Kabinett Cuno*, p. 192.

49   Keynes's positions were shaped by his passion for Carl Melchior,
the German financier and reparations expert whom he met during
negotiations at Spa shortly after the armistice. John Maynard
Keynes, *Two Memoirs: Dr. Melchior, A Defeated Enemy, and My Early
Beliefs* (New York, 1949); Stephen A. Schuker, review of *Collected
Writings of John Maynard Keynes*, Vols 17 and 18, in *Journal of Economic
Literature*, Vol. 18 (March 1980), p. 126.

50   Taylor shows less insight about war debts, but that is little wonder
in view of the inadequacy of the literature.

51   Taylor claims (pp. 31, 48) that France retarded reparations
settlements in hopes of remaining on the Rhine. It would be more
accurate to say that, after German bad faith had been demonstrated
by numerous defaults on deliveries in kind, French leaders argued
that, until Germany was in compliance with the Versailles treaty, the
5–10–15 year terms for the Rhineland occupation would not begin to
run. This argument, which revealed France's preoccupation with
security, was not endorsed by any other power and was a casualty of
the 1924 London reparations settlement.

52   Taylor, *Origins*, p. 38.

53   Taylor confuses Germany's economy, healthy compared to those
of continental victors, with its fiscal and monetary shambles. It
perhaps would be more judicious to say that, for a variety of
political, economic, and diplomatic reasons (including reparations), successive German cabinets let the financial situation
slide. After the summer of 1921, reparations payments in cash
quickly dwindled to a trickle, chiefly financed as earlier by foreign
loans, later repudiated by Hitler. There were substantial defaults
on payments in kind as well. In purely economic terms, aside from
the export advantage, Germany actually made a profit (approximately equal to all reparations paid in cash and kind through
1923) on the inflation until mid-1922, thanks to foreign speculation in the mark which, owing to its depreciation, amounted to a
direct capital transfer to German benefit. See Karl-Ludwig Holtfrerich, "Internationale Verteilungsfolgen der deutschen Inflation, 1918–1923", *Kyklos*, vol. 30 (1977/2), pp. 271–91. For a
wider-ranging analysis focusing on American capital transfers
but taking the same line, see Stephen A. Schuker, "American
'Reparations' to Germany, 1919–1933", in Gerald D. Feldman
(ed.), *Die Nachwirkungen der Inflation auf die deutsche Geschichte,
1924–1933* (Munich, 1985), pp. 237–68.

54   There is much disagreement about when Poincaré decided to
enter the Ruhr. Archival evidence suggests that he still hoped the

British could be persuaded to united, lesser action until 4 January 1923. See also Stephen A. Schuker, *The End of French Predominance in Europe* (Chapel Hill, NC, 1976), pp. 21–5.

55   The American element in the front was, on the whole, not governmental but rather the financiers, notably J. P. Morgan, Jr.

56   For the pressures on Poincaré see Schuker, *French Predominance*, pp. 20–1.

57   The profits were held on reparations account for all the victors but, for technical reasons, most of the money went to Belgium. Sorting out the Ruhr accounts was probably the most complex financial transaction attempted before the arrangements in 1981 for release of American hostages in Iran. Net profits (after Ruhr and Rhineland occupation costs) amounted to nearly 900 million gold marks (*FRUS PPC*, Vol. 13, pp. 487, 785). A cautious, precise Belgian reparation commission official put the net receipts at just over a milliard gold marks. See Gaston Furst, *De Versailles aux experts* (Nancy, 1927), p. 336. These figures should not be compared to the defunct London Schedule but to the four year moratorium on payments which Britain had demanded at the January 1923 Paris conference. The Ruhr episode generated a British economic boom caused by the elimination of German competition (Saint-Aulaire, *Confession*, p. 651). Board of Trade figures confirm this fact, which British officials refused to face.

58   On the French financial crisis of 1924, Schuker, *French Predominance*, is definitive.

59   The published literature has not yet fully elaborated the situation in all its complexity but, in essence, Poincaré faced pressures of varying intensity from Britain, the United States, Belgium, Italy and Germany.

60   Schuker, *French Predominance*, pp. 386, 392.

61   Jacques Bariéty, *Les Relations franco-allemandes après la première guerre mondiale* (Paris, 1977), and Schuker, *French Predominance*, provide detailed accounts of the London negotiations. Herriot agreed with them about the bankers (Edouard Herriot, *Jadis*, 2 vols (Paris, 1948–52), Vol. 2, pp. 155–8).

62   The extent of France's defeat was evident to contemporary observers. See Bariéty, *Les Relations franco-allemandes* (quoting Jacques Bainville's *Journal, 1919–1926*), p. 718; Sally Marks, "The myths of reparations", *Central European History*, vol. 11 (September 1978), p. 249 (quoting dispatch of Sir Eric Phipps, chargé at the British embassy in Paris, to MacDonald, 29 August 1924).

63   Taylor, *Origins*, p. 54.

64   For Briand's first effort toward a British treaty in 1921–2, see Sally Marks, "Ménage à trois: the negotiations for an Anglo-French-Belgian alliance in 1922", *International History Review*, vol. 4 (November 1982), pp. 524–52. For attitudes of the Quai d'Orsay and Briand in 1925, ibid., p. 551.

65 Taylor, *Origins*, p. 58.
66 They both crowed: Stresemann, in a speech in Berlin on 14 December 1925, about the humiliation of Poland and Czechoslovakia (Gustav Stresemann, *Vermächtnis*, 3 vols (Berlin, 1932), Vol. 2, p. 243); Chamberlain literally, but out of euphoria in general, in a telegram to the Foreign Office from Locarno after the conference.
67 *DDB*, Vol. 2, p. 213. Remark of a German diplomat attending a conference at Geneva in June 1925.
68 Stresemann, *Vermächtnis*, Vol. 2, p. 233.
69 Great Britain, Parliament, Parliamentary Command Paper [hereafter Cmd.] 2525 (1925) provides the text of the treaty; for Stresemann's interpretation, see *Vermächtnis*, Vol. 2, pp. 232–3, and especially Manfred J. Enssle, *Stresemann's Territorial Revisionism* (Wiesbaden, 1980), pp. 109–12.
70 *DDB*, Vol. 2, p. 399.
71 Enssle, *Stresemann's Territorial Revisionism*, pp. 85–6, 104, 113, 126, 128. Briand was aware of Stresemann's interpretation and challenged it through diplomatic channels but glossed over it publicly in order not to jeopardize German ratification of the treaties.
72 Taylor, *Origins*, p. 57.
73 ibid., p. 62.
74 ibid., p. 63.
75 ibid., p. 58.
76 ibid., p. 54.
77 Jon Jacobson, *Locarno Diplomacy* (Princeton, 1972), Part 4.
78 The decision was solemnized at Geneva in September 1928. For the text of the Geneva communiqué see *DBFP*, Series 1A, Vol. 5, p. 335. For the texts of the Young Plan and Hague conference documents, see Denys P. Meyers, *The Reparations Settlement* (Boston, 1929 [1930]) or Cmd. 3484 (1930), Cmd. 3763 (1931), and Cmd. 3766 (1931).
79 For text of his proposal, see *DBFP*, Second Series, Vol. 1, pp. 314–24.
80 Taylor, *Origins*, pp. 54–5.
81 In addition to several solid studies of aspects of the peace conference having little or nothing to do with the German problem, there are: Seth P. Tillman, *Anglo-American Relations at the Paris Peace Conference of 1919* (Princeton, 1961); Harold I. Nelson, *Land and Power: British and Allied Policy on Germany's Frontiers, 1916–19* (Toronto, 1963); Arno J. Mayer, *Politics and Diplomacy of Peacemaking* (Knopf, 1967); Inga Floto, *Colonel House in Paris* (Åarhus, Denmark, 1973); Kay Lundgreen-Nielsen, *The Polish Problem at the Paris Peace Conference* (Odense, Denmark, 1979); Sally Marks, *Innocent Abroad: Belgium at the Paris Peace Conference of 1919* (Chapel Hill, NC, 1981); and Klaus Schwabe, *Woodrow Wilson, Revolutionary Germany, and Peacemaking, 1918–1919* (Chapel Hill, NC, 1985).

82   For example, Royal J. Schmidt, *Versailles and the Ruhr* (The Hague, 1968); David Felix, *Walther Rathenau and the Weimar Republic* (Baltimore, 1971), and, to a degree, Hermann J. Rupieper, *The Cuno Government and Reparations, 1922–1923* (The Hague, 1979).

83   Hans W. Gatzke, *Stresemann and the Rearmament of Germany* (Baltimore, 1954) and Annelise Thimme, "Stresemann and Locarno" in Hans W. Gatzke (ed.), *European Diplomacy Between Two Wars, 1919–1939* (Chicago, 1972).

84   Taylor, *Origins*, p. 183.

85   For example, David Marquand, *Ramsay MacDonald* (London, 1977).

86   The situation emerges clearly in the archival material, particularly concerning the autumn of 1923. See also Schuker, *French Predominance*, pp. 365–7, 385.

87   For a recent study making judicious use of the Italian archives as well as those of many other countries, see Carole Fink, *The Genoa Conference: European Diplomacy, 1921–1922* (Chapel Hill, NC, 1984). The standard work on Italian policy in this era, Alan Cassels, *Mussolini's Early Diplomacy* (Princeton, 1970), was written before the Italian archives opened. Though it uses some German archival material, it rests chiefly on the copious supply of printed Italian documents available in Mussolini's *Opera omnia* and the Italian government's series, *I documenti diplomatici italiani*.

88   Czech files are open only to Czech citizens. The Poles are more obliging. The situation as to Russian records needs no comment.

89   W. M. Jordan, *Great Britain, France, and the German Problem* (London, 1943).

90   D. C. Watt, "Some aspects of A. J. P. Taylor's work as diplomatic historian", *Journal of Modern History*, vol. 49 (March 1977), p. 30.

91   Nobody has yet attempted a full-scale synthesis of the era. The only English-language survey based upon archival research is Sally Marks, *The Illusion of Peace: International Relations in Europe, 1918–1933* (London, 1976). Major monographic studies in English of various aspects of the period include Piotr S. Wandycz, *France and Her Eastern Allies, 1919–1925* (Minneapolis, 1962); Jacobson, *Locarno Diplomacy*; Charles S. Maier, *Recasting Bourgeois Europe* (Princeton, 1975); Schuker, *French Predominance*; and the concluding section of Marks, *Innocent Abroad*. Other books useful for some aspects of the era include Gatzke, *Stresemann*; Anne Orde, *Britain and International Security, 1920–1926* (London, 1978); Derek H. Aldcroft, *From Versailles to Wall Street, 1919–1929* (Berkeley, 1977); and Keith L. Nelson, *Victors Divided* (Berkeley, 1975).

92   Taylor, *Origins*, p. 28.

93   F. H. Hinsley, "The origins of the Second World War", in Louis, *Origins*, p. 72; Gerhard L. Weinberg, "The defeat of Germany in 1918 and the European balance of power", *Central European History*, vol. 2 (September 1969), pp. 248–60.

94   Edward W. Bennett, *German Rearmament and the West, 1932–1933* (Princeton, 1979), which covers a more extended period than the title indicates.

95   Taylor, *Origins*, p. 50.

96   ibid., p. 49.

97   Among English-language works dealing with reparations with varying emphases, accuracy and intelligibility, are: Maier, *Recasting Bourgeois Europe*; Schuker, *French Predominance;* Rupieper, *The Cuno Government*; Marc Trachtenberg, *Reparation in World Politics* (New York, 1980); Dan P. Silverman, *Reconstructing Europe after the Great War* (Cambridge, Mass., 1982); and Gerald D. Feldman, *Iron and Steel in the German Inflation, 1916–1923* (Princeton, 1977). See also the debate in *Journal of Modern History*, vol. 51 (March 1979); Marks, "The myths of reparations"; and Schuker, "American 'Reparations' to Germany".

98   Sally Marks, "Reparations reconsidered: a rejoinder", *Central European History*, vol. 5 (December 1972), p. 360.

99   The 50 milliard was composed of A Bonds (representing the 12 milliard unpaid balance on what Germany was supposed to have paid by 1 May 1921) and B Bonds. The nebulous C Bonds constituted the remainder of the 132 milliard ostensible figure, subject to arithmetic adjustments. One or two historians, concentrating only on technicalities and dismissing political and emotional factors as well as the considerable inducements written into the London Schedule itself to render the C Bonds uncollectable, have argued that some or all of them could have been issued and paid.

100 See the debate in *Journal of Modern History*, vol. 51 (March 1979). Beyond this, little has been written about the emerging historiography of the 1920s except for Jon Jacobson's two review articles, both dealing substantially with reparations, "Strategies of French foreign policy after World War I", *Journal of Modern History*, vol. 55 (June 1983), pp. 78–95, and "Is there a new international history of the 1920s", *American Historical Review*, vol. 88 (June 1983), pp. 617–46. In addition, Charles S. Maier, "Marking time: the historiography of international relations", pp. 355–87, in Michael Kammen (ed.), *The Past Before Us* (Ithaca, 1980), surveys some of the literature although its chief emphasis is on aspects of American diplomacy.

101 Taylor, *Origins*, p. 32.

102 This view is subscribed to in varying degrees by Joel Blatt, Fink, Marks, Schuker, and Tractenberg.

103 Taylor, *Origins*, p. 61.

104 ibid., p. 32.

105 ibid., p. 48.

106 ibid., p. 60.

107 For the text, see *DBFP*, Second Series, Vol. 1, pp. 487–8.

108 ibid., Vol. 1, p. 502.

109 See Gerhard L. Weinberg, *The Foreign Policy of Hitler's Germany*, 2 vols (Chicago, 1970, 1980), Vol. 1, pp. 13–14.
110 *Hitler's Secret Book* (New York, 1961), pp. 139, 145.
111 ibid., pp. 144–5; Gerhard Weinberg, "Friedenspropaganda und Kriegsvorbereitung", in Wolfgang Treue and Jürgen Schmädeke (eds), *Deutschland 1933* (Berlin, 1984), pp. 121–2.
112 Taylor, *Origins*, p. 23.
113 ibid., p. 70. See also p. 71.
114 Gerhard L. Weinberg, *World in the Balance* (Hanover, 1981), pp. 76, 81–4, 89–90, and "Die Deutsche Politik gegenüber den Vereinigten Staaten im Jahr 1941", in Jürgen Rohwer and Eberhard Jäckel (eds), *Kriegswende, Dezember 1941* (Frankfurt-am-Main, 1984), pp. 73–9.
115 Taylor, *Origins*, p. 267.

2

The End of Versailles

STEPHEN A. SCHUKER

When did the Versailles system break down? A. J. P. Taylor never quite makes up his mind in *The Origins of the Second World War*. He devotes almost a third of his book to charting the successive stages in the disintegration of the peace settlement over the course of fifteen years. But he attaches at most secondary importance to these epiphenomena. He approaches the subject on the assumption that the Versailles treaty "lacked moral validity from the start".[1]

That does not necessarily reflect his own judgment, Taylor insists (not wholly convincingly). It represents rather the view of the Germans and the many people in the Allied countries who came to sympathize with them.[2] The essence of the matter lay in the balance of demography and economic resources. These criteria indicated that Germany remained potentially by far the greatest power on the European continent after 1919; indeed the disappearance of Austria–Hungary, the withdrawal of Russia from international affairs, and the exhaustion of France and Italy rather worsened the disparity compared with relative strengths before the war. All Germans, Taylor notes, meant to shake off some part of the peace treaty as soon as it proved convenient to do so. They differed at most over timing.[3] The conclusion seems to follow with disarming simplicity. The treaty was doomed from the moment that the Allies agreed to make it with a united Germany – with the great unified state created by Bismarck. "Given a great Germany . . . the only question was whether the settlement would be revised, and Germany become again the greatest Power in Europe, peacefully or by war."[4]

Was the course of events then foreordained once the Allies had failed to march on Berlin in 1918 and to impose a dictated peace? Is Taylor not forgetting the caveat of the distinguished medievalist F. W. Maitland – which he quotes elsewhere to telling effect – that historians should avoid "after-mindedness" and remember that "events now long in the past were once in the future"?[5] Taylor, however, is not so easily pinned down. In 1919 the danger lay "in a hypothetical future; and who could tell what the future would hold?" Out-of-office Frenchmen might peddle separatism by the back door. "High-flying historians" might lament that the work of Bismarck remained intact. Yet after every great war alarmists had feared that the defeated power would strike again. It did so rarely, or half-heartedly.[6]

Here is one example, among many, of the quintessential Taylor method. He rivets one's attention with an extraordinary claim, and then qualifies it, or contradicts it, before objections are raised. Like a bantam-weight boxer, ever nimble on his toes, he lands a darting blow here, executes a clever feint there, and dances away to the next subject before the reader knows what has happened. He stands as the master of history presented as a seamless web of aphorisms: "Everything about Fascism was a fraud." "The greatest masters of statecraft are those who do not know what they are doing."[7] Does it not seem churlish to ask for proof or to inquire about documentation? Usually diplomatic historians rely on the inductive method. They are fussy, even obsessive, about sources. But other ways exist of apprehending reality. "One should absorb the color of life", Oscar Wilde once remarked, "but one should never remember its details. Details are always vulgar."

As a matter of fact, Taylor offers no footnotes for his interpretation of events before 1932. He provides but a handful for the period before 1935. Perhaps this does not matter much. He aims in his first chapters principally to set the stage for his discussion of Hitler's motives and of the proximate origins of the Second World War. And those are the subjects too with which his critics have exclusively concerned themselves. Not a single contributor to the collections edited by E. M. Robertson and William Roger Louis deals at any length with Taylor's analysis of European diplomacy before Hitler's assumption of power.[8] Yet Taylor evidently accords considerable significance to what happened earlier. This emerges by implication from the "Second Thoughts" that he prepared for the 1963 reissue of his work. "My book has really little to do with Hitler," he protests. "The vital question, it seems to me, concerns Great Britain and France." If Germany naturally sought to become a great power again, " 'why did the victors not resist her'?"[9]

Clearly, this formulation suggests the importance of an

inquiry into the shift in the power balance that began in the first years after the Versailles treaty came into force. When Taylor published *The Origins of the Second World War* in 1961, however, historians had available to them hardly any reliable data about policy formulation in the 1920s. Even for the 1930s, Taylor found little enough to go on – mainly the published volumes of British and German diplomatic documents, supplemented by statesmen's memoirs. The "extraordinary paucity" of original records, he concedes in his own memoirs with as much frankness as grace, "makes my book a period piece of limited value".[10] For the 1920s the situation then appeared even more discouraging. Only the defeated Germans had been forced to open their archives. Elsewhere (except in the United States) the "fifty-year-rule" still held sway. Moreover, given the intense public interest in the immediate causes of the latest world catastrophe, European governments had relegated publication of official documentary collections on the 1920s to a lower and distant priority. Taylor had perforce to rely for the early period on secondary accounts – and his bibliography suggests that most of these were general surveys not informed by primary research. What could he do but to mediate the impressions garnered from these works through his own experience of the 1920s as a politically conscious young man?

By his own account, Taylor came from an unusual family of Nonconformist Lancashire cotton merchants. With a competence of £100,000 sterling, his father had retired from business to join the gas workers' union, deserted Liberalism for the Independent Labour Party, and for twenty years displayed his militancy on the local Trades and Labour Council, hoping to transform himself into an authentic working man. His mother, not to be outdone, progressed from anti-conscription agitation in the First World War to a romantic communism that did not exclude acting as a conduit for Soviet funds to the British Communist Party. Taylor himself was a seventeen–year-old fifth-former of decidedly progressive views at Bootham, the Quaker-run public school, when Poincaré occupied the Ruhr in 1923. He had become a Labour firebrand at Oxford who thrilled to the "revolutionary enthusiasm of the common people" in Russia by the time that the frock-coated representatives of the Western powers negotiated the Locarno agreements two years later. When Hitler took over the Reich chancellery in 1933, Taylor had already won local notoriety as the brilliant university lecturer who served as chief spokesman for the Manchester Anti-War Council.[11]

Of course, no one with Taylor's temperamental independence

and iconoclasm could remain in an intellectual straitjacket of any sort for long. Still, hardly anyone from this background in interwar Britain had a good word to say about the Versailles treaty. None would have defended the sanctity of international obligations or expostulated on the justice of reparations and war-debt payments. Few would have grasped the importance of a strong military establishment for Britain, let alone for France. Significantly, Taylor opposed rearmament by the National Government until the mid-1930s because he feared that Britain might take Hitler's side in a war against Russia. When his anti-Nazi sentiments overcame these scruples and he swung round on rearmament in 1936, he lapsed into political inactivity. To favor armament expenditure, whatever the circumstances, was an impossible position for a man of the left![12] The wonder is not that vestigial traces of interwar Labour views turn up in Taylor's treatment of the period. The marvel is that Taylor the mature historian has so far transcended the sentiments of his youthful milieu that he approaches objectivity at all.

Yet one must explain somehow a perceptible inconstancy in Taylor's interpretation of the 1920s. Can one speculate that this derives from the tension between Taylor's youthful recollections and his subsequent reflections as a historian? How else can the reader account for his disconcerting tendency to write on both sides of almost every issue? Let us examine, for example, Taylor's successive statements on the question with which we started – when and how the Versailles system broke down.

The German army had ceased to exist as a major fighting force after the war, Taylor tells us; no one had to worry about armed conflict with the Reich for years to come. Nevertheless, measures of coercion against Germany could not ultimately work. The decision whether to comply with the treaty remained in German hands.[13] At each confrontation from the 1918 armistice to the 1923 Ruhr occupation, it became more and more difficult for the Allies to threaten the application of force. Yet in fact by 1921 much of the peace treaty was being enforced.[14] Resentment against the treaty increased with every passing year, largely owing to reparations. On the other hand, appeasement began not with Neville Chamberlain, but with Lloyd George, who carried it through successfully. "Even reparations were constantly revised, and always downward, though no doubt the revision dragged out tiresomely long."[15] The Locarno treaties of 1925 ended the First World War and ushered in a period of "peace and hope". Indeed, the most popular cry in

Germany, as late as 1929, was "No More War". All the same, appeasement was not achieved, and when the occupying forces left the Rhineland in 1930, German resentment bulked larger than ever.[16]

The conflict between France and Germany seemed bound to continue, Taylor asserts further, so long as the illusion persisted that Europe remained the center of the world. On the other hand, it appeared that "treaty revision would go on gradually, almost imperceptibly, and that a new European system would emerge without anyone noticing the exact moment when the watershed was crossed".[17] The French had "never possessed" a mobile army capable of independent offensive action against the Reich in case of need. Consequently, French foreign policy stood in fundamental contradiction with French strategy. The system of security against Germany, however, as devised in the Versailles treaty, remained intact in 1929.[18]

More of this follows. No reason existed why the Depression should have increased international tension. In depressions most nations turn away from foreign affairs. The Brüning government in Germany, however, had to seek successes abroad in order to counterbalance the hardships imposed by deflation at home, and the Japanese had a good case also for invading Manchuria because their trading interests had suffered devastation there. "Men who are well off forget their grievances; in adversity they have nothing else to think about."[19] No real negotiations were possible at the 1932–3 disarmament conference because the German government needed a "sensational success". Yet men "rightly feared" the collapse of Germany, not German strength, in the midst of the Depression; and actually the Reich remained "virtually disarmed" even when Hitler came to power. On the other hand, one could not assure security for France and equality of status for Germany at the same time. By insisting upon this fact, nevertheless, the French "fired the starting pistol for the arms race", though characteristically they failed to run it.[20] As for Hitler himself, finally, he merely took over the policies of his predecessors and indeed of virtually all Germans. In principle and doctrine, he seemed "no more wicked and unscrupulous than many other contemporary statesmen". If truth be told, he did not concern himself much with foreign affairs initially, but spent the bulk of his time at Berchtesgaden "dreaming in his old feckless way". Still, with little talent on the showing here other than his gift for patience, he somehow within two years had broken the Franco-Polish alliance, foiled an

"Eastern Locarno", made a first move to subvert Austria, reclaimed the Saar, and reintroduced conscription. The artificial security system of Versailles was dead. But never mind these achievements! They merely proved that "a system cannot be a substitute for action, but can only provide opportunities for it".[21]

Paradox after paradox – the mind reels as Taylor presses onward with his pellucid prose and opaque meaning. Yet Taylor reports in his memoirs that Boswell's *Life of Dr. Johnson* became his favorite book in public school and has remained so ever since.[22] Did he never, when fashioning his epigrams, recall the advice that Johnson ascribes to a college tutor: "Read over your compositions, and wherever you meet with a passage which you think is particularly fine, strike it out"? Of course, we would have been the poorer for it if he had done so. All the same, the best-advised passengers on this historical journey will take pleasure in the gems along the path and suspend belief about the destination.

Enough has been said of the artifices by which Taylor contrives to sustain the reader's interest. Let us pass to an analysis of his fundamental views – in so far as we can distinguish them from the pyrotechnic accompaniments. Taylor rightly points out that the history of Europe between the wars revolved around the German problem.[23] Italian irredentism, Hungarian revisionism, the territorial squabbles among the Habsburg successor states, and the continuing colonial rivalries of the Entente powers grew from local conflicts into serious threats to peace only when they impinged on the overriding issue – how to reconcile Germany to Versailles. Historians since Taylor have questioned his assumption that Soviet Russia abandoned its efforts to undermine other governments after 1920. They have further explored the raw competitive underside to Anglo-American co-operation, particularly outside Europe; and they have emphasized the difficulties caused by the rapid change in the Far Eastern balance of power.[24] Generally, however, they have confirmed Taylor's judgment that international relations on the European continent turned on the two conventional topics – reparations and security.

Taylor recognizes that reparations figured as the dominant problem in the first years after 1919. But he devotes limited space to this complicated issue – perhaps out of discretion. Lord Palmerston had joked of the nineteenth-century Schleswig-

Holstein dispute that only three men had ever understood it; and he, the only one who had not gone mad or died, had forgotten all about it.[25] Before the research of the last decade, reparations appeared to many as the Schleswig–Holstein question of the interwar period. Taylor demonstrably makes no pretence of joining the intitiates' circle; still, his instincts are right as often as they are wrong, and that rates as no mean accomplishment for a book published in 1961.

Taylor shrewdly concludes that Etienne Mantoux had the better of his controversy over reparations with John Maynard Keynes.[26] The reparations actually required from Germany – as distinguished from that country's legal liability – amounted to approximately 6 per cent of German national income under the 1921 London Schedule of Payments.[27] That would have represented an appreciable claim on German resources, roughly comparable to the burden imposed on some Western economies as a result of the explosion in oil prices during the 1970s. To transfer such a sum would have required genuine sacrifices. But it would not have constituted an insuperable burden for a nation resolved to limit domestic consumption sufficiently to meet the levy. It would not have reduced Germany, in the picturesque phrase that Taylor borrows from Keynes, to "a state of Asiatic poverty".[28] In fact, the London Schedule marked the abandonment of the unrealistic proposals bandied about by some of the British and French delegates at the Paris peace conference and adjustment of the bill to German capacity to pay.

Taylor does not deal specifically with the London Schedule. He outlines with only the barest of brush strokes the many disputatious conferences of 1920–2 at which the French endeavored to compel payment, the Germans sought to evade it, and the British twisted uneasily between the two, increasingly coming to favor concessions with the hope of reviving their export trade. But he correctly suggests what the archives have since confirmed: that Poincaré occupied the Ruhr as a last resort in 1923 in order to oblige Germany to meet its financial obligations, and not with a view to promoting the disintegration of the Reich.[29] He shows how France snatched defeat from the jaws of victory. Germany found itself obliged to abandon government-sponsored "passive resistance" in the Ruhr. France, however, could muster neither the financial strength nor the will to go it alone. Almost inevitably, fresh negotiations within an inter-allied framework led to a new reduction of the reparations bill. The moral seemed to be that the Allies could reach a stable accommodation with Germany only by engaging the latter's voluntary co-operation, and not through compulsion.[30]

Taylor does not traffic in economic statistics, but he perceptively observes that Germany emerged in the end as a net gainer through the financial transactions of the 1920s.[31] Subsequent calculations give emphasis to his analysis. The Dawes Plan of 1924 provided a four-year partial moratorium and reduced the projected reparations levy afterward to 3·3 per cent of national income. The Young Plan of 1929 marked a further limitation of the claim on German resources, effectively to 2·6 per cent. Moreover, the Reich never paid these sums in full. In 1932 the Lausanne conference cancelled reparations altogether. For the whole period 1919–31, Germany transferred to the Allies in cash and kind together an average of only 2·0 per cent of national income. At the same time, Germany experienced a windfall profit resulting from the devaluation of foreign-owned mark-denominated assets during the 1919–23 inflation. Then, after 1931, it defaulted on most private foreign investment. These items combined yielded a unilateral transfer equal to a startling 5·3 per cent of German national income for 1919–31. On balance, the United States and to a lesser extent the European Allies subsidized Germany during the Weimar era, and not the other way round.[32]

So far Taylor has gotten it right – as his hero Evelyn Waugh might say, "up to a point, sir!"[33] Characteristically, he then reverses field. The foreign subsidy of the German economy, he asserts, provided "little consolation to the German taxpayer, who was not at all the same person as the German borrower".[34] Hence the average German held the "more or less rational belief" that reparations pointed down the road to ruin.

The United States "complicated the problem", Taylor argues further, by insisting on repayment of Allied war debts. Thus Allied taxpayers obtained little relief from reparations because they saw the proceeds immediately transferred across the Atlantic. In addition, reparations fanned international suspicion and resentment all around. This happened in part because the French "cheated": some of them did not wish to be paid, and attempted to exploit the situation instead to keep troops in the Rhineland or ruin Germany forever. Yet ultimately reparations did almost as much damage to democracy in France, where they caused people to lose faith in the political leadership, as they did across the Rhine. More than any other issue, in sum, reparations "cleared the way for the Second World War". Economically, however, they produced but one effect after the various capital flows were balanced against each other: "to give employment to a large number of bookkeepers".[35] Here we have, in short compass, a distillation of every cliché that nourished self-righteous sentiment on the part of subscribers to the fashionable intellectual weeklies and readers of the *Manchester Guardian* in Britain between the wars. Each of the substantive claims, however, turns out upon further scrutiny to be seriously misleading.

The careful reader will observe here some gratuitous pulling of Uncle Sam's beard. Actually the American debt settlements of 1923–6 required no more than token payments during the first decade from the continental Allies, and the British could not reasonably complain about an annuity claiming a mere 0·8 per cent of their foreign investment portfolio. An examination of the magnitudes involved does not substantiate the common references to a circular flow of funds.[36]

But Taylor's misconceptions go beyond technical economics. He appears to have lost from sight the point of reparations in the first place – to repair damage wrought in a war for which Germany bore primary responsibility. He starts from the premise that both sides in the conflict "found it difficult to define their war aims", that both fought only for victory.[37] No one who had assimilated Hans Gatzke's findings in *Germany's Drive to the West* could have sustained that point of view even in 1961.[38] Studies published since then have rendered it wholly implausible. The discoveries of Fritz Fischer and his students, and the revelations from the diary of Chancellor Bethmann-Hollweg's assistant, Kurt Riezler, have underscored the almost megalomaniacal annexationism of the German leadership, civilian as well as military, from the "September Program" of 1914 down to the end of the war.[39] Scholars of Allied war aims have uncovered nothing comparable.[40] Taylor acknowledges this disparity in the "Second Thoughts" prepared for his 1963 edition. Indeed, with not atypical overstatement he now accuses Bethmann-Hollweg of nurturing more extreme aims than Hitler, because the former sought *Lebensraum* in the west as well as the east.[41] Unfortunately, Taylor gives no outward sign of thinking through the implications of the new evidence. If the nations of Europe had in 1914 blundered into war by mistake, a peace of reconciliation involving a sharing of financial burdens might have helped bind up the wounds. If, however, the elites of the new republican Germany inherited the territorial appetites of their Wilhelminian predecessors, such largesse would prove neither expedient nor wise.

At no point does Taylor state clearly the issue: that whether Germany paid reparations and how much it paid would largely determine the European balance of power in the 1920s. The costs of the most destructive conflict in history had already been incurred. Someone would have to pay for the treasure spent, the foreign investment lost, the land laid waste, the ships destroyed, and the men cut down on the battlefield at the start of their productive years. Someone would have to care for the maimed, the widowed, and the orphaned. War also spurs economic growth, of course. But in this case the greatest development had taken place in Asia and the Americas, and the burgeoning manufacturing capacity outside Europe would dislocate trade patterns and make recovery for the belligerents more rather than less difficult.[42]

At the peace conference European statesmen had maneuvered to induce the United States to subsidize victors and vanquished alike by cancelling war debts and purchasing reparations bonds on commercial markets. American officials, however, had declined to fall in with these schemes. Some Wall Street bankers acknowledged that their country's new-found creditor status imposed special responsibilities. But the United States remained remarkably self-sufficient economically (compared, for example, with the situation obtaining after the Second World War). Political leaders in Washington, mindful that their constituents had already spent $40 billion on the war effort, recognized from the spring of 1919 on that public sentiment would not tolerate disbursing any more.[43] Europeans had to face the question squarely: would the taxpayers, bondholders, savers, and consumers of Germany assume the main burden of reconstruction, or would their counterparts in France, Britain, and other Allied nations have to foot the bill?

Taylor explains with his habitual eloquence how reparations took on symbolic importance for Germans outraged by the punitive aspects of the peace.[44] If the German government won its test of wills with the Allies and undermined the reparations clauses of the Versailles treaty, it would assume a stronger moral position in its efforts to revise the territorial provisions of the European settlement. Taylor neglects to add, however, that reparations also involved the transfer of real resources, which assumed critical importance in the boom-and-bust cycle and the prolonged period of trade disruption that followed the war.

If France, most importantly, could obtain sufficient coal, coke, and capital on reparation account, it might hope to rebuild its devastated districts and to promote economic revival without overstraining the nation's rickety tax and financial system. In the generation before 1914 Germany had rapidly pulled ahead of France and Britain in industrial capacity. It had quadrupled its steelmaking capacity – the key to military power. Could France, having secured Lorraine minette ore and Saar coal through other Versailles treaty provisions, now deploy its reparation entitlement to make a comparable leap forward?[45]

Despite the deficient mechanisms in the Paris bureaucracy for shaping long-term economic policy, certain French officials perceived this challenge clearly. That is why Jacques Seydoux of the Foreign Ministry, for example, pressed so hard in the postwar years for reparations in kind and, far from trying to "ruin Germany", vainly sought to find a formula that would link the steel, coal, potash, and chemical industries of the two nations to their mutual advantage.[46]

Taylor evinces no demonstrable interest in such technical negotiations, possibly because he believes that in any case a united Germany would have come to dominate Europe again.[47] Admittedly, the prospects for any outcome other than this appeared slim from the beginning. France would have had to create an industrial infrastructure enabling it to sustain permanently the diplomatic position secured for the moment by a paper treaty. For that purpose reparations appeared indispensable, yet insufficient. France would also have had to maintain an unshakeable alliance with Britain. But the economic interests of the two erstwhile Allies diverged. If the United States refused to act as *deus ex machina* by providing loans to Germany, how could one reconcile these interests? The British suffered from their own form of "devastated areas". Two million unemployed queued disconsolately for the dole in the Midlands, on Clydeside, and in Wales. Once war passions cooled, Britain could neither tolerate the transfer of cash reparations large enough to reduce the German standard of living nor encourage deliveries in kind coupled with Franco-German industrial linkages: both prospects might further reduce the Central European market for British goods. British difficulties in fact derived as much from the wrong mix of industries, unprofessional management, and backward labor relations as they did from the state of world trade. But few discerned this at the time.[48] The Franco-British conflict over reparations steadily deepened, and, as it festered, all hope of forcing compliance with the treaty as a whole slipped away.

If Taylor were writing today, presumably he would make more of the connections between economics and political power. In the past generation, practitioners of diplomatic history have changed the face of the discipline by investigating questions of this sort. Today it is a commonplace to say that reparations determined the outcome of the struggle for power in Europe between France and Germany. The war-debt controversy similarly figured as a central element in the duel between Britain and the United States for dominance in world finance. But, for all his brilliance, Taylor approaches diplomacy the old-fashioned way. He therefore mentions the 1924 London conference only in passing. He focuses instead on the Locarno meeting fourteen months later as the turning point of the era between the wars.[49] Today, looking back, we see clearly that the London conference provided the first unmistakable augury of the demise of the Versailles system.[50]

At London, France agreed to evacuate the Ruhr without any significant quid pro quo. Germany might meet its reduced obligations under the Dawes Plan or successor schemes for a while. It would never subsequently pay reparations on a scale sufficient to change power relationships. And when it defaulted, France in effect pledged not to take unilateral action again. Moreover, the last chance slipped by to strike a deal on coal and steel before Germany recovered its tariff sovereignty and took advantage of its natural strengths to dominate European heavy industry. In addition, France conceded a heretofore disputed legal point with an important bearing on security. The Allies confirmed that, whether Germany had met its disarmament obligations or not, the Rhineland occupation clock had begun to run. The occupation henceforth constituted a wasting asset. French troops would have to withdraw by 1935 in any case. Why squander scarce military resources and exacerbate ill will by remaining until the final hour?

Taylor would have us believe that, after Germany had freely accepted the Locarno accords, the French could think of no logical justification for preserving reparations or perpetuating one-sided disarmament of the Reich.[51] Actually, few Frenchmen suffered from a bad conscience – that malady principally afflicted their friends across the English Channel. But, owing to financial weakness and national lassitude, they had already made the decisive concessions. When they fussed about arrangements for leaving the Cologne zone in 1926, fumed about minor conditions for terminating Allied military control in 1927,

and jockied tiresomely for reparations advantages before withdrawing the last skeletal divisions from the Rhineland in
1929–30, they knew that they were engaged in desperate rear-
guard actions.[52]

In discussing security problems of the 1920s Taylor offers his
habitual admixture of good sense and artful obfuscation. He
makes a surprisingly favorable evaluation of the Versailles territorial settlements. The new borders, even in eastern Europe,
rested in his judgment on the "principles of natural justice, as
then interpreted".[53] Germany only lost land, Taylor adds, to
which it held no entitlement on national grounds. With facile
insouciance he dismisses even the most bitterly voiced German
grievances: the Polish Corridor had a predominantly Slavic
population; the arrangements for railway communications
across that area to East Prussia seemed adequate; and the lost
colonies had proven a drain rather than a source of profit.[54]

Other historians do not on the whole confirm the claim that
the mass of Germans expressed indifference to an Austrian
Anschluss in 1919 or that they cared little about the fate of
German-speaking minorities in the Sudetenland and elsewhere (though undoubtedly German plenipotentiaries at the
peace conference had to rank their objectives and concentrate
their fire).[55] But ultimately it makes little difference how much
German resentment against the new boundaries originated in
1919 and how much developed later. No treaty enforces itself.
Certainly the Versailles treaty could not do so. The Congress of
Vienna a century earlier had reached a modicum of consensus by
appealing to the universally acknowledged principles of legitimacy and compensation, suitably diluted with the equally familiar values of convenience and hypocrisy. The world of 1919
comprised too many ideological divisions to hope for a similar
consensus. Only the application of superior force had won the
war. Only the threat of force – whether applied through a Wilsonian "concert of right" or through the cruder equilibration of the
balance of power – could keep the peace.

Taylor, however, bends all his ingenuity to showing why the
Allies could not maintain a preponderance of power on their
side. He deprecates security arrangements as "artificial"
expedients that "ran against the common sense of mankind".
He embraces, apparently as his own, the reasoning of the
(British) man in the street: "The war had been fought to settle
things. What was the good of it if now there had to be new

alliances, more armaments, greater international complexities than before the war started?"[56] One by one, Taylor dismisses every solution for maintaining the status quo. German disarmament could only work if the Germans chose to make it work. The Anglo-American guarantee of France, even if the American Senate had not tabled it without action, constituted no more than a long-term promise to liberate France after Germany had overrun it again. France erred in seeking a substitute for the prewar Russian alliance through arrangements with Poland and the Little Entente, since those states had backward and ill-equipped armies and would require assistance rather than provide it.[57] Some truth exists in these claims – although French planners understood their dilemma and the narrow range of possible solutions rather better than Taylor suggests. But does it follow that just a single option remained: to appease the Reich sufficiently to win the Germans over, and to allow German statesmen to set the diplomatic agenda and define the terms?[58]

Two possibilities that Taylor excludes from discussion also merit attention. He does not dwell on the fact that France had renounced separation of the Rhineland from Germany in return for the Anglo-American guarantee, nor explore whether the French government should have returned to an aggressive Rhineland policy – as some military men and local agents urged – in the absence of such a guarantee. He assumes, finally, that a British government with aspirations to enlarge the welfare state and resolved to defend the empire as well could make no meaningful "Continental commitment". The wish is clearly father to the thought. "It is easy to understand why the British felt distinct from the Powers of Europe", Taylor volunteers discreetly here, "and why they often wanted to withdraw from European politics."[59] In his subsequent biography of Lord Beaverbrook the hidden agenda emerges. He records his conviction that a policy of isolation, free of European alliances, figured as "the wisest course to follow in a world full of dangers" and seemed "also more honourable than to distribute guarantees which we could not fulfill".[60]

It is evident why Taylor ranks Gustav Stresemann, the foreign minister in the middle years of the Weimar Republic, as "a great German, even as a great European, statesman".[61] Stresemann sought to recover Danzig, the Polish Corridor, and Upper Silesia, to bring about *Anschluss*, and to protect ethnic Germans living outside the borders of the Reich. But he would go about this in a peaceful way, for the present generation, and leave the West alone. He would pose no threat to British interests.[62] Taylor waxes enthusiastic over the Locarno treaties because they reconciled, at least on paper, Franco-British friendship with France's eastern alliances.[63] We can now show more explicitly than Taylor did that the treaties were meant to open the way for territorial revision in the East. If France went to the assistance of its Polish ally, and Germany then attacked France, the British guarantee of the western frontiers would not apply. The British Cabinet expected the French, in consequence, to adopt a defensive military strategy and to limit their eastern commitments. The Poles and the Czechs would draw closer to the German economic orbit. Forces would be set in motion that would gradually lead to peaceful change and stabilize the continent.[64]

It is never easy, however, to manage peaceful change. British Foreign Office planners did not reckon with the increased urgency of German revisionism in the Depression, nor did they expect the Poles to ignore the relationships of power and to become ever more obdurate as time went on. All the same, the British government did not issue a blank check, in 1925 or later. Taylor does not stand on firm ground in drawing a direct comparison between Stresemann and Hitler, either when he argues that Hitler merely sought satellites and not territorial gains, or when he asserts in contradictory fashion that Hitler aspired to restore the great eastern conquests of Brest-Litovsk, but that many in the West accepted this as natural, even desirable.[65]

If Taylor had wished to strengthen his case for the continuity of Weimar and Nazi foreign policy, he would have done better to focus more attention on the years 1930–3. The Brüning, Papen, and Schleicher cabinets did seek more radical concessions in foreign policy than their predecessors, both to provide distraction from the pain of deflation and to head off the growing Nazi electoral menace. We now have more proof than Taylor did of the quantum leap in the *Reichswehr*'s military preparations in 1931–2.[66] One rubs one's eyes in disbelief at Taylor's portrayal of Arthur Henderson as a latter-day Austen Chamberlain, anxious to "reconcile disarmament and security" and to use disarmament as a "lever for increasing British commitments to France".[67] The Cabinet secretary, Sir Maurice Hankey, was nearer the mark when he noted in September 1931 that British pacifism and disarmament policy drew inspiration less from idealism than from realization of the country's exhaustion and economic weakness, and that this derived in turn from "our insistence on maintaining a much higher standard of living than our economic circumstances justify".[68]

Whatever the mix of motives, Great Britain, like the United States, supported "equality of rights" for Germany throughout the Geneva disarmament conference of 1932–3. They tried to persuade France to reduce its forces to a level that Germany was already planning to exceed. American leaders considered the balance of power immoral; British statesmen failed to perceive where the balance really lay. Taylor makes much of the slow pace of German rearmament in 1933–5 and speaks slightingly of the "false alarms" issued by Churchill and others.[69] One wishes he had coupled this with an analysis of unreadiness in the British and French armed forces over the same period and an explanation of how Depression-era budgetary constraints determined the glacial pace of improvement.[70] Most Englishmen, Taylor notes, believed in the early 1930s that "great armaments were themselves a cause of war".[71] Once they acted on that belief, the European structure erected at the Paris peace conference was bound to crumble. And crumble it did.

None of the newest objections made to *The Origins of the Second World War* – least of all those to the early chapters – will bother Taylor a whit. In reply to earlier criticism, he pleaded the simplest of motives. He sought to produce "a straightforward piece of hack diplomatic history".[72] He tried to write without thinking that he was English or a radical or a socialist. He took no delight, "impish or otherwise", in shocking readers; he just put down what seemed to him right without worrying whether it would appear orthodox or not. If inconsistencies turned up, they usually resulted from his having learned better afterward.[73] Doubtless these explanations represent much of the truth. The French Socialists used to remark about Aristide Briand, one recalls, that he was "so guileful one ought not to believe the opposite of what he says".[74] Yet elsewhere Taylor observes, half in jest, that we have left the era of Ranke behind; nowadays we read diplomatic history "for purposes of entertainment".[75] If the office of history is to amuse, then Taylor stands without peer. A quarter century after publication of *The Origins of the Second World War*, students still read the book avidly. No doubt they will continue to do so a quarter century hence, when the learned rebuttals of critics lie moldering on library shelves. Such scholarly longevity speaks for itself. André Gide, when asked whom he considered the greatest French poet, replied, "Victor Hugo, hélas." Taylor's sternest critics will scarcely improve the line.

NOTES

1 A. J. P. Taylor, *The Origins of the Second World War* (London, 1961), p. 28. Citations in this essay are to the latest American edition (New York: Atheneum, 1983), which uses arabic pagination as in the original, but employs roman pagination for the "Preface for the American Reader" (dating from 1966) and the 1963 Foreword, "Second Thoughts".
2 Taylor, *Origins*, p. xi.
3 ibid., pp. 24, 28.
4 ibid., p. 51.
5 See Taylor's reference in ibid., p. 234; Maitland on after-mindedness in H. M. Cam (ed.), *Selected Historical Essays of F. W. Maitland* (London, 1957), p. xix.
6 Taylor, *Origins*, pp. 23, 25.
7 ibid., pp. 56, 72.
8 E. M. Robertson (ed.), *The Origins of the Second World War: Historical Interpretations* (London, 1971); W. Roger Louis (ed.), *The Origins of the Second World War: A. J. P. Taylor and His Critics* (New York and London, 1972).
9 Taylor, *Origins*, p. xiv.
10 A. J. P. Taylor, *A Personal History* (New York, 1983), p. 233.
11 Taylor, *Personal History*, pp. 23–4.
12 ibid., pp. 125–8.
13 Taylor, *Origins*, pp. 42, 29.
14 ibid., pp. 28, 42.
15 ibid., pp. 42, 48.
16 ibid., pp. 55, 57, 59.
17 ibid., pp. 58, 59.
18 ibid., pp. 59–60, 61.
19 ibid., pp. 61, 62.
20 ibid., pp. 67, 74, 77.
21 ibid., pp. 68, 71–2, 86.
22 Taylor, *Personal History*, p. 60.
23 Taylor, *Origins*, p. 40.
24 On Russian policy, see the standard synthesis by A. B. Ulam, *Expansion and Coexistence* (New York, 1968); J. Braunthal, *History of the International*, Vol. 2, *1914–1943* (New York, 1967); and the meticulously compiled evidence on Soviet subversion in Germany in W. T. Angress, *Stillborn Revolution* (Princeton, 1963). But E. H. Carr, *Twilight of the Comintern, 1930–1935*, (New York, 1982) still portrays Soviet policy as defensive, and some younger scholars agree. See, for example, J. Haslam, *Soviet Foreign Policy, 1930–1933* (New York, 1983). Helpful works on co-operation and competition in Anglo-

American relations include C. Parrini, *Heir to Empire* (Pittsburgh, 1969); M. J. Hogan, *Informal Entente* (Columbia, Mo., 1977); M. G. Fry, *Illusion of Security* (Toronto, 1972); and S. V. O. Clarke, *Central Bank Cooperation, 1924–1931* (New York, 1967). K. Burk, *Britain, America and the Sinews of War, 1914–1918* (London, 1985) provides background. R. N. Kottman, *Reciprocity and the North Atlantic Triangle, 1932–1938* (Ithaca, 1968); C. A. MacDonald, *The United States, Britain and Appeasement, 1936–1939* (New York, 1981); and D. Reynolds, *The Creation of the Anglo-American Alliance, 1937–1941* (Chapel Hill, 1981), carry the story on. On the Far East, the best works include A. Iriye, *After Imperialism* (Cambridge, Mass., 1965); M. D. Kennedy, *The Estrangement of Great Britain and Japan, 1917–1935* (Manchester, 1969); I. H. Nish, *Alliance in Decline* (London, 1972); R. Dingman, *Power in the Pacific* (Chicago, 1976); and J. Neidpath, *The Singapore Naval Base and the Defence of Britain's Eastern Empire, 1919–1941* (Oxford, 1981).

25 Quoted in E. Eyck, *Bismarck and the German Empire* (London, 1958), pp. 77–8.

26 Taylor, *Origins*, p. 44; cf. J. M. Keynes, *The Economic Consequences of the Peace* (London, 1919), and the still less temperate *A Revision of the Treaty* (London, 1922), with E. Mantoux, *The Carthaginian Peace* (London, 1946; reprint Pittsburgh, 1965).

27 On the London Schedule, Taylor could have consulted, but apparently did not, E. Weill-Raynal, *Les Réparations allemandes et la France*, 3 vols (Paris, 1947), esp. Vol. 1, pp. 618–702. C. Holtfrerich, *Die deutsche Inflation 1914–1923* (Berlin 1980), p. 221, summarizes recent work reconstructing German national income for the period. S. Marks provides the best orientation to the reparation problem in "Reparations reconsidered", *Central European History*, vol. 2 (1969), pp. 356–65, and "The myths of reparations", *Central European History*, vol. 11 (1978), pp. 231–55.

28 Taylor, *Origins*, p. 44.

29 ibid., p. 50; cf. S. A. Schuker, *The End of French Predominance in Europe* (Chapel Hill, NC, 1976), pp. 20–6; J. Bariéty, *Les Relations franco-allemandes après la première guerre mondiale* (Paris, 1977), pp. 101–8; W. A. McDougall, *France's Rhineland Diplomacy* (Princeton, 1978), pp. 214–49. For the latest work summarizing the copious literature on passive resistance, see J.-C. Favez, *Le Reich devant l'occupation franco-belge de la Ruhr en 1923* (Geneva, 1969).

30 Taylor, *Origins*, pp. 44, 50; on negotiation of the Dawes Plan and French financial problems, see Schuker, *French Predominance*, pp. 31–231; and Bariéty, *Relations*, pp. 289–320.

31 Taylor, *Origins*, p. 44.

32 For economic analysis and statistics, see S. A. Schuker, *American "Reparations" to Germany* (Princeton, 1986).

33 Quoted in A. J. P. Taylor, *Beaverbrook* (London, 1972), p. 678n.

34 Taylor, *Origins*, p. 44. Exactly what Taylor means by this remains

puzzling, since the German states and municipalities – the greatest borrowers in 1925–8 – would otherwise have had to draw upon tax revenue, directly or indirectly, for the services they provided.

35 Taylor, *Origins*, pp. 27, 32, 44–5, 47. Keynes produced the original formulation: "The engravers' dies, the printers' forms are busier. But no one eats less, no one works more." See "The progress of the Dawes scheme", 11 September 1926, in E. Johnson (ed.), *The Collected Writings of John Maynard Keynes* (London, 1978), Vol. 18, pp. 277–82.

36 See B. D. Rhodes, "The United States and the war debt question, 1917–1934", PhD thesis, University of Colorado, 1965, and "Reassessing Uncle Shylock", *Journal of American History*, vol. 55 (1969), pp. 783–803; M. P. Leffler, "The origins of Republican war debt policy, 1921–1923", *Journal of American History*, vol. 59 (1972), pp. 585–601. On linkage of the debts with other issues, note R. A. Dayer, "The British war debts to the United States and the Anglo-Japanese Alliance, 1920–1923", *Pacific Historical Review*, vol. 45 (1976), pp. 569–95; E. Wandel, *Die Bedeutung der Vereinigten Staaten von Amerika für das deutsche Reparationsproblem 1924–1929* (Tübingen, 1971); and especially the magisterial work by W. Link, *Die amerikanische Stabilisierungspolitik in Deutschland 1921–1932* (Düsseldorf, 1970).

37 Taylor, *Origins*, pp. 19–20.

38 H. W. Gatzke, *Germany's Drive to the West* (Baltimore, 1950).

39 F. Fischer, *Griff nach der Weltmacht* (Düsseldorf, 1961), and *Krieg der Illusionen* (Düsseldorf, 1969) [trans. as *Germany's Aims in the First World War* and *War of Illusions* (New York, 1967 and 1975)]; I. Geiss, *Der polnische Grenzstreifen 1914–1918* (Lübeck and Hamburg, 1960); K. Riezler, *Tagebücher, Aufsätze, Dokumente*, (ed.) K. D. Erdmann (Göttingen, 1972). For a spirited attack on the *Sonderweg* thesis, however, see D. Calleo, *The German Problem Reconsidered* (Cambridge, 1978).

40 Standard works in this still growing field include V. H. Rothwell, *British War Aims and Peace Diplomacy, 1914–1918* (Oxford, 1971); D. Stevenson, *French War Aims against Germany, 1914–1919* (Oxford, 1982); M. Palo, "The diplomacy of Belgian war aims during the First World War", PhD thesis, University of Illinois, 1977; S. Marks, *Innocent Abroad* (Chapel Hill, NC, 1981), pp. 5–102. On the earlier period, see also D. C. B. Lieven, *Russia and the Origins of the First World War* (London, 1983); and J. F. V. Keiger, *France and the Origins of the First World War* (London, 1983).

41 Taylor, *Origins*, p. xxv. Such a comparison appears unduly harsh in light of the appreciation by K. H. Jarausch, *The Enigmatic Chancellor* (New Haven, 1973).

42 D. H. Aldcroft, *From Versailles to Wall Street, 1919–1929* (Berkeley, 1977), pp. 11–77. For reflections on war as a stimulus to technological change and growth, see also A. S. Milward, *War, Economy and Society, 1939–1945* (Berkeley, 1977), pp. 1–17.

43   M. Leffler, *The Elusive Quest* (Chapel Hill, NC, 1979), pp. 3–39; D. Artaud, *La Question des dettes interalliées et la reconstruction de l'Europe, 1917–1929*, 2 vols (Lille, 1978), Vol. 1, pp. 66–324; F. Costigliola, *Awkward Dominion* (Ithaca, 1985).

44   Taylor, *Origins*, pp. 44–5.

45   J. Bariéty, "Das Zustandekommen der Internationalen Rohstahlgemeinschaft als Alternative zum misslungenen 'Schwerindustriellen Projekt' des Versailler Vertrages", in H. Mommsen, D. Petzina, and B. Weisbrod (eds.), *Industrielles System und politische Entwicklung in der Weimarer Republik* (Düsseldorf, 1974), pp. 552–68; "Le Rôle de la minette dans la sidérurgie allemande et la restructuration de la sidérurgie allemande après le traité de Versailles", in *Centre de Recherches Relations Internationales de l'Université de Metz,* vol. 3 (1975), pp. 233–77; S. A. Schuker, "Frankreich und die Weimarer Republik", in M. Stürmer (ed.), *Die Weimarer Republik* (Königstein, Ts., 1980) pp. 93–112.

46   G. Soutou has written numerous articles on this subject, among them "Problèmes concernant le rétablissment des relations économiques franco-allemandes après la première guerre mondiale", *Francia*, vol. 2 (1974), pp. 580–96; and "Die deutschen Reparationen und das Seydoux-Projekt 1920–21", in *Vierteljahrshefte für Zeitgeschichte*, vol. 23 (1975), pp. 237–70. See also P. Krüger, *Deutschland und die Reparationen 1918/19* (Stuttgart, 1973), pp. 134–7; and M. Trachtenberg, *Reparation in World Politics* (New York, 1980), pp. 155–91.

47   Taylor would have had available to him only the excessively technical treatment of reparations in kind by Weill-Raynal, *Réparations allemandes*, Vol. 1, pp. 368–592. Documentation on the political significance of the subject became available only subsequently.

48   For a helpful introduction to this now vast field, see S. Pollard, *The Development of the British Economy, 1914–1967* (London, 1969); also N. K. Buxton and D. H. Aldcroft (eds.), *British Industry between the Wars* (London, 1979). On the process of recognizing the structural problems, S. Howson and D. Winch, *The Economic Advisory Council, 1930–1939* (Cambridge, 1977), proves suggestive.

49   Taylor, *Origins*, pp. 53–4.

50   Schuker, *French Predominance*, pp. 295–382; Bariéty, *Relations*, pp. 475–747. For the subsequent negotiations on trade and economic issues, 1925–7, see also K.-H. Pohl, *Weimars Wirtschaft und die Aussenpolitik der Republik 1924–1926* (Düsseldorf, 1979); B. Weisbrod, *Schwerindustrie in der Weimarer Republik* (Wuppertal, 1978); and the insightful C. S. Maier, *Recasting Bourgeois Europe* (Princeton, 1975), pp. 516–45.

51   Taylor, *Origins*, p. 58.

52   The basic work on the whole period remains J. Jacobson, *Locarno Diplomacy: Germany and the West, 1925–1929* (Princeton, 1972). New material has appeared in C. A. Wurm, *Die französische Sicherheitspoli-*

tik in der Phase der Umorientierung 1924–1926 (Frankfurt, 1979). On military aspects, see M. Salewski, *Entwaffnung und Militärkontrolle in Deutschland, 1919–1927* (Munich, 1966); and J. M. Hughes, *To the Maginot Line* (Cambridge, Mass., 1971). Many of the essays in G. Schmidt (ed.), *Konstellationen internationaler Politik 1924–1932* (Bochum, 1983), also address these questions.

53   Taylor, *Origins*, p. 26.
54   ibid., p. 47.
55   Given the confusion in Germany during 1918–19 and the illusions of German statesmen about what was achievable at the peace conference, it is not surprising that scholars have not yet reached a consensus on the relative importance of these objectives. K. Schwabe provides the most reliable general overview in *Deutsche Revolution und Wilson-Frieden* (Düsseldorf, 1971), revised version as *Woodrow Wilson, Revolutionary Germany, and Peacemaking, 1918–1919* (Chapel Hill, NC, 1985). For public opinion throughout the subsequent period, see C. Höltje, *Die Weimarer Republik und das Ostlocarno-Problem 1919–1934* (Würzburg, 1958); and E. Hölzle (ed.), *Die deutschen Ostgebiete zur Zeit der Weimarer Republik* (Cologne, 1966). C. M. Kimmich, *The Free City* (New Haven, 1968) covers Danzig; F. G. Campbell, *Confrontation in Central Europe* (Chicago, 1975), and R. Jaworski, *Vorposten oder Minderheit?* (Stuttgart, 1977), deal with the German minority in Czechoslovakia from different points of view. N. Krekeler, *Revisionsanspruch und geheime Ostpolitik der Weimarer Republik* (Stuttgart, 1973), covers assistance to minorities in Poland; K.-H. Grundmann, *Deutschtumpolitik zur Zeit der Weimarer Republik* (Hanover, 1977), treats the Baltic. One cannot even speak with categorical assurance about policy toward Austria: see S. Suval, *The Anschluss Question in the Weimar Era* (Baltimore, 1974), pp. 3–20; and A. D. Low, *The Anschluss Movement 1918–1919 and the Paris Peace Conference* (Philadelphia, 1974).
56   Taylor, *Origins*, pp. 27–8.
57   ibid., pp. 31–9. On the Anglo-American guarantee, see L. Yates, *The United States and French Security, 1917–1921* (New York, 1957). The fundamental book on the eastern alliances, P. Wandycz, *France and Her Eastern Allies, 1919–1925* (Minneapolis, 1962), emphasizes the importance of the Polish and Czech connections. But numerous recent articles in *Relations internationales*, the *Revue d'histoire de la deuxième guerre mondiale* and other journals have pointed to the frustrations experienced by the French in training armies or trying to turn a profit on their investments in eastern Europe. P.-E. Tournoux, *Défense des frontières* (Paris, 1960), examines the successive strategic plans of the French army and confirms what Taylor suspected – that they became steadily more defensive in the 1920s.
58   See J. M. King, *Foch versus Clemenceau* (Cambridge, Mass., 1960); and McDougall, *Rhineland Diplomacy*. There exists a large literature, much of it contentious in tone, evaluating the seriousness with

which the French viewed this option at various points. See K. D.
Erdmann, *Adenauer in der Rheinlandpolitik nach dem Ersten Weltkrieg*
(Stuttgart, 1966), still the most solid account; E. Bischof, *Rheinischer
Separatismus 1918–1924* (Bern, 1969); Centre de Recherches Rela-
tions Internationales de l'Université de Metz, *Problèmes de la Rhé-
nanie 1919–1930/Die Rheinfrage nach dem Ersten Weltkrieg* (Metz, 1975);
G. Steinmeyer, *Die Grundlagen der französischen Rheinlandpolitik
1917–1919* (Stuttgart, 1979); and H. Köhler, *Novemberrevolution und
Frankreich* (Düsseldorf, 1980).

59 Taylor, *Origins*, p. 41. For a survey of the subject from a broad
perspective, see M. Howard, *The Continental Commitment* (London,
1972).

60 Taylor, *Beaverbrook*, p. xiii.

61 Taylor, *Origins*, p. 51.

62 For useful discussions of Stresemann's aims, as set out in his 7
September 1925 letter to Crown Prince Wilhelm, see Hans Gatzke,
Stresemann and the Rearmament of Germany (Baltimore, 1954); and
Gaines Post, *The Civil-Military Fabric of Weimar Foreign Policy* (Prince-
ton, 1973). W. Michalka and M. M. Lee (eds.), *Gustav Stresemann*
(Darmstadt, 1982), group twenty essays by leading specialists who
over the past quarter century have evaluated various aspects of
Stresemann's policies.

63 Taylor, *Origins*, p. 54.

64 For the explicit formulations by Cabinet members and by the
Foreign Office legal adviser, see Schuker, *French Predominance*,
pp. 389–90; note also the discussion in J. Jacobson, *Locarno Diplomacy*, pp. 12–44; and S. E. Crowe, "Sir Eyre Crowe and the Locarno
pact", *English Historical Review*, vol. 87 (1972), pp. 49–74.

65 Taylor, *Origins*, pp. 70, 80. On the growing rigidity of Polish policy,
see R. Debicki, *The Foreign Policy of Poland, 1919–1939* (New York,
1962); J. Korbel, *Poland between East and West* (Princeton, 1963); and
L. Radice, *Prelude to Appeasement: East European Central Diplomacy in the
Early 1930s* (Boulder, 1981). On French frustration with the Poles,
see the review article by H. Rollet, "Deux mythes des relations
franco-polonaises entre les deux guerres", *Revue d'histoire diplomatique*
(1982), pp. 225–48. G. Weinberg, *The Foreign Policy of Hitler's
Germany: Diplomatic Revolution in Europe, 1933–36* (Chicago, 1970),
esp. pp. 1–24, puts to rest in elegant fashion the notion of Hitler as
a traditional diplomat. Neither J.-B. Duroselle, *La Décadence
1932–1939* (Paris, 1979), nor any of the monographs on which he
based his synthesis, offer support for Taylor's quixotic notion that
"most" Frenchmen came to favor German dominance of Russia on
the model of the 1918 Brest-Litvosk treaty.

66 On foreign and military policy of the Reich in 1931–2, see particularly E. W. Bennett, *Germany and the Diplomacy of the Financial Crisis,
1931* (Cambridge, Mass., 1962), and *German Rearmament and the West,
1932–1933* (Princeton, 1979). The seriousness of German rearma-

ment in these years remains disputed. Much depends whether one examines industrial mobilization or immediate readiness, and short- or long-term planning. G. Meinck, *Hitler und die deutsche Aufrüstung, 1933–1937* (Wiesbaden, 1959), minimizes earlier efforts under Schleicher; M. Geyer, "Das Zweite Rüstungsprogramm (1930–1934)", *Militärgeschichtliche Mitteilungen* Vol. 16 (1975), pp. 125–72, and *Aufrüstung oder Sicherheit: Die Reichswehr in der Krise der Machtpolitik 1924–1936* (Wiesbaden, 1980), esp. pp. 237–362, emphasizes elements of continuity. Note also E. W. Hansen, *Reichswehr und Industrie* (Boppard am Rhein, 1981), which explores industrial rearmament; and T. Vogelsang, *Reichswehr, Staat und NSDAP* (Stuttgart, 1962), which concentrates on political questions. G. Schulz's introduction to I. Maurer and U. Wengst (eds.), *Politik und Wirtschaft in der Krise: Quellen zur Ära Brüning*, 2 vols (Düsseldorf, 1980), Vol. 1, pp. ix–civ, reviews the growing literature on Brüning's foreign economic policy.

67   The latest findings shed a less unkindly light on Prime Minister Ramsay MacDonald than they do on Henderson, although there is ample discredit to go around. See D. Carlton, *MacDonald versus Henderson: The Foreign Policy of the Second Labour Government* (London, 1970) and D. Marquand, *Ramsay MacDonald* (London, 1977).

68   S. Roskill, *Hankey: Man of Secrets*, Vol. 2, *1919–1931* (London, 1972), pp. 544–5.

69   Taylor, *Origins*, p. 75. The debate over the pace of German rearmament before 1936 still continues. The latest entry is the semi-official history, W. Deist, M. Messerschmidt, H.-E. Volkmann, and W. Wette, *Das Deutsche Reich und der Zweite Weltkrieg*, vol. 1, *Ursachen und Voraussetzungen der deutschen Kriegspolitik* (Stuttgart, 1979). On the difficulties of using nominal figures to evaluate German offensive strength in the air, see R. J. Overy's suggestive "German air strength, 1933 to 1939", *Historical Journal*, Vol. 27 (1984) pp. 465–71.

70   For Britain, see N. H. Gibbs, *Grand Strategy*, Vol. 1 (London, 1976); B. Bond, *British Military Policy between the Two World Wars* (Oxford, 1980), esp. pp. 161–214; G. C. Peden, *British Rearmament and the Treasury, 1932–1939* (Edinburgh, 1979); and R. P. Shay, *British Rearmament in the Thirties* Princeton, 1977). For France, see M. Vaisse, *Sécurité d'abord* (Paris, 1981), esp. pp. 597–615; and R. J. Young, *In Command of France* (Cambridge, Mass., 1978), pp. 13–75.

71   Taylor, *Origins*, p. 64. For a notable example of the pro-disarmament mentality of the era, see P. Noel-Baker, *The First World Disarmament Conference, 1932–1933, and Why It Failed* (New York, 1979). M. Ceadel, *Pacifism in Britain, 1914–1945* (Oxford, 1980), is also suggestive.

72   Taylor, *Personal History*, p. 234.

73   Taylor to E. B. Segal, 21 November 1964, in Louis, *Origins*, pp. 26–7.

74   Quoted in D. B. Goldey, "The disintegration of the *Cartel des*

Gauches and the politics of French government finance, 1924–1928", D.Phil. thesis, Oxford University, 1961, p. 110.
75 Cited by E. B. Segal in Louis, *Origins*, p. 14.

3

Switching Partners:
Italy in A. J. P. Taylor's
Origins of the
Second World War

ALAN CASSELS

The second World war was, in large part, a repeat performance of the first. There were obvious differences. Italy fought on the opposite side, though she changed back again before the end.[1]

Given the reverberations that it has produced, A. J. P. Taylor's *The Origins of the Second World War* is a remarkably short book. Take for comparison the most cogent and up-to-date statement in the English language of Hitler's prime responsibility for 1939 – the view Taylor set out to refute. G. L. Weinberg's two volumes, *The Foreign Policy of Hitler's Germany*,[2] require 1,125 pages to cover the years 1933–9. Taylor's *Origins*, on the other hand, occupies fewer than 300 pages, and the period 1933–9 is subsumed in just over 200 pages of text. Such brevity demands concentration on the main German theme and short shrift for some other nation states. One of the latter is Italy which flits in and out of Taylor's account of diplomacy between the two world wars. Any consideration of his treatment of Italo-German, and above all fascist-Nazi, relations thus becomes as much a matter of what perforce has been left out as what has been said.

But there are perhaps other and subjective reasons why Italy does not figure so prominently in *Origins* as one might expect of an allegedly major European power. British historians, more than North American, have tended to be censorious of modern Italian public life. One thinks, for example, of Denis Mack Smith's acerbic reflections on Italy's politicians from the *risor-*

gimento to fascism.[3] This trait may derive from a classical educational upbringing which instills a deep appreciation of the Italian peninsula's cultural richness. Conversely, set against the golden ages of classical, Christian and Renaissance art, modern Italian civilization is cast into dark relief. In particular, the politics of united Italy appear a mixture of corruption and comicality, and not to be taken seriously. In Taylor's case he arrived late at a first-hand acquaintance with Italian artistic treasures because, as a young man, he refused to visit Italy under Benito Mussolini.[4] To an ingrained British disposition to slight Italian politics in general, then, must be added Taylor's visceral antifascism and his antipathy towards Italian nationalism. At the end of the Second World War, in fact, he was active in the campaign to wrest Trieste from Italy in Yugoslavia's favor.[5] Not surprisingly, in *Origins*, fascist Italy is written off in a fine burst of Taylorian denunciation:[6]

> Everything about Fascism was a fraud. The social peril from which it saved Italy was a fraud; the revolution by which it seized power was a fraud; the ability and policy of Mussolini were fraudulent. Fascist rule was corrupt, incompetent, empty; Mussolini himself a vain, blundering boaster without either ideas or aims.

The characterization of a strictly lightweight regime prepares the way for its relegation to the periphery of the interwar diplomatic story: "The most Italy could do was to hit the headlines, not raise an alarm".[7]

In accusing fascist Italy of lacking logic and purpose in its foreign policy Taylor echoes the taunt of Mussolini's contemporary critics – from Gaetano Salvemini to Carlo Sforza.[8] These critics seemed vindicated by the collapse of fascist diplomacy and fascism itself in 1943, and their opinion held sway immediately after the Second World War. For that matter, the portrayal of Mussolini as a bumbling opportunist and no more still goes on.[9] However, the past quarter century has also witnessed the quiet growth of other schools of thought that find the blanket dismissal of Mussolinian statecraft too easy and cavalier. These writings are not fascist apologiae, for to find some pattern in Mussolini's foreign policy is not to condone it nor to deny its final bankruptcy. Some of these revisionist views will be noticed later in this essay.[10]

Commentators of every stripe, though, are agreed on one thing: the verdict on fascist diplomacy must turn on its handling, or mishandling, of the German nationalist question. And the nature and scope of German nationalism under Hitler is, after all, the essence of Taylor's *Origins*. For the sake of convenience, Italo-German relations between the wars may be divided into three sections: (1) from the post-First World War settlement, which played its part in bringing Mussolini to power, up to Hitler's appointment as German chancellor in 1933; (2) from 1933 to the diplomatic revolution of 1936, which was marked by the enunciation of a Rome–Berlin axis; (3) from 1936 to the transformation of the Nazi-fascist *rapprochement* into a firm alliance, just in time for the outbreak of the Second World War.

Arguably, the single most potent factor in the foreign policy of united Italy was resentment: resentment at Italy's very unification by the efforts of foreign powers more than the exertions of Italians themselves; resentment at Italy's failure to win any glittering prizes in the colonial scramble, epitomized by the ignominious expulsion from Ethiopia after the battle of Adowa in 1896; and climactically, resentment at the refusal of the Paris peace conference to meet all of Italy's post-First World War demands.[11] Mussolini profited enormously from Italian umbrage at the so-called "mutilated victory" of 1918–19. On the one hand, the fascist leader offered strong, even authoritarian, government and social cohesion at home as a platform for a vigorous foreign policy. On the other, a number of Italians, including many in the diplomatic corps, believed that they could use the "wild" Mussolini to frighten the Western powers into concessions.[12] Taylor acutely observes that Italy felt emboldened to indulge in wrangling with its wartime partners because it was not directly confronted with the "German problem". The disappearance of the Habsburg empire provided "an illusory security".[13] Yet any drive for "parity" within the Allied camp entailed some challenge to the settlement of 1919 – in other words, "international revisionism". And revisionism inevitably suggested bringing Germany into play as a counterweight to Anglo-French hegemony. In light of Italian fascism's origins and promise to assuage injured national pride, this became a greater temptation once Mussolini reached office in 1922. Predictably, the first decade of the fascist era was punctuated by numerous Italian overtures to exploit German nationalism. Unremarked by Taylor, they proved harbingers of Italy's eventual alliance with Germany in the 1930s.

The year 1923 appeared to Mussolini a suitable moment to

approach Berlin. Germany and France were locked in the imbro-
glio of the Ruhr occupation, while the fascist Duce was resolved
to impose Italian sovereignty on Fiume in defiance of Yugoslavia
which presumably would turn to France for sympathy and
support. In September, Mussolini asked whether Germany
"would be in a position to immobilize part of the French army on
the Rhine". But the German chancellor, Gustav Stresemann,
was not interested in an open Italo-German alliance.[14] Fascist
Italy was thus left free to pursue an alternative and probably
preferred stratagem to enlist Germany in Italy's cause. This
consisted of cultivating the goodwill of German nationalists on
the right of the political spectrum in expectation that sooner or
later they would assume direction of German policy. Ties were
established with Germany's Nationalist party and its paramili-
tary arm, the *Stahlhelm*; German generals were approached and
wooed with secret supplies of arms for the *Reichswehr* in violation
of the Versailles treaty. The *sub rosa* nature of this activity dictated that it be conducted mainly through unofficial emissaries
rather than formal diplomats. Mussolini's man in Berlin, Major
Giuseppe Renzetti, was unquestionably more aware of all the
ramifications of the Duce's German policy than the Italian
ambassador himself.[15]

Included amongst the German right-wing nationalist groups
to receive Mussolini's favours was the Nazi party. Fascist Italian
money almost certainly flowed into the Nazi treasury. Mussolini
may have encouraged Adolf Hitler's Beer Hall *Putsch* in 1923,
and in its wake afforded a comfortable sanctuary for some of the
Nazi fugitives, most famously Hermann Goering.[16] Despite the
ignominious outcome of Hitler's first bid for power, fascist Italy
continued to pay close attention to the Nazi movement,[17] for on
two counts at least the Nazis stood out and apart from the
run-of-the-mill German nationalists. They called themselves
fascist, admittedly a nebulous term, but the presumptive imitation flattered Mussolini's thirsty ego.[18] Of much greater importance, however, was Hitler's unequivocal stand on the Alto
Adige. The Paris peace conference's delimitation of the Austro-
Italian border at the Brenner Pass had consigned more than
200,000 German-speaking former Habsburg subjects to the
mercy of an intolerant Italian state. Hence German nationalists,
not excepting Hitler, referred to the region south of the Brenner
by its German name of the South Tyrol. But whereas all other
pan-Germans put the South Tyrol/Alto Adige high on their
irredentist list for inclusion in a future Reich, Hitler consistently

repudiated any such ambition. In *Mein Kampf* he castigated imperial Germany's diplomacy before 1914 for allowing Italy to slip out of the Triple Alliance; in future an Italian alliance would have to be bought by abandoning the South Tyrol. This line of argument he reiterated publicly in speeches and in the *Völkischer Beobachter*, as well as privately to Mussolini.[19] Taylor points out that for Hitler, an Austrian pan-German, this was an unusually hard promise to make and to keep.[20]

The South Tyrol, of course, would remain safely Italian only as long as Austria continued independent and weak. *Mutatis mutandis*, Austrian union with Germany, *Anschluss*, posed an automatic threat to Italy's principal reward for the sacrifices of the First World War. Mussolini, as heir to Italian nationalist tradition, was obligated to impose a harsh program of Italianization on the South Tyrol, and to protest loudly whenever the *Anschluss* issue was raised. All of which, indeed, was comprehended in fascist Italy's public polity throughout the 1920s.[21] And yet, at the same time, there were hints of laxness. In 1925, Mussolini turned down an offer to include a guarantee of the Brenner frontier in the Locarno accords. Granted, he feared that *Anschluss* might turn out to be the price of a Brenner guarantee; even so, it was a hasty and questionable decision.[22] Then, after Locarno, the Duce stepped up his intrigues in the Danube valley to destroy the Little Entente and exclude French influence. These involved him with the Balkan revisionists, and no doubt instigated his notorious public endorsement of revisionism in 1928: "I have sometimes had occasion to point out that the treaties of peace are not eternal . . . Is there anyone who dares argue that the peace treaties . . . are a work of perfection?"[23] The statement could be made to justify *Anschluss* in principle if not in intent. Fascist Italy's Balkan designers had further repercussions. They widened the breach with France and, by extension, with the Western democracies at large (a fact obscured in the late 1920s by the Duce's cordial relationship with the British foreign secretary[24]). If Italian security on the Brenner was best served by collaboration with the West, then Mussolini's temptation of fate and *Anschluss* began in the 1920s.[25]

But there was one way Mussolini might have his cake and eat it too. Were Nazism to capture the German state, fascist Italy could continue to traffic in revisionism, theoretically secure in Hitler's disclaimer of interest in the South Tyrol. That the Duce had come to count on this contingency perhaps betokened a keen prescience of the course of German politics. Nor was this

policy a random fishing in troubled waters, as the old anti-
fascists used to allege; it possessed some inner coherence. On
the other hand, it was a policy which threatened to reduce room
for maneuver and left little scope for error. The international
situation of the 1920s let fascist Italy pursue revisionism without
foreclosing other options; this was the course which Dino
Grandi, Italian foreign minister from 1929 to 1932, recommended and was permitted to follow.[26] The next decade,
however, would tax more severely Mussolini's ability to maintain a balance and freedom of choice.

Hitler's advent to power in 1933 found Mussolini persisting in
his policy of moderate revisionism and "equidistance".[27] As one
who had anticipated the resurgence of a nationalistic Germany,
it was appropriate that the fascist Duce should be the first to
advance a plan to cope with the new exigency. His Four Power
Pact predicated embracing – and controlling – Nazi Germany
within a new concert of Europe (thereby undercutting the
League of Nations, a Mussolinian *bête noire*). As inducement,
some revision of the postwar settlement was proffered; parity in
armaments was openly touted, adjustment of Germany's frontiers hinted at. It was this degree of revisionism in the offing
which in the end killed Mussolini's proposal. "Nevertheless",
writes Taylor, "it remained the basis of Italian policy for some
years."[28] Debate remains alive, though, over exactly how long
Mussolini struggled to cling to the balanced approach embodied
in the Four Power Pact.

Of necessity, the touchstone of fascist-Nazi relations in the
1930s was the double-edged problem of Austrian integrity and
the sanctity of Italy's Brenner frontier. Whatever promise Hitler
might make about the South Tyrol, his program envisaged *Anschluss* in due course. For his part, Mussolini's concern to preserve
an independent Austria as a buffer state was translated into
patronage of Engelbert Dollfuss, the Austrian conservative and
quasi-fascist chancellor. The latter, with the Duce's encouragement, proceeded to attack the Austrian socialists, thus precipitating a state of tension in his country which caused Mussolini
and Hitler to meet in Venice in June 1934. But, in Taylor's
phraseology, "the meeting did not come up to expectations";
the two leaders' conflicting desiderata in Austria were hidden
amid the persiflage of mutual fascist propaganda.[29] The inherent misunderstanding sprang into the open the next month
when the Viennese Nazis murdered Dollfuss in a coup intended

to bring about *Anschluss*. Circumstantial evidence implicates Hitler more deeply in this Vienna *Putsch* than Taylor allows.[30] None the less, he backed down at once when Mussolini reacted violently to the point of threatening military intervention in Austria. Having preached the need for Italian friendship for fifteen years, the Führer remained true to his precept; the Austrian Nazis were left to stew in their own juice, thereby postponing *Anschluss*.[31]

Notwithstanding this success, Mussolini was shaken by the Dollfuss murder and its revelation of the fragility of Austrian independence. This was apparent in his gravitation back towards the Western powers, and specifically in fascist Italy's hospitality to the British and French government heads at Stresa on Nazi Germany's announcement of conscription. The rebuke administered to Hitler by this Stresa Front in April 1935 was in itself ineffectual, but Mussolini's signature on the communiqué ran counter to his tolerance of German rearmament in the Four Power Pact. Moreover, the anti-German gesture at Stresa was backed up by Franco-Italian staff talks.[32] The French premier, Pierre Laval, "flattered himself that Mussolini was now cured by the Austrian affair of any revisionist longings".[33] It required the Ethiopian crisis to set fascist Italy back on the road towards revisionism and liaison with Nazi Germany.

At first glance, Italy's assault on Ethiopia in 1935 seems a diversion from the critical Brenner frontier. In reality, however, the two issues were linked. With *Anschluss* temporarily on hold, the moment was propitious to implement military plans which had been in preparation since 1932.[34] The notion of a glorious imperial triumph achieved in time to resume guard on the Brenner before the Austrian question flared up again is not nearly so "nonsensical" as Taylor presumes.[35] Reports of internal dissension involving the military and other weaknesses in the Third Reich could not help but reassure Mussolini.[36] In addition, we now have ample indication that a conscious appraisal of the European balance was made in Rome, and the conclusion drawn that so favorable an opportunity to strike at Ethiopia might not soon reappear.[37] In the Balkans an Italo-Austrian-Hungarian bloc was still extant, while volatile Italo-Yugoslav relations had entered an unusually amicable phase. The two powers with colonial territory bordering Ethiopia, France and Britain, appeared propitiated by Mussolini's rupture with Hitler over Austria, and implied as much at Stresa.[38] Furthermore, Italy's military intelligence service purloined from the British embassy in Rome a copy of the Maffey report, an interdepartmental study made in London which concluded that Italy's conquest of Ethiopia would not jeopardize vital British interests.[39]

Besides the contemporary international situation, the internal state of Italy undoubtedly entered into Mussolini's calculations.[40] On this score, Taylor is again succinctly dismissive: "Revenge for Adowa was implicit in Fascist boasting; but no more urgent in 1935 than at any time since Mussolini came to power in 1922. Conditions in Italy did not demand a war. Fascism was not politically threatened; and economic circumstances in Italy favoured peace."[41] This, it must be said categorically, represents a grave misjudgment. In the first place, it assumes that Mussolini acted out of cold, rational calculation – always a dubious supposition where the Duce was concerned. Even more serious, it ignores totally the changing dynamics of Mussolini's regime. By the mid-1930s whatever social reforming zeal Italian fascism had initially possessed was exhausted. The Great Depression disclosed this clearly enough and, *pace* Taylor, did give rise to a fair amount of working-class unrest. "Fascismo-regime" was an institutionalized series of Mussolinian bargains with Italy's power structure.[42] Having completed such an accommodation and to reinject some energy into his flagging regime, Mussolini in 1931 embarked on a program of "reaching out to the people".[43] A paramount device to promote a greater degree of social mobilization than hitherto was the cult of Rome. Mass enthusiasm was to be kindled by the romantic vision of a third Roman empire succeeding those of the caesars and the popes.[44] In a sense, military imperialism supplanted social change as the *raison d'être* of Italian fascism. Alternatively, it has been argued that Mussolini, like Hitler, saw conquest abroad and revolution at home as complementary; only through war could the dead hand of the old guard be prised loose.[45] (It is worth recalling that Mussolini had advocated Italy's intervention in the First World War as a "revolutionary war".)[46] But in any event, empire was not a means to material profit, which was never there for the taking from Italy's "collection of deserts", but to national regeneration.

It is in this context that the Ethiopian crisis must be perceived. War and conquest were desirable in themselves to the Duce. Hence, his rude rebuff of Anthony Eden's attempt to buy him off with part of Ethiopia before the outbreak of hostilities.[47] During the Italo-Ethiopian war Mussolini was made a similar but more generous offer in the Hoare–Laval plan, the publication of whose terms in the French press aborted both the proposal and League of Nations sanctions.[48] Mussolini's opinion of the putative Hoare–Laval plan is still a matter for conjecture; evidence which has come to light since Taylor wrote calls into question his flat assertion that Mussolini "was ready to accept it".[49] The Duce's purposes were just as well served by victory on the battlefield.

The Ethiopian affair was the occasion for Mussolini's return to the German revisionist orbit, but not necessarily the cause.[50] For one thing, Hitler was decidedly hostile at the outset to the fascist adventure in East Africa because it promised to distract Italy from her appointed role in the Führer's grand scenario – the containment of France in the Mediterranean.[51] Italo-German relations thereupon lapsed into what Mussolini termed "a state of cold neutrality".[52] During the actual war German arms continued to reach Ethiopian forces; and although refusing to participate in League of Nations sanctions against Italy, Germany did not markedly step up strategic supplies to Italy to fill the sanctions gap.[53] In the meantime, Hitler was able to take advantage of the Ethiopian crisis for his own use; the damage done to collective security and to Italy's relationship with the Western democracies facilitated the remilitarization of the Rhineland in March 1936.[54] But all in all, the Führer's demeanour and conduct throughout the Italo-Ethiopian conflict did not furnish much to arouse the Duce's gratitude. At its close in May 1936, there was no objective reason why Mussolini should not have returned to the Stresa Front. The British and French by halfheartedly dragging the League of Nations into the fray had hardly impeded, and certainly not prevented, Italy's conquest of Ethiopia. Nothing "forced [Mussolini] on to the German side", as Taylor puts it. In fact, Taylor goes on to describe the unremitting clash of Italo-German interests, particularly in the Danube valley, which should have kept Rome and Berlin apart.[55]

The decision to keep up the quarrel with Britain and France, and to find solace in a détente with Nazi Germany, was Mussolini's own. To some extent, the Duce was driven by personal pique – his reflex to Britain's "mad sanctionist policy", and to barbed remarks about himself expressed in London government circles that reached him by means of security leaks.[56] Additionally, however, one must take into account his private conception of international politics. Taylor comments on Mussolini's vaunted "freedom from accepted standards",[57] but he does not specify the raw Social Darwinism that informed all his actions. Mussolini's simplistic division of the powers into "rising" and "declining" states seemed validated by the events of 1935–6. The feebleness of British and French opposition to his Ethiopian venture was at hand to testify to the "decadence" of these nations. In contrast stood Nazi Germany's "virility" in outfacing the First World War victors – over rearmament and in the Rhineland.[58] Fascists worshipped strength, and what Mussolini called a fascist foreign policy meant in effect siding with the strongest power. In an avowed effort to "fascisticize" Italian diplomacy, the Duce appointed his son-in-law, Galeazzo Ciano, foreign minister in June 1936. Needless to add, at this point Ciano was fervidly pro-German.[59]

The Spanish civil war, following on the heels of the Ethiopian affair, reaffirmed Mussolini's Social Darwinist predilections. The Anglo-French campaign to stave off foreign intervention was vacillating and ineffectual. Mussolini's determination to have his way in Spain, on the other hand, was firm. Indeed, his commitment to the anti-republican cause in Spain was much stronger than Taylor conveys, which throws doubt on the contention that Italy (and Germany) would have ceased to intervene if challenged forcefully by the democracies. (Limitation of Italian submarine activity around the Balearics after the establishment of an Anglo-French naval patrol is hardly sufficient evidence.)[60] The Spanish civil war also heightened the ideological temper of international affairs. Foreign intervention made it appear, however fallaciously, a contest between international communism and *universal fascismo*. Such oversimplification appealed to Mussolini's mentality and thus operated to draw the two fascist nations closer together. Appropriately, as Taylor correctly says, it was "ideological similarity" that was stressed when, on 1 November 1936, the Duce informed the world of a Rome–Berlin "axis around which may revolve all European states with a will for cooperation and peace".[61] No substantive agreement was signed at this juncture to lend weight to the Axis. A secret protocol for Italo-German collaboration, which Ciano had signed on a visit to Berlin at the end of October, was notable for its generalities. A joint stand was pledged against communism and the Popular Front governments in Madrid and Paris and also against the League of Nations; but the gist was rhetorical.[62] On the other hand, Mussolini, an arch propagandist himself, was ever prone to swallow whole these simple ideological statements. And it should be noted that it was the Italian Duce who devised the Rome–Berlin Axis, just as it was he who had made all the running for an Italo-German *rapprochement* throughout 1936. (By comparison, Hitler did very little to launch the Axis.) In his fashion, Mussolini was simply returning to the path he had followed until halted by the murder of Dollfuss, but now he risked being sucked into the quicksand of revisionism beyond hope of escape.

As usual, the most accurate barometer of the Rome–Berlin connection was to be found in the Austrian question. The distinct Italo-German frigidity of the early weeks of the Ethiopian war dissipated in proportion as the dispute between Mussolini and the Anglo-French combination escalated. Nevertheless, Hitler could scarcely have anticipated the bonus he was about to receive. In January 1936, right after the failure to reconcile fascist Italy with the Western powers by the Hoare–Laval plan, the German ambassador in Rome reported Mussolini as saying that "if Austria as a formally quite independent State were . . . in practice to become a German satellite, he would have no objection".[63] After initial scepticism Hitler seized on this hint to effect a change in Austria's status. A personal Hitlerian message of solidarity with Mussolini, conveyed by Hans Frank, laid the groundwork for a midsummer bargain.[64] In June Berlin promised diplomatic recognition of fascist Italy's Ethiopian empire; the next month, on 11 July, an Austro-German "gentleman's agreement" was concluded with Mussolini's blessing.[65] This latter declared Austria to be "a German state" whose foreign policy must henceforth accord with that of the Third Reich, while also providing for the entry of pro-*Anschluss* elements into the Viennese cabinet. Patently, the agreement compromised Austrian integrity; in Taylor's words, Mussolini now "was content with the shadow – the preservation of Austria's name".[66]

Anschluss was a logical consequence of the 1936 "gentleman's agreement". None the less, the Germans took care to confirm Italian benevolence. Joachim von Ribbentrop, soon to become Nazi foreign minister, visited Rome in November 1937 to sign a tripartite anti-Comintern pact and took the opportunity to raise the Austrian issue too. He was pleased to hear Mussolini confess that he "was tired of mounting guard over Austrian independence".[67] *Anschluss* was duly accomplished the following March. Regardless of the genesis of the actual *Anschluss* crisis,[68] Mussolini's desertion of Austria was foreordained; Hitler's effusive thanks ("Tell Mussolini I shall never forget this ... Never, never, never") were perhaps superfluous.[69] The Führer's gratitude found further outlet on a visit to Italy in May when he delighted his hosts by re-emphasizing the inviolability of Italy's Brenner frontier.[70] But none of this could disguise the measure of Mussolini's subservience to Hitler once Nazi troops were stationed on Italy's northern border. Symptomatic of the real situation was fascist Italy's sudden and official adoption of racism. The Manifesto of the Race of July 1938 was Mussolini's invention; it did not result from Hitlerian pressure, yet the imitation of the Nazi Nuremberg Laws was not lost on the mass of Italians.[71] Open mimicry of foreign models did not bode well for a regime that by now staked its popular repute on fulfillment of frustrated Italian nationalism. In Taylor's view, however, Mussolini's acceptance of *Anschluss* and Nazi tutelage – given the exhaustion of Italy's resources in Ethiopia and Spain – bespoke a "realist".[72] Other than reflecting the actual state of affairs in 1938, this connotes an oddly perverse judgment on the Duce whose policies for two years had worked steadily to put his country at such a disadvantage.

Far from being a realist the Duce, with his infinite capacity for self-delusion, apparently went on believing in the wake of *Anschluss* that he could still play an "equidistant" role amongst the powers.[73] After announcing the Rome–Berlin Axis in November 1936, Mussolini had swiftly come to a paper understanding with Britain to respect the Mediterranean status quo; now, after *Anschluss*, Rome and London at Easter 1938 reached another "gentleman's agreement" concerning the Mediterranean and the Red Sea.[74] Furthermore, in the Sudetan crisis Mussolini's support of Hitler's bellicosity, while verbally staunch, proved in the final analysis less than unflinching. On 28 September, he seconded the pleas addressed by Britain and the United States to Hitler to postpone mobilization and have recourse to an international conference.[75] Hitler's compliance permitted Mussolini to pose as peacemaker, but whether the Führer's eleventh-hour retreat from war was due to Mussolini's call remains moot. Taylor argues that his volte-face arose from Hungarian and Polish reluctance to join in an attack on Czechoslovakia.[76] Be that as it may, Mussolini's *arbiter mundi* image was burnished again at the Munich conference itself where an Italian proposal formed the basis of the actual Sudeten settlement. In truth, the scheme had been drafted in Berlin; the Duce was no more than the messenger.[77]

In other words, Mussolini's equidistance did not signify a median point between Nazi Germany and the Western powers. Rather, he sided more with the former in order to blackmail the latter into making colonial concessions. To this end, a staged demonstration in the Italian parliament in November 1938 raised a clarion demand for the French possessions of Tunisia, Corsica, Nice and Savoy. The British prime minister, Neville Chamberlain, was invited to Rome in January in the hope of persuading him to exert pressure on France. The tactic availed nothing.[78] One reason was that, although Mussolini's immediate colonial claims were for French territory, his long-term and larger goals could only be obtained at the expense of the British empire and British naval supremacy. This could be read between the lines of a memorandum which the Duce submitted to the Grand Council of Fascism on 4 February 1939. Herein was sketched the design for a new Roman empire stretching from the Atlantic to the Indian Ocean. Its precondition was, of course, realization of the old Italian nationalist dream of a Mediterranean *mare nostrum*, which entailed displacement of the British "sentinels" at Gibraltar and Suez. In short, since empire had become the ideology of fascism, geopolitics prescribed Anglo-Italian conflict.[79]

Failure to wring colonial sacrifices from the West left Mussolini with two choices – either to give up or to step up his blackmail. But the former option of a genuine reconciliation with the democracies was not only out of character, it was virtually out of the question after *Anschluss*. So the Duce resolved to count even more on the Axis. A slight hiccup occurred in March 1939 when Nazi Germany seized the body of Czechoslovakia without consulting Rome; "Italy . . . was now on the sidelines", writes Taylor.[80] However, wounded fascist pride was appeased by annexing Albania (although the country had been a virtual Italian protectorate since 1926), whereupon Mussolini resumed his movement towards a formal alliance with Germany. A fascist-Nazi alliance had been bruited since the morrow of *Anschluss*. It had hitherto foundered partly on Mussolini's vestigial adherence to equidistance, partly on the Nazi fear that Italian quarrelling with France might precipitate the wrong war at the wrong time, and partly on Berlin's preference for a tripartite arrangement embracing Japan. Japan's insistence that such a triple alliance be directed against the Soviet Union did not suit Hitler's plans in 1939, leaving an Italo-German pact as the sole practicable possibility. Meanwhile, Mussolini had determined on an alliance in early January, even before Chamberlain's Rome visit. His eagerness increased during the spring – or so one must deduce both from the Pact of Steel's negotiation and its terms. The Duce and Ciano accepted wholesale what the Nazis placed before them; with the signing of the pact on 22 May, Hitler and Ribbentrop secured a comprehensive undertaking without the customary diplomatic reservations about a defensive *casus belli*. If either party went to war for any reason, the other was contracted to "immediately come to its assistance as an ally and support it with all its military forces on land, on sea and in the air".[81]

"No doubt Mussolini hoped that the Pact woud give him some say in German counsels."[82] Taylor's observation refers to the oral understanding, which accompanied the Pact of Steel, that no war was contemplated until 1942 or 1943. This would afford Italy ample time to use the strengthened Axis in a fresh campaign to browbeat Britain and France into meeting Mussolini's colonial desiderata. But as for influencing Hitler's decision-making, the vast economic and military disparity between the Axis partners constituted a formidable stumbling-block. Most German military experts, well aware of fascist Italy's dependence on German coal and overall unpreparedness for war, wrote off Italy as a useful ally and discounted Italian opinion. Yet, this was not necessarily Hitler's estimate. The personal and ideological affinity between Führer and Duce, reaching back almost two decades, predisposed the Nazi leader to attach weight to the Italian counter in the diplomatic balance far beyond what statistics and *Realpolitik* warranted.[83] For example, in a corollary to the Pact of Steel Hitler bowed to Italian susceptibilities by authorizing the transfer of as many Germans from the South Tyrol as were willing to be resettled.[84] More important, in the Danzig crisis of August 1939, Hitler appeared to set uncommonly great store by Italian help. Although his threatened attack on Poland violated the tacit promise to keep the peace for several years, Hitler nevertheless expected Mussolini to honour his signature on the Pact of Steel. Portents that Italy would not fight were to be gleaned from Ciano's words in some uncomfortable meetings with Ribbentrop and Hitler at Salzburg and Berchtesgaden on 11, 12 and 13 August.[85] However, when on 25 August under cover of requesting immense quantities of German supplies Mussolini revealed Italy's prospective neutrality, Hitler registered shock. The date for the *Wehrmacht*'s invasion of Poland was put back to 1 September (it had been advanced to 26 August). Although Taylor is anxious to minimize its effect, the scholarly consensus holds that Mussolini's desertion (coupled with the simultaneous conclusion of an Anglo-Polish treaty) was regarded in Berlin as a severe setback.[86].

Fascist Italy's option for neutrality was only one instance of Axis disarray. Mussolini's decision received some retroactive justification when Rome found out that Hitler, even before learning of Italian neutrality, had offered Britain a global package with anti-Italian implications in the colonial sphere. In tit-for-tat style, Ciano then surreptitiously let the British know of Italy's intended neutrality – an invaluable piece of information in the Anglo-German war of nerves.[87] As hostilities became imminent the Duce dreamed of saving face by returning to his Munich conference posture. On 31 August he proposed an international conference. Some in French ruling circles were interested, but the British and ·German governments prevaricated. After 1 September diplomacy was no longer feasible unless Nazi forces withdrew from the Polish Corridor, and Mussolini had no leverage to obtain this.[88]

In successive years, 1938 and 1939, Mussolini was prevailed upon to admit fascist Italy's economic and military deficiencies, and to steer clear of impending war. "Mussolini, despite all his boasting, strove desperately to keep out of war", is Taylor's comment.[89] But this is a partial truth. The Duce's aversion to war came and went. He who had relished bloodshed and violence in Africa and Spain underwent no conversion in the Sudeten and Danzig crises.[90] Rather, Mussolini was ashamed of the weakness that Italy was forced to display in choosing peace. This was particularly so on the outbreak of the Second World War. Not only was nonbelligerence (Mussolini's preferred word) incompatible with fascist martial valour, but the parallel with the neutrality of despised liberal Italy of 1914 was too embarrassing to suffer for long. Hence, in the first weeks of the Second World War, Mussolini began to look for an opportunity to intervene.[91] Taylor's narrative in *The Origins of the Second World War* stops on 3 September 1939, but personal characteristics unveiled after that date cannot be ruled out in examining motives and conduct beforehand. This is true of Hitler, and no less so of Mussolini. The Duce of the winter of 1939 was a war lover chafing at the bit; it was the same persona who had with great reluctance – not with officious striving – shunned war earlier.

Italy's gradual shift over the twenty interwar years from the victorious Allied bloc to the vanquished enemy camp comprises a mere subplot in Taylor's work. Inevitably, there are elisions and omissions. Little or no space has been accorded, for example, to the roots of Italian nationalism in liberal Italy, the diplomacy of Mussolini in the 1920s, or the significance of Ciano's appointment in the 1930s. This is not to say that Taylor's outline of Italian foreign policy is inaccurate – far from it in one respect at least, for there is a sharp appreciation throughout of the revisionist tendencies in Italy's foreign policy after the First World War. Pursuit of international revisionism, incidentally, supplies a unifying thread that belies Taylor's initial dictum regarding the incoherence of fascist diplomacy.

If there is a major flaw in the treatment of Italy, it is a reflection of the approach of *The Origins of the Second World War* as a whole. Probably the most trenchant of all objections to *Origins* is that it deals with foreign policy *in vacuo*. Typical of a legion of critics is T. W. Mason who comments:[92]

> Mr. Taylor reduces the international relations of the period to the obsolete formula of independent states pursuing intelligible national interests with varying degrees of diplomatic skill . . . Yet Mr. Taylor's formula largely excludes the profound causes [of 1939] from consideration; it seems unable to accommodate political movements and ideologies.

What is above all absent from the account of German foreign policy after 1933 is any recognition of the ideological drive of National Socialism – to the great majority of historians a self-evident feature of all walks of life in the Third Reich. Of course, Taylor is compelled to disregard the racial factor and its expansionist concomitant, the hunt for *Lebensraum*, if he is to present Hitler the statesman as no more than opportunist and *Realpolitiker*.[93] In his prefatory "Second Thoughts" in later editions of *Origins*, the author states more openly than in the first edition the irrelevance of Nazism's racial ideology to its diplomacy: "He [Hitler] gave orders, which Germans executed, of a wickedness without parallel in civilized history. His foreign policy was a different matter."[94] Sauce for Nazi Germany is sauce for fascist Italy. Mussolini's foreign policy, too, is presented without any informed reference to its domestic background.

The idea that Mussolini was a realist surrounded by irresponsible fascists is an especially bizarre misconception.[95] If anything, the very opposite was the case, as some of the more cautious nationalists in his entourage (Giuseppe Bastianini,

Giuseppe Bottai, Dino Grandi, among others) tried tentatively and vainly between 1938 and 1940 to restrain a madcap Duce.[96] Mussolini was no more a rational statesman than Hitler. True, he never subscribed to the cosmic ideology of racism in the way that Hitler did. Nevertheless, Mussolini had his *idées fixes*, and with the passage of time he grew more fatalistic, trusting in providence to provide.[97] In other words, the Social Darwinist laws of the universe, rather than coal and guns, would ensure the third Roman empire. For Mussolini was gullible, and he was not least susceptible to his own propaganda.[98] Occasionally, he retreated in the face of overwhelming evidence of fascist Italy's woeful lack of readiness for war. Yet, in the last resort – namely, Italy's intervention in the Second World War on 10 June 1940 – he acted as if fascism had magically transformed his country into an authentic great power. This was the ultimate fantasy of the well-known "regime of gestures". But then propaganda and myth were the stuff of Mussolini's entire career. Taylor apprehends perfectly well the emptiness of Italian fascism. The fault rests on his expectation of a rational interpretation of the deeds of so pretentious a movement and its leader.

Italy figures most prominently in the chapter of *Origins* entitled "The Abyssinian Affair and the End of Locarno". This chapter has often been praised,[99] although mostly, one suspects, because it enables Taylor to depict Hitler at his most opportunistic in seizing unexpected advantage of the Italo-Ethiopian war. Its content therefore is grist to the author's thesis of the *realpolitik* nature of Nazi diplomacy. But as a recital of the crucial episode in fascist Italian policy, the chapter illustrates all the shortcomings of Taylor's limited perspective. As to why the Duce became embroiled in Africa when he did, he rules out several credible interpretations and then avows: "At any rate, for reasons which are still difficult to grasp, Mussolini decided in 1934 to conquer Abyssinia."[100] On the other salient issue of why Mussolini, on emerging victorious from the Ethiopian war, chose to throw in his lot with Hitler, Taylor advances no discernible explanation at all.[101] The point is that the answers to these questions lie in the internal workings of the fascist regime and in the recesses of the Duce's personality. Such matters rarely surface in the diplomatic documents from Europe's chancelleries. Moreover, much of our present understanding of the structure and dynamics of Italian fascism flows from the scholarship of the twenty-five years since the first appearance of *The Origins of the Second World War*. Yet these factors hardly excuse Taylor's willful refusal to take cognizance of the fascist ambience in which diplomatic decisions were taken, no matter how tentative conclusions would have been in 1961. An argument can be made that Italian history between the world wars exemplifies *das Primat der Aussenpolitik*, but in no way is it advanced by foreign policy's divorce from the rest of historical reality.

NOTES

1   A. J. P. Taylor, *The Origins of the Second World War* (London, 1961), p. 18. Citations throughout this essay are to the first British edition, unless stated otherwise.

2   G. L. Weinberg, *The Foreign Policy of Hitler's Germany*, Vol. 1, *Diplomatic Revolution in Europe, 1933–1936*; Vol. 2, *Starting World War II, 1937–1939* (Chicago and London, 1970, 1980).

3   D. Mack Smith, *Italy: A Modern History* (rev. edn, Ann Arbor, 1969); *Victor Emanuel, Cavour and the Risorgimento* (London and New York, 1971); *Mussolini* (London, 1982).

4   A. J. P. Taylor, *A Personal History* (London, 1983), pp. 240–1, 258–9; and *An Old Man's Diary* (London, 1984), pp. 69–70, 81.

5   Taylor, *Personal History*, pp. 158, 173.

6   Taylor, *Origins*, p. 56.

7   ibid., p. 40.

8   G. Salvemini, *Opere*, III, *Scritti di politica estera*, Vol. 3: *Preludio alla seconda guerra mondiale*, ed. A. Torre (Milan, 1967), pp. 263–84; C. Sforza, *Pensiero e azione di una politica estera italiana* (Bari, 1924), p. 283; L. Zeno Zencovich, *Ritratto di Carlo Sforza* (Florence, 1975), pp. 113–30.

9   An excellent example is D. Mack Smith, *Mussolini's Roman Empire* (London and New York, 1976).

10 For an interim appraisal of this scholarly revisionism, see J. Petersen, "Die Aussenpolitik des faschistischen Italien als historiographisches Problem", *Vierteljahrshefte für Zeitgeschichte*, vol. 22 (1974), pp. 417–57.

11 The historical growth of this national sense of outrage is signposted in F. Chabod, *Storia della politica estera italiana dal 1870 al 1896*, Vol. 1, *Le premesse* (Bari, 1951), pp. 179–323, 529–62; R. J. Bosworth, *Italy: The Least of the Great Powers* (London, 1979), pp. 1–67, 418–20; R. Vivarelli, *Il dopoguerra in Italia e l'avvento del fascismo, 1918–1922*, Vol. 1, *Dalla fine della guerra all'impresa di Fiume* (Naples, 1967), pp. 1–53, 84–114.

12 R. Guariglia, *Ricordi, 1922–1946* (Naples, 1950), pp. 14–16; Legatus (R. Cantalupo), *Vita diplomatica di Salvatore Contarini* (Rome, 1947), pp. 73–8.

13 Taylor, *Origins*, pp. 32–3.

14 A. De Bosdari, "Memorie", September 1923, in *I documenti diplomatici italiani* [*DDI*], Series 7, Vol. 2, p. 238, n. 3; Mussolini–De Bosdari, 14 September 1923, ibid., no. 360; De Bosdari–Mussolini, 17 September 1923, ibid., no. 373.

15 G. Carocci, *La politica estera dell'Italia fascista, 1925–1928* (Bari, 1969), pp. 190–1, 196–7; A. Cassels, *Mussolini's Early Diplomacy* (Princeton, 1970), pp. 160–6; K–P. Hoepke, *Die deutsche Rechte und der italienische Faschismmus* (Düsseldorf, 1968), pp. 243–8, 292–5, 306–9. See also *DDI*, Series 7, Vol. 7, no. 372; Vol. 8, nos 420, 478, 492; Vol. 9, nos 193, 267.

16 Cassels, *Early Diplomacy*, pp. 166–74; Hoepke, *Die Deutsche Rechte*, pp. 125–33, 304–6; M. Paulumbo, "Goering's Italian exile, 1924–25", *Journal of Modern History*, vol. 50 (March 1978), D1035.

17 Instances of Italian interest in the Nazis are to be found in *DDI*, Series 7, Vol. 5, no. 680; Vol. 6, no. 322; Vol. 7, nos 413, 576; Vol. 8, nos 367, 377, 384; Vol. 9, nos 180, 254, 262, 289.

18 Use of the generic name, "fascism", papered over the substantive differences in ideological inspiration between the Italian and the German movement; witness the failure to establish a fascist international: M. A. Ledeen, *Universal Fascism: Theory and Practice of the Fascist International, 1928–1936* (New York, 1972).

19 A. Hitler, *Mein Kampf*, trans. R. Manheim (New York, 1943), pp. 128–30, 628–30, 655–6; cf. *Hitler's Secret Book*, intro. by T. Taylor (New York, 1961), pp. 178–208. See also Hoepke, *Die Deutsche Rechte*, pp. 159–65; E. Jäckal, *Hitler's Weltanschauung* Middletown, 1972), p. 30; D. J. Rusinow, *Italy's Austrian Heritage, 1919–1946* (New York, 1969), pp. 215–18.

20 Taylor, *Origins*, pp. 80, 194.

21 Carocci, *Politica estera*, pp. 182–90; Cassels, *Early Diplomacy*, pp. 272–5, 279–83; Rusinow, *Austrian Heritage*, pp. 179–84.

22 Cassels, *Early Diplomacy*, pp. 275–9; S. Marks, "Mussolini and Locarno", *Journal of Contemporary History*, vol. 14 (1979), pp. 423–39.

23 Senate speech, 5 June 1928, Mussolini, *Opera omnia* [*00*], eds E. and D. Susmel, 44 vols (Florence, Rome, 1951–80), Vol. 23, pp. 176–7.

24 Cassels, *Early Diplomacy*, pp. 310–14; P. G. Edwards, "The Austen Chamberlain–Mussolini meetings", *Historical Journal*, vol. 14 (1971), pp. 153–64.

25 This thesis is argued by H. J. Burgwyn, *Il revisionismo fascista: La sfida di Mussolini alle grande potenze nei Balcani e sul Danubio, 1925–1933* (Milan, 1979).

26 ibid., p. 235.

27 F. D'Amoja, *Declino e prima crisi dell'Europa di Versailles, 1931–1933* (Milan, 1967), pp. 213–58.

28 Taylor, *Origins*, p. 78, where, on the other hand, it is wrongly stated that the Four Power Pact "was never ratified"; it was

ratified by Italy and Britain but not by Germany and France (K. Jarausch, *The Four Power Pact, 1933* (Madison, 1965), p. 217, n. 71). See also D'Amoja, pp. 259–354; G. Giordano, *Il Patto a Quattro nella politica estera di Mussolini* (Bologna, 1976).

29   Taylor, *Origins*, p. 83, and comment by R. Sontag in W. R. Louis (ed.), *The Origins of the Second World War: A. J. P. Taylor and His Critics* (New York, 1972). Also Weinberg, *Diplomatic Revolution*, pp. 100–101.

30   Taylor, *Origins*, p. 83; cf. Weinberg, *Diplomatic Revolution*, pp. 102–5.

31   J. Gehl, *Austria, Germany and the Anschluss, 1931–1938* (London, 1963), pp. 101–4; Weinberg, *Diplomatic Revolution*, pp. 105–7.

32   L. Noel, *Les illusions de Stresa* (Paris, 1975), pp. 93–8, 183–7, 201–3.

33   Taylor, *Origins*, p. 85.

34   G. Rochat, *Militari e politici nella preparazione della campagna d'Etiopia* (Milan, 1971), pp. 26–33.

35   Taylor, *Origins*, p. 88.

36   Italian Ministry of Interior reports for Foreign and War Ministries, 18 September 1935, 10 October 1935, Italy, Archivio Storico del Ministero degli Affari Esteri, Serie affari politici [ASME], "Germania", busta 26 (1935), fasciolo 2.

37   This is best argued in E. M. Robertson, *Mussolini as Empire Builder: Europe and Africa, 1932–1936* (London, 1977).

38   What was actually said and what left unspoken at Stresa may be pieced together from R. Mori, *Mussolini e la conquista dell'Etiopia* (Florence, 1978), pp. 20–3; R. A. C. Parker, "Great Britain, France and the Ethiopian crisis of 1935–1936", *English Historical Review*, vol. 89 (1974), pp. 295–7; E. Serra, "La questione italo-etiopica alla conferenza di Stresa", *Affari Esteri*, vol. 9 (1977), pp. 313–39; G. Thompson, *Front-Line Diplomat* (London, 1959), pp. 97–9. The best overall synopsis is R. Quartararo, *Roma tra Londra e Berlino: Politica estera fascista dal 1930 al 1940* (Rome, 1980), pp. 118–29. Possibly the most credible depiction of Mussolini's devious tactics is Mack Smith, *Mussolini*, pp. 193–4.

39   Quartararo, *Politica estera fascista*, pp. 143–7; M. Toscano, *Designs in Diplomacy* (Baltimore, 1970), pp. 412–14.

40   G. W. Baer, *The Coming of the Italian-Ethiopian War* (Cambridge, Mass., 1967), pp. 29–35; R. De Felice, *Mussolini il Duce*, 2 vols (Turin, 1974–81), Vol. 1, *Gli anni del consenso, 1929–1936*, pp. 605–16; R. Mori, "Delle cause dell'impresa etiopica mussoli-niana", *Storia e Politica*, vol. 17 (1978), pp. 663–706.

41   Taylor, *Origins*, p. 87.

42   De Felice, *Il Duce*, Vol. 1, chs 1–3 *passim*.

43   Speech in Naples, 25 October 1931, *00*, Vol. 25, p. 50; V. De Grazia, *The Culture of Consent* (Cambridge, 1981), pp. 51–9.

44   De Felice, *Il Duce*, Vol. 2, *Lo Stato totalitario, 1936–1940*, pp. 254–330 *passim*; Mack Smith, *Roman Empire*, pp. 32–4, 42–3, 84–6, 120.

45 M. Knox, "Conquest, foreign and domestic, in fascist Italy and Nazi Germany", *Journal of Modern History*, vol. 56 (1984), pp. 26–57.
46 R. De Felice, *Mussolini il rivoluzionario, 1883–1920* (Turin, 1965), pp. 288–361 *passim*; D. D. Roberts, *The Syndicalist Tradition and Italian Fascism* (Chapel Hill, NC, 1979), pp. 113–14.
47 M. Toscano, "Eden's mission to Rome on the eve of the Italian-Ethiopian conflict", in A. O. Sarkissian (ed.), *Studies in Diplomatic History and Historiography* (London, 1961), pp. 126–52.
48 Apropos the role played by the League of Nations, Taylor's statement that Ethiopia was admitted to the League in 1925 is incorrect; it was in 1923 (Taylor, *Origins*, p. 88; F. P. Walters, *A History of the League of Nations* (London, 1952), Vol. 1, p. 258).
49 Taylor, *Origins*, p. 94. Mori, *Conquista dell'Etiopia*, pp. 217–20, flatly contradicts Taylor, but for the most judicious handling of the ambiguous evidence, see De Felice, *Il Duce*, Vol. 1, pp. 718–24.
50 This proposition is advanced by M. Funke, *Sanktionen und Kanonen: Hitler, Mussolini und der Abessinienkonflikt, 1934–1936* (Düsseldorf, 1970), pp. 174–7. Funke is disputed, and Ethiopia's causal importance maintained, by G. Buccianti, "Hitler, Mussolini e il conflitto italo-etiopico", *Il Politico*, vol. 37 (1972), pp. 415–28; and by J. Petersen, *Hitler–Mussolini: Der Entstehung der Achse Berlin-Rome 1933–1936* (Tübingen, 1973), pp. 447–54, 493–502.
51 Hitler, *Mein Kampf*, pp. 617, 620, 664–5; *Hitler's Secret Book*, pp. 173–4.
52 Mussolini-Cerruti, 31 August 1935, ASME, "Germania", busta 28 (1935), fasc. 2. Further Mussolinian strictures on Germany in Mussolini–Attolico, 8 October 1935, ibid.
53 Funke, pp. 48–81.
54 Understandably, Mussolini refused to join Britain and France in considering sanctions against Germany in the Rhineland affair so long as these powers subscribed to League sanctions against Italy (Mussolini–Grandi, 23 March 1936, Mussolini–Attolico, 2 April 1936, ASME, "Germania", busta 31 [1936], fasc. 1; Suvich-Cerruti, 28 Mar. 1936, ASME, "Etiopia-fondo di guerra," busta 145 [1936], fasc. 4).
55 Taylor, *Origins*, pp. 108, 110.
56 Mussolini–Grandi, 13 April 1936, ASME, "Germania", busta 31 (1936), fasc. 1; Mack Smith, *Roman Empire*, pp. 71, 96.
57 Taylor, *Origins*, p. 106.
58 Mack Smith, *Mussolini*, pp. 208–9, 220; and *Roman Empire*, pp. 71, 92–5.
59 G. B. Guerri, *Galeazzo Ciano, una vita, 1903–1944* (Milan, 1979), pp. 161–3.
60 Taylor, *Origins*, pp. 120–1, 126–7. Cf. J. F. Coverdale, *Italian Intervention in the Spanish Civil War* (Princeton, 1976), pp. 171–2, 263–4, 306–16, 388–91; De Felice, *Il Duce*, Vol. 2, pp. 432–6.
61 Taylor, *Origins*, p. 111; speech in Milan, 1 November 1936, *00*,

vol. 28, pp. 69–70. The axis metaphor was not new in Mussolini's vocabulary; he had once described Germany alone as the axis of world affairs (Preface to R. Suster, *La Germania repubblicana* (Milan, 1923), *00*, vol. 20, p. 31).

62   G. Ciano, *Ciano's Diplomatic Papers*, ed. M. Muggeridge (London, 1948), pp. 52–60; Quartararo, *Politica estera fascista*, pp. 306–7; Weinberg, *Diplomatic Revolution*, pp. 334–7.

63   Hassell-Neurath, 7 January 1936, *Documents on German Foreign Policy, 1918–1945 [DGFP]*, Series C, Vol. 4, no. 485.

64   Aloisi *aide-mémoire*, 4 April 1936, ASME, "Germania", busta 34 (1936), fasc. 1; Weinberg, *Diplomatic Revolution*, pp. 266–7.

65   Text of "gentleman's agreement", 11 July 1936, *DGFP*, Series D, Vol. 1, no. 152. See also Ciano, *Diplomatic Papers*, pp. 8–9; Weinberg, *Diplomatic Revolution*, pp. 270–71, 333. Berlin's diplomatic recognition of Italian Ethiopia was announced on 24 October 1936.

66   Taylor, *Origins*, p. 110.

67   Ciano, *Diplomatic Papers*, p. 146; Weinberg, *Starting World War II*, p. 286.

68   On whether Hitler opportunistically grasped the chance for *Anschluss* or orchestrated the crisis in 1938, see respectively Taylor, *Origins*, pp. 131–50, and Weinberg, *Starting World War II*, pp. 287–303.

69   Quoted in Taylor, *Origins*, p. 148.

70   M. Domarus (ed.), *Hitler: Reden und Proklamationen, 1932–1945*, 2 vols (Neustadt, 1962), Vol. 1, pp. 860–1.

71   M. Michaelis, *Mussolini and the Jews: German-Italian Relations and the Jewish Question in Italy, 1922–1945* (Oxford, 1978), pp. 107–91.

72   Taylor, *Origins*, p. 139.

73   The theme of equidistance is emphasized in De Felice, *Il Duce*, Vol. 2, pp. 467ff., and Quartararo, *Politica estera fascista*, pp. 376ff.

74   Olla P. Brundu, *L'equilibrio difficile: Gran Bretagna, Italia e Francia nel Mediterraneo 1930–1937* (Milan, 1980), pp. 159–206; D. Bolech Cecchi, *L'accordo di due imperi: L'accordo italo-inglese del 16 aprile 1938* (Milan, 1977).

75   Weinberg, *Starting World War II*, pp. 409–14, 452–6.

76   Taylor, *Origins*, p. 183. For an alternative explanation, see Weinberg, *Starting World War II*, pp. 450–64.

77   Taylor, *Origins*, pp. 184–5.

78   ibid., p. 200; P. R. Stafford, "The Chamberlain–Halifax visit to Rome: a reappraisal", *English Historical Review*, vol. 98 (1983), pp. 61–100.

79   Mussolini's memorandum to the Fascist Grand Council is printed in full in De Felice, *Il Duce*, Vol. 2, pp. 321–3.

80   Taylor, *Origins*, p. 222.

81   Text of Pact of Steel, 22 May 1939, *DGFP*, Series D, Vol. 6, no. 426. For the negotiations leading up to the pact, see T.

Sommer, *Deutschland und Japan zwischen den Machten, 1935–1940*
(Tübingen, 1962), pp. 116–239 *passim*; M. Toscano, *The Origins of
the Pact of Steel* (Baltimore, 1967); D. C. Watt, "An earlier model
for the Pact of Steel: the draft treaties exchanged between Germany and Italy during Hitler's visit to Rome in May 1938",
International Affairs, vol. 33 (1957), pp. 185–97; Weinberg, *Starting
World War II*, pp. 565–77; E. Wiskemann, *The Rome–Berlin Axis* (rev.
edn, London, 1966), pp. 163–86.

82 Taylor, *Origins*, p. 222.

83 W. Murray, *The Change in the European Balance of Power, 1938–1939*
(Princeton, 1984), pp. 5, 110–18, 254–5; D. C. Watt, "The Rome–
Berlin Axis, 1936–1940: myth and reality", *Review of Politics*, vol.
22 (1960), pp. 519–43.

84 C. F. Latour, *Südtirol und die Achse Berlin–Rom, 1938–1945* (Stuttgart, 1962), pp. 30–42.

85 *Procès-verbaux* of Ciano talks with Ribbentrop and Hitler, 11–13
August 1939, *DDI*, Series 8, Vol. 13, nos 1, 4, 21. See also G. Ciano,
Diario, ed. R. De Felice (Milan, 1980), pp. 326–7.

86 Taylor, *Origins*, pp. 269–70. For the conventional wisdom, see S.
Aster, *1939: The Making of the Second World War* (London, 1973),
pp. 334, 338; F. Siebert, *Italiens Weg in den Zweiten Weltkrieg* (Frankfurt, 1962), pp. 301–3; C. Thorne, *The Approach of War, 1938–1939*
(London, 1967), pp. 184–6; Weinberg, *Starting World War II*,
pp. 636–9.

87 Ciano, *Diario*, 27 and 31 August 1939, pp. 335–6, 339; De Felice, *Il
Duce*, Vol. 2, pp. 665–6.

88 De Felice, *Il Duce*, Vol. 2, pp. 666–70; Quartararo, *Politica estera
fascista*, pp. 509–18; Siebert, *Italiens Weg*, pp. 304–44; P. R. Stafford, "The French government and the Danzig crisis: the Italian
dimension", *International History Review*, vol. 6 (1984), pp. 48–87;
Taylor, *Origins*, p. 276; Thorne, *Approach of War*, pp. 196–202.

89 Taylor, *Origins*, p. 103.

90 On Mussolini's appetite for war, see Mack Smith, *Mussolini*,
pp. 173–4, 195, 201–2, 205, 207, 227; and *Roman Empire*,
pp. 15–16, 39–41, 68, 78–81, 95, 190–1.

91 M. Knox, *Mussolini Unleashed, 1939–1941* (New York, 1982), pp.
44–59.

92 T. W. Mason, "Some origins of the Second World War", *Past and
Present*, no. 29 (December 1964), pp. 67–8.

93 For Taylor's dismissal of *Lebensraum*, see *Origins*, pp. 105–6.

94 Taylor, *Origins* (Harmondsworth: Penguin, 1964), p. 27. For an
interpretation combining Hitlerian opportunism and long-range
planning based on a racial imperative, see A. Bullock, "Hitler and
the origins of the Second World War", in Louis, *A. J. P. Taylor and
Critics*, pp. 117–45.

95 See above, n. 72.

96 G. Bastianini, *Uomini, cose, fatti* (Milan, 1959), pp. 70–6, 180–2; De

Felice, *Il Duce*, Vol. 2, pp. 671–4, 776, 789–93; G. Guerri, *Giuseppe Bottai: Un fascista critico* (Milan, 1976), pp. 209–10; Quartararo, *Politica esterafascista*, pp. 579–81, 606–7.

97   Knox, "Conquest, foreign and domestic", pp. 7–26; and *Mussolini Unleashed*, pp. 5–6.

98   Mack Smith, *Mussolini*, pp. 130, 239; and *Roman Empire*, pp. 169–89 *passim*, 203–5.

99   For example, G. A. Craig, comment in Louis, *A. J. P. Taylor and Critics*, p. 110; Mason, "Some origins", p. 67.

100   Taylor, *Origins*, p. 88.

101   ibid., pp. 110–11.

4

A. J. P. Taylor
and the
Problem with France

ROBERT J. YOUNG

Rereading the *Origins of the Second World War*, twenty-five years after its first appearance, is like bumping into a familiar face at some school reunion. Years ago we, the new boys, had been cautioned about this celebrity. Our mentors distrusted his judgment, though they admired his "style" – in part a temperament distinguished by audacity, in part an inspired pen that too often made the complex appear simple. It was clear to us then, even if the reasoning behind it was less so, that Taylor's *Origins* had passed some tests magnificently and failed others rather miserably. Whatever the final assessment of his peers, we undergraduates knew that Taylor had been responsible for an historical event of its own kind. Twenty-five years later that publishing event of 1961 remains, as Taylor said of the war itself, "a matter of historical curiosity".[1]

It is a mark of this book's impact to be able to say that it remains central to a debate that continues to bubble away over the war's origins. Of course, scholars may persist in saying, as they have for a quarter of a century, that Taylor got it wrong, or at least much of it. They will continue to insist, as indeed they must, that his evidence is often inadequate for his case, if not overtly incompatible with it. An historical *agent provocateur*, he has invited the blows of those who find his grasp of economics rudimentary, his interest in ideology moribund, his predilection for contrived aphorisms excessive. And yet he has never been chased from the field, never made to surrender. They may work around him, for a while they may even ignore him, but in the end they have to return to his field.

Taylor opened the first edition of *Origins* with a chapter entitled "Forgotten Problem". It was here that he acknowledged some of the archival obstacles that he had encountered and which, by his own admission, may have contributed to the "perhaps misleading impression that international relations between the wars were an Anglo-German duologue".[2] Misleading or not – and it was – this is what Taylor concentrated on. Accordingly, it was here that one might have expected him to vent his enthusiasm. He did not disappoint. Taylor tackled Hitler's Germany and Chamberlain's England with the zeal of an iconoclast. Hitler, contrary to all that had been said, had no great design, plan or blueprint, but succeeded. Chamberlain, contrary to popular wisdom, had a plan, knew what he wanted, but failed. Hitler was no man of action, but rather a procrastinator, one who excelled in waiting. Chamberlain was no chinless temporizer, but rather a resolute decision-maker who was impatient for peace. After Taylor, many of the old truths looked decidedly shop-worn. One of the greatest lovers of paradox since Karl Marx, Taylor played games with all previous judgments, often agreeing with two opposing views and so discrediting both. "Though the object of being a Great Power is to be able to fight a great war, the only way of remaining a Great Power is not to fight one."[3] The Rhineland crisis of March 1936 was a turning point in that it "opened the door for Germany's success" though it also "opened the door for her ultimate failure". What better paradoxical illuminations could one seek, unless it be that "the defect of this explanation is that, since it explains everything, it also explains nothing"?[4]

This is vintage Taylor, unconventional insight articulated by means of paradox, and sometimes through riddle-like aphorism. "Only a country which aims at victory can be threatened with defeat." "Wars, when they come, are always different from the war that is expected. Victory goes to the side that has made fewest mistakes, not to the one that has guessed right." "After all, standing still is the best policy for anyone who favours the *status quo*, perhaps the only one." As Taylor himself once said of Metternich, "most men could do better than this when shaving", for what do such maxims really mean?[5] Are they intended to instruct, or merely titillate? Explanation alone could make or unmake their profundity. Until then one is only reminded of Captain Corcoran's response to a torrent of enigmas: "Though to catch your drift I'm striving. It is shady – it is shady."

Frankly, this is an overlooked quality of *Origins*. It is a rare and

singular gift which permits Taylor to be as controversial when he
is being abstruse as when he is being crystal clear. For example,
one can understand the picture of Hitler as day-dreamer, a
man who had no desire or plan for war, a man whose international goals were more modest than those of his predecessors.
One may object, protest, but the point is clear enough, But
precisely what is one to understand from the way Taylor bran-
dishes the vocabulary of morality in international affairs? Here,
the point is not at all clear. Sometimes we are led to believe that
fascism had such a corrupting effect that the leaders of Britain
and France were beset by a "moral and intellectual fog", so
much so that they "came to believe that an unscrupulous policy
was the only resource". So far so good. Yet appeasement, by
Taylor's telling, was the work of a British government whose
motives were "of the highest" and who made this "high-minded
attempt at the impartial redress of grievances".[6] Then, presumably, the fog rolled in again, for by the time of the Munich conference, appeasement "had lost its moral strength". And then it
lifted, just in time to make it obvious that for the British "morality
counted for a great deal", and that a British prime minister had
actually succeeded in getting the French, even the Czechs, "to
follow the moral line".[7]

One such illustration normally would be enough to demonstrate the frequent patches of confusion, but in this instance the
point is too important for doubts to be allowed to linger. This is a
study which purports to be addressed more to Britain and
France than to Germany, and to the question of why they did not
resist Hitler. As such, the issue of their moral motivation certainly became very central to the book, despite Taylor's claim
that he never mixed business with morality.[8] The historian, so
he assured critics of his first edition, must only elucidate, never
judge – an admirable counsel of self-restraint, providing one is
sure of being able to distinguish one from the other. When it
comes to his remarks on the French, however, Taylor's claim
seems a little tarnished. From where he sits, beside the Thames,
the fog never seems to lift over Paris. Never do the French catch
sight of even a few errant rays of moral enlightenment, except of
course when they are hoodwinked into following "the moral
line". How all of this fits into Premier Daladier's despairing
protestations is anyone's guess, for it seems to have been he, in
April and September 1938, who resisted the very principle of
appeasing Hitler at the expense of "independent peoples".[9]

As he was to do with the British and the Germans, so Taylor

would do with the French, stirring up the water with a great stick in an effort to catch a glimpse of the foreign policy of the Third Republic and the attitudes behind it. Paradoxically, however, the less certain he was of the French, the less he wrote, and the less he wrote, the greater was his impact. In the case of Britain and Germany, on which he wrote immeasurably more, Taylor has been challenged and corrected, repeatedly. In the case of France, has anyone bothered? In 1961, or subsequently, one would not have turned to *Origins* for a considered, measured analysis of French policy; but for a provocative and witty study of the coming of a world war, why not? Accordingly, hundreds of thousands read Taylor, while a few score looked for something better on France, in some cases even works written in French. Two and a half decades later, it still shows.

Some years ago I commented on those many studies of international relations which had skimmed over interwar France with only the most imperceptible of retards. A Great Power by the standards of the day, France had been duly located on the right side of the Channel and then dismissed with comments which were as dogmatic as they were brief. Yet every such passage left a trail of slips and innuendos, all of them suggesting a country that had lost its way, that had become unmistakably degenerate.[10] At the time, A. J. P. Taylor was far from my thoughts. Today, on rereading *Origins*, the conviction grows that his work had contributed substantially to that earlier impression. Certainly when it came to the French, Taylor was no revisionist. Quite the reverse. An Englishman, as he says, "by birth and preference",[11] Taylor tended to confirm what his compatriots had known for a century or two, namely that the French were a thoroughly difficult lot. One might choose to upend any number of previously cherished interpretations, even give Stalin the benefit of the doubt, but some truths were indeed self-evident and needed defending.

Some historians of France are certain to dislike Taylor's treatment of the interwar Third Republic. Much of what he has to say about the French will seem questionable in the extreme, whether it is when he sees fit to link them with the British or when he is more determined to disassociate them from the high-minded thinking of Whitehall. In the former case a series of examples comes to mind: "western policy mainly turned" on Britain; "western statesmen strove to keep them [the Americans] out"; "British and French statesmen . . . sincerely believed . . . that Hitler would be content and pacific if his claim were met"; both "Great Britain and France in 1938 were for 'peace at any price'".[12] Unlike the second and third of these extraordinary assertions, the first and last are only half mistaken. Fundamentally, however, what is offputting is the assumed ease with which the French can be packaged with the British, when it is convenient to do so.

Sometimes, of course, it is altogether too inconvenient. For whatever this means to the "western" policy above, appeasement is presented very much as an English invention. The French do not subscribe to it as a positive way of reconciling differences, Rather, for them, it is merely an expedient to get them off the hook and free them from the obligation to defend the Czechs, "not a dangerous . . . but perhaps an ignoble policy".[13] In other ways, too, the French were different and had to be assessed by Taylor in quite discrete ways. For example, he says they made "no attempt to protect the French frontier with Belgium", with the same assurance that he claims the Baldwin government imposed a Spanish non-intervention policy on Léon Blum.[14] Neither has the evidence on its side. Nor is there substance, indeed credibility, to the claim that the French failed to appreciate the significance of Germany becoming "the dominant Power in Eastern Europe". And whatever could have possessed Taylor to say that the French "did not fear defeat if war were thrust upon them" in 1938?[15] Such affirmations, all of them, are baseless, at least as they are so tersely expressed in *Origins*. In fact, the French stepped up their fortification program along the Belgian frontier in 1936. They actually initiated the policy of non-intervention in Spain, instead of buckling under to pressure from London. They were only too conscious of what the consequences might be for their own security if Germany acquired the resources of eastern Europe. They certainly did fear military defeat at the hands of the Germans in 1938, *if* they were to face Germany on their own, without benefit of an Allied coalition. Taylor's inability to appreciate this point alone, suggests such a degree of misunderstanding that one cannot help but be frankly puzzled. Surely something has obscured the vision of this often remarkably insightful and undeniably gifted historian.

Part of his problem with the French is source-related. He knew from the start that there were difficulties to overcome, in particular the unevenness of the published diplomatic documentation, rich on the British and German sides but impoverished on the French and Russian.[16] Consequently, compensating as he could with a mixed array of other published sources, Taylor took the plunge, as he had to, assuring himself that there was little to be gained by waiting for the release of further archival material. In fairness, who would have wished otherwise? Nevertheless, it is also fair to suggest that Taylor – intent as he was on working with a broad, continental canvas – did not come close to exhausting the supply of very important French materials. By all appearances he did consult Paul-Bancour, Bonnet and Flandin, but he overlooked Baudouin, Cot, Fabry, Laval, Monzie, Reynaud, Tardieu and Zay. General Gamelin he read, but evidently not Armengaud, Bourret, Gauché, Jacomet, Minart, Nollet, Prételat, Réquin or Weygand. More remarkable, the eleven volumes of reports and testimonies produced by a French parliamentary commission just after the war seemed to have escaped Taylor's attention.[17] Though such criticism may be mistaken for cavil by some, the scholar will surely acknowledge the point. The fact is that Taylor, for all his Anglo-German research, made no extraordinary or even great effort to consult many of the French sources which were available to him and which he would have found instructive.

Another part of the problem comes from what one is tempted to call a cultural bias. In a word, it is this which makes it easy for many English to think ill of the French, a state of mind which is known to have been reciprocated by the French when given half a chance. The trick, of course, is to be able to sort out informed from uninformed bias, a service sometimes afforded by one historian to another. The "despairing cynicism" of the French in the 1930s, Taylor writes, their "lack of faith in their leaders and in themselves", had a "long and complicated origin which has often been dissected by historians".[18] Reassured by the reasoned analyses of these entirely unidentified scholars, and satisfied by the very predecessors whose other judgments he was in the process of discarding, Taylor was ready to confront the French. What ensued was a scattering of cryptic, unflinching, unsubstantiated, judgmental remarks about the French. Indeed, *Origins* is peppered with the language of some apprehensive day-tripper to Calais.

"Characteristically", the French failed to see the implications of their decisions on disarmament policy in April 1934. Faced with a renascent Germany, they "looked plaintively to London". Weak in spirit and devoid of resolution, they were responsible for "dragging the British down with them", for as everyone knows, "weakness is infectious".[19] Daladier, when not being "sullen", either "gave way" or "wriggled and dodged". He, the

"most representative of French politicians" led a people who
regularly had "acquiesced in" or "allowed" one German challenge to succeed after another, a people who had "supposed all
along that the advantages won in 1919 and subsequently . . .
were assets which they could supinely enjoy, not gains which
they must fiercely defend".[20] Indeed, for all of his assurance that
appeasement was a positive policy, generated by Chamberlain
without reference to military calculations, Taylor writes of the
prime minister's dilemma before the Commons in September
1938: "He could not stress the unwillingness of the French to
fight, which had been the really decisive weakness on the
western side."[21] Despite gallant attempts to be the impartial
exponent, and not the judge, there is little doubt that Taylor was
manifestly more successful when it came to treating England's
enemy than her ally.

Force of assumption, undiminished by a really thorough
reading of French source materials, does much to explain Taylor's handling of France. As a result, he is not merely unpredicta-
ble, he is often unreliable. It is, however, a tribute to his native
perspicacity and instinct that he can be as insightful as he
sometimes is. He is error-prone, he demonstrates no profound
sense of France's plight between the wars, and yet he still saw
what so many others did not. It was he who recognized the fact
that the Hoare–Laval proposal of December 1935 was not a
wicked French invention, indeed not French at all and only
arguably wicked. He also saw that the absence of a French
military reaction in March 1936 was the result of a deliberate
government policy, arranged in advance of the German initiative, and not the panic-induced paralysis of a government taken
by surprise. In a similar vein, Taylor's few sentences on the
subject correctly implied that the French government had no
intention of doing anything about the *Anschluss* in March 1938.
And he did not miss the fact that the Daladier government
assumed more and more of the diplomatic initiative in the wake
of the Munich conference, and especially after the fall of Prague
and the guarantee to Poland.[22] Each of these examples he may
have read perversely, in ways that were consistently unflattering
to the French; nevertheless, on the surface, when it came to
specific policy at specified moments, Taylor was indeed able to
"get things right" much of the time.[23] Considering the liabilities
with which he was working in the late 1950s – some more
avoidable than others – that is a respectable record. Indeed, it
may have been far better than many comparable studies which

noticed France only through peripheral vision. But clearly, it was not good enough.

I have suggested that Taylor, even when he gets it "right", demonstrates little interest in interwar France and, accordingly, no great understanding. Two illustrations come to mind: his practiced inability to see either skill or acumen behind French foreign policy in the 1930s; his failure to ask why the French seemed so anxious to keep in step with Britain, why they were "terrified at losing even the thin shreds of British support".[24] Both deficiencies derive from the same source – the ineradicable impression that, at worst, the French were craven and, at best, that they had been reduced to some catatonic state by the spectre of a new war. Out of this leaps the argument that the British were forced to take the initiative, forced to sort everything out, with the French "dragging protestingly along behind".[25]

The first illustration concerns Foreign Minister Pierre Flandin in March 1936. Taylor says, fairly, that the Sarraut government had decided in advance not to resist a German remilitarization of the Rhineland with force. Yet Flandin went to London and threatened to use the army unless the British government offered some new and further assurances for French security. Taylor says that this was mere bravado and that Flandin simply caved in when Baldwin condemned the notion of any kind of military riposte. After all, Flandin had never been serious about such action in the first place. Fair again, but all that Taylor can discern in this is a typical Frenchman "concerned to take his responsibility across the Channel and to leave it there".[26] He makes no connection between Flandin's apparent change of heart and the British decision of the same week to commit Britain "for the first time in her history – to peacetime alliance with a continental Great Power"; no connection between this milestone – designed only for restraining France, for "ceaselessly holding her back" – and Flandin's triumphant return to Paris where he announced the dawning of a new day in Anglo-French relations. If ever he suspected it, Taylor certainly never acknowledged even the possibility that a British government had been finessed. As for the retort that it was the French who had been finessed and unwittingly harnessed, one has only to invoke Taylor's murmured aside: "not that the French needed much restraining".[27] If not, then what explains his "alliance", unless Flandin's bluff had worked and the British government had felt compelled to defuse the situation?

Edouard Daladier receives similar treatment in the course of the Czech crisis of 1938. After Chamberlain's meeting with Hitler at Berchtesgaden, a series of Anglo-French meetings took place in London in the last two weeks of September. Daladier, by Taylor's record, had proven obstreperous. However much he "wriggled", he seemed to have a nasty habit of "returning to the question of principle". For their part, the British "were urging the French not to take the offensive". They even declined the possibility of a last minute meeting between Chamberlain and Daladier, just on the eve of the Munich conference, for fear that the French premier "would once more try ineffectually to coordinate resistance".[28] The trick was to keep the pressure on Daladier until he was trapped, but the premier had demanded something in exchange, one "essential condition". His acquiescence was contingent upon a British agreement to share in a formal guarantee to the forthcoming, rump Czech state. Chamberlain, the moralist, balked at such a commitment but finally relented. Daladier, Taylor's weak cynic, though "convinced in his heart that Germany was aiming at something far greater", had stood firm. As a result, he managed to commit Britain "to opposing Hitler's advance in the east". No mean achievement this, had it been deliberate; but of course it was not, not by Taylor's light. Rather, Daladier "had built better than he knew".[29] In short, he had succeeded by blunder and pure chance – a familiar Taylor motif – unaware of what he had done, or why. How many times can one afford to lift the glass to the blind eye?

There was something else that Daladier had demanded, and got, in London. This was the inauguration of more formalized staff talks with the English. Indeed, this was the one thing that Daladier was really after. All of his grudging concessions to Chamberlain, over a period of several months, need to be considered in the light of his determination to put some teeth into the "alliance" with Britain. This conclusion, to be sure, makes sense only if one rejects yet another of Taylor's contentions – namely that military considerations were not central to British policy in 1938 and that neither Britain nor France seriously envisaged the possibility of being defeated by Germany in 1938. This is not the place, nor is there space, to argue this point. Sometimes, à la Taylor, it is enough to rely on simple refutation. Recent research certainly raises many questions about his judgment of British policy – even to some extent where Chamberlain himself is concerned – and who but Taylor would suggest that the French were incapable of admitting the possibility of defeat?[30] Clearly, they were not. Accordingly, they were intensely interested in promoting joint Anglo-French planning through the medium of extended staff talks. To secure agreement here, the French government was prepared to adopt a policy in which it did not believe, and which it actually considered to be inimical to the peace of Europe. Taylor, distracted by seeing the French "dragged helplessly behind", catches little if any of this.[31]

But what made Britain so important to the French? Here is the second illustration of the problem Taylor has with France. For him the answer lies in the tirelessly repeated assertion that they were resolved to avoid war at any cost. This, of course, is neither argued nor substantiated, only reiterated. The combination of this technique, and the cultural bias previously discussed, means that the French emerge gutless from Taylor's mold. In the absence of clear historical exposition, there would appear to be no rhyme or reason to their fear of finding themselves at war. But just as there is another construction that can be placed on Flandin and Daladier, so there is another that may illuminate further the condition of France between the wars. Since the argument has been advanced before, and more thoroughly than is possible here, it should be sufficient to sketch its outline – namely that French foreign and military policy may be profitably appraised with some reference to the "guerre de longue durée".

This notion of a long war of attrition, similar to that which ended in 1918, was central to French official thinking between the wars.[32] Little wonder, therefore, that they found the prospect of some future war both awesome and repellent. Nevertheless; for twenty years the conviction endured that the Germans were bent on revenge, that France would be the principal adversary and the first victim of German attack. In the absence of outside assistance, the struggle would be uneven. Indeed, Germany was likely to win, thanks to its superior industrial and demographic resources. Short of resigning themselves to such an outcome – an alternative that even Taylor discards when he says they did not fear defeat – the French had to rebuild a coalition of allies, one that could be used to deter Germany from an act of revenge, or to defeat it if deterrence should fail. To that end, with very mixed results, the government of the Third Republic sought to enlist the co-operation of Belgium, Poland, Czechoslovakia, Romania, Yugoslavia, Italy and Russia. Each, for a time, was part of what is often called the French alliance "system". The term, though an exaggeration, is probably better than having French policy confused with alleged attempts to establish a new continental imperium. This was not what the French were after. Rather they wished to have at the ready allies who would help to defend France. As such, the contradictions between their reciprocal undertakings to each "ally" and their much remarked upon "defensive" military strategy, are perhaps more apparent than real.

The keystone of this system, however, was supposed to be Britain. It was to Britain that successive French governments turned for economic and financial support. The delayed onslaught of the depression in France had presaged a similarly delayed recovery, one that was not very apparent until the last quarter of 1938. Accordingly, French governments depended heavily on British fiscal co-operation and accommodation in order to engineer the economic recovery which the German danger had made imperative. Without that recovery, and the attendant acceleration of French rearmament, the chances of deterring Germany were reckoned to be slight. If deterrence failed, the argument for an Anglo-French alliance was all the more compelling.[33] In the event of an actual German attack, the best the French could hope to do by themselves was to secure a military stalemate. Thereafter, and in theory, the resources of the allies could be brought to bear against the initial German siege, and latterly to permit a war-winning strategic offensive. But all of this would take time, indeed, several years: time during which British coal could be delivered to France's wartime industries; time for essential raw materials from the French and British empires to be carried to France in British merchant ships; time for the British navy to join with that of France in an economic blockade of Germany, and to assist in the passage of troops from North Africa to France, or from France to some future theatre of military operations in eastern Europe. In short, British assistance was more than simply desirable, it was held to be indispensable. And this is what Taylor chooses not to explore, the possibility that something other than moral lethargy lay behind French behavior.

Certainly he was right to say that General Gamelin expressed confidence in military victory in 1938 – a victory entirely and expressly predicated on the presence of a broad, anti-German coalition. But this did not exist, as the general, and the premier, well knew. The British government, in particular, refused to contemplate a military confrontation with Germany in 1938.

That said, it was understandable why the French themselves declined to run the risk of war without firm and prior assurances of British support. They were alarmed not merely at the prospect of war itself – which overall they were more prepared to counten- ance than Chamberlain – but also by the possibility, even the likelihood, that they would be defeated in a strictly bilateral war with Germany. Far from craven, some might call it common sense. Others, were they to follow Taylor's own nostrum, might even see French policy as a coarse mix of principle and pragma- tism, and as such the work of "every statesman of any merit".[34] Certainly it is unclear why we should call "ignoble" Daladier's grudging consent to something he knew to be wrong, when Chamberlain's refusal to admit to any kind of wrong-doing is deemed to be "high-minded".

Nevertheless, the spell of A. J. P. Taylor endures. Even we, his sometime critics, see him as mentor and follow his example. Even as we are provoked by him, we may be inclined to reply in kind, over-accenting our arguments, implying a degree of self- assurance and of consensus that may not be there. The foregoing analysis is a case in point, for the fact is that it remains a maverick view, shared by a minority of scholars and a very tiny minority of general readers. In other words, Taylor still reigns, the lion whose tail is occasionally bitten by some mouse; but to use Donald Watt's sobering metaphor, "the mouse remains a mouse and the lion a lion".[35] It may be just as well, for the mice too have their differences.

Precisely what these differences are is rather difficult to say. Indeed, that which is most obvious is but the *appearance* of controversy among current scholars of interwar France. Real or apparent, however, central to any discussion and still presiding over it, is the distinguished French historian J.-B. Duroselle – lately retired professor at the Sorbonne, former director of the Institut d'Histoire des Relations Internationales Contempo- raines, and supervisor of some of the finest doctoral work done in France in the past two decades. It was in 1979 that Professor Duroselle published his massive study of French foreign policy in the 1930s which he entitled *La Décadence*. At first glance there is no mistaking the interpretive cast, one that had been familiar to A. J. P. Taylor twenty years earlier.

The actual theory of decadence is only expressly addressed in the book's sixteen-page introduction.[36] Here we find a survey of the principal flaws which pulled the republic down to ignominy in the 1930s. To begin with, there was a fundamental structural problem manifested in an overly powerful legislature and an emasculated executive branch; this accounted for the sixteen different governments that presided over France's destiny between 1932 and 1940. From this chronic upheaval came the associated problem of long-range planning for the purpose of international affairs. Hence we have Professor Duroselle's root cause of the uncertainty and indecisiveness which he detects in the country's foreign policy, but there is something more, something more serious. He is reluctant to suggest some kind of lethal blemish in the "national character", and is only slightly more willing to attribute this suspected decadence to the self-seeking, bourgeois governing class. Much more credible, he finds, is the prospect of linking whatever was wrong with France to the already discredited Marshal Pétain, the defeated and dismissed General Gamelin, the exiled and forever taciturn Alexis Léger. Here is proof, in some symbolic form, that the carnage of the First World War had denied the country of really first-class leadership when it came to facing her destiny in the interwar period. Here, in the Third Republic, "men proved weaker than fate".

Another voice has been added to that of Professor Duroselle, the voice of his successor at the Sorbonne and at the Institut, René Girault. In him we find a new and firm endorsement of the notion of decadence. "The perception of French power, among all decision-makers, was based on a strong sense of impotence. Decay was in the air. They were preparing for defeat." For Girault, the lack of will-power is at the heart of this decadence, at once symptom and cause of it. Like Duroselle, he is convinced that internal political divisions had proven so fractious that there was no longer one France but two, two nations divided over an ideological vision of where the greatest danger lay. Hence, there was no unified, single, national will; and in its absence, France gave to all observers the impression of being the new sick man of Europe.[37]

Clearly, Taylor would be quite at home with all of this, entirely familiar with the broad outline of this extraordinarily enduring view of interwar France. What could be more encouraging than to have the support of two such eminent French historians? Together, and expressly, they have ensured that the brief but sweeping judgments of *Origins* will retain their relevance for some years to come. Appraised in this light, therefore, one would have to grant that Taylor's version of France remains very much in the historical mainstream, despite the dissident and detracting comments that have been recorded earlier in these pages.

It would take a debunker of Taylor's talent and stature to overturn all of the dismal verdicts that have been pronounced on the failures of interwar France. Indeed, no one has tried, and no one seems likely to. The instances of brilliant policy brilliantly conducted are rare in human affairs, at least such is the impression left by generations of very tough-minded historians. This is neither more nor less true of France than elsewhere, despite the disturbing proclivity of some observers – French and foreign – to see France as perpetually exceptional. Common sense, to invoke one of Taylor's favourite devices, would tell us that interwar France, like prewar or postwar France, is likely to disclose a rather mixed legacy: on the one hand, oversights, mistakes, missed opportunities; and on the other hand, instances of success and achievement, some delivered through good planning, others through good fortune. Not surprisingly, this is indeed what we do find. The moment one discards the blurring vocabulary of French decadence – doubtfully appropriate when measured against the gulags of Stalin and the death camps of Hitler – one detects beneath the surface of this apparent historical controversy a consensus that in fact does not sit very comfortably with Taylor's understanding of France.

As Taylor himself recognized, popular morale in France of 1939 was not defeatist; but for him, the public mood was distinguished by an indecisive fatalism. They "were at a loss what to do; they therefore decided to let things happen".[38] None other than Professor Duroselle has hastened to correct that impression. In fact, a French public opinion poll taken shortly after Munich discovered that 70 per cent of the respondents believed that Britain and France ought to resist any subsequent demands from Berlin. Moreover, a later poll suggested that a very substantial majority of Frenchmen, once again, were in favor of military action if Germany chose to annex the Baltic port of Danzig by force. So it was, in Duroselle's opinion, that the French faced the approach of war in 1939 "with sadness but with resolution".[39] Pacifism, which had been in the ascendant in 1938, had become the refuge of a minority in 1939, as the public mood swung in favor of resistance. Though incapable of regenerating the enthusiastic but naive spirit of belligerence of 1914, the French nation grimly accepted the coming of war in August 1939.

The growing mood of resistance was in turn associated with

the very considerable upswing of the French economy between 1938 and 1939. Indeed, so substantial was the acceleration of industrial production between October 1938 and June 1939 that Professor Duroselle has concurred with the contemporary judgment of the London *Times*. It was a form of "miracle"; and from it came, among other things, the "remarkable" progress which was made in the area of aerial rearmament.[40] Two economic historians, Jean Bouvier and Robert Frank, have added their assent. More than this, they have used this economic renaissance to explain the contrast between French international policy in 1938 and 1939. In 1938 the overall economic situation was so troubled that Daladier could not accept the risk of war. A year later, when the economic mood was so much brighter, there was an appreciable increase in the nation's determination to check Hitler.[41] Such conclusions render two services, First, they credit the Daladier government with an actual *reason* for having gone along with Chamberlain in 1938. Secondly, they certainly imply that the spirit of resistance, far from extinguished in France, was quickly rekindled once there were some identifiable grounds for renewed economic optimism.

Similar conclusions are suggested by a look at the related field of military rearmament. Far from shunning war on principle – without any reference to the details of the military situation in 1938 – the French government was simply appalled by the "flagrant imbalance" that had arisen between French and German military capacities. This conclusion, reached by a highly competent team of French scholars under the direction of the army's historical director, adds further to the list of legitimate reasons why Daladier acted as he did in 1938. By the same token, the progress in rearmament, which was recorded between 1938 and 1939, especially in the air, certainly contributed to the government's decision to accept war only a year after the Munich conference.[42] France remained vulnerable, and doubtless unprepared for any major offensive, but the combination of its growing gains, the recent loss of Czechoslovakia and the threatened loss of Poland, made both its potential and its need for resistance that much more obvious. By the spring of 1940 the rhythm of its rearmament production had become even more impressive, yet another omen for those who would be captivated by French despair, resignation, or apathy.

If this proves insufficient, attention may be shifted to some recent works in the area of French military planning – from grand strategy to military doctrines, from rearmament administration to tactical theory. The French high command was not, so it seems, a group of doddering incompetents. No one is speaking of brilliance, but often of foresight and more often still of a highly-trained professionalism. This is the conclusion of Jeffery Gunsburg. Neither he nor Henri Michel – who has written a foreword for Gunsburg – is much drawn to the decadence thesis, the "moral decay" argument. Gunsburg, in fact, is struck by the technical proficiency of the French army in 1940, and explains its collapse within the much broader context of an Allied defeat.[43] Martin Alexander's recent study of General Gamelin also rejects the notion that France's problems can be neatly reduced to an allegedly timid and abject general staff. Rather, he argues, the generals of the 1930s were constantly confronting the problem of material shortages which had arisen from the 1920s, and which rightly sobered them whenever there was any question of a new war with Nazi Germany.[44] More recently still, Robert Doughty's work on French mechanized forces has convinced him that France fell in the course of the war, not before it began. Not for him the attribution of defeat to the "spiritual and political failure of the French people".[45] Nevertheless, as each of these works expressly acknowledges, the view of a France that was all thumbs seems quite unshaken. How ironic that some should see 1940 as the logical end of a long line of French blunders, when Taylor can attribute the Germany victory to a purely fortuitous blunder on Hitler's part.[46]

Still other works lend support to the view of a reviving France. Recent research by Serge Berstein on French political parties in the 1930s makes two important points. First, Daladier was seen by a majority of deputies from the centre and centre-right to be a "strong man", the kind of resolute leader who could preside over the recovery from uncertainty to confidence. Secondly, the premier enjoyed a quite remarkable popularity, not simply the momentary acclaim he received when he landed at Le Bourget after the Munich conference but rather a widespread and enduring public respect. In 1938–9 it was he who was seen as the symbol of a recovering France, of a republic rediscovering its self-confidence. It is for this reason that Berstein sees 1939 as "producing an undeniable psychological turning-point. Thanks to Daladier's vigour, the parties of the centre and right considered that the process of decline had been halted and that a revival was underway."[47] Again, no one believed that the country was out of the woods, with all of its problems behind it. Rather, what was believed was that France was on the road to recovery. Having been mired in a particularly acute economic depression, which had taken its toll on the franc, on industrial production and on class harmony, the country was beginning to find its feet.

Other recent work is also instructive on this point, partly because it generally forswears the language of decadence, and partly because it documents from a variety of perspectives a society that has retained much of its confidence and sense of purpose. Rediscovered financial optimism was part but not all of it. School textbooks in the 1930s, for instance, hardly inculcated defeatism or despair in the minds of schoolchildren. Indeed, if anything, the shock of 1940 was greater for the fact that French youth had not been fed on notions of Germany's power and invincibility. A significant current of French cinema, it is true, often expressed and perhaps spread a mood of despair and cynicism. But the officially-sponsored cinema combated the current with equal enthusiasm and imagination, drumming home the greatness of France and of its armed forces. And the foreign ministry, through its *Service des Oeuvres Françaises à l'Etranger*, steadily increased its expenditures from 1936 onward in order to reassert the cultural influence of France, even and particularly in the threatened areas of eastern Europe.[48] In short, the sense of revival which was articulated by the French financial attachés in 1938–9, or in the pages of the magazine *Marianne*, did not emerge from a period of unmitigated malaise and ennui.[49]

The mood of resistance that was becoming more prominent in 1939 clearly found more and more room for expression in the government's foreign policy.[50] Taylor did not miss this entirely, but he was at a loss to explain it in terms other than those of panic and desperation. Professor Duroselle, too, documents all of this with considerable care. Having been careful to disassociate Daladier and Bonnet from any of Chamberlain's illusions about Hitler, he goes on to recall the French refusal to follow political appeasement with any form of economic appeasement, and to deny that Bonnet washed his hands of eastern Europe during the talks with Ribbentrop in December 1938. So too does Duroselle record how firmly Daladier, in particular, resisted all British efforts to win Italy over by means of concessions from France, and how both he and Bonnet assumed more and more of the diplomatic initiative in the halting negotiations with Russia in the summer of 1939.[51] In other words, whether one looks to foreign policy or to the economy, to cultural policy or rearmament, to popular, parliamentary or party opinion, 1939 turns up as much evidence to question the theme of decadence as it does to endorse it. Perhaps the more striking, Professor Duroselle's own picture of a France with new-found courage in 1939 accords well with the findings of scholars who see the period from 1938 to 1940 as one of rejuvenation rather than of unbroken malaise.

Whether or not one believes that there was something fundamentally and peculiarly wrong with France in the 1930s, as Taylor did, there remains a final bone of contention. In his "Second Thoughts" of 1963 he prescribed that the historian's "sole duty is to find out what was done and why". A related dictum, however, proscribes the historian from considering "what ought to have been done".[52] The argument, though he offers none, presumably is that otherwise we would spend too much of our time fecklessly speculating on the historical "what ifs". Many will share this legitimate concern, but many may also worry that such a proscription on some occasion might disguise irresponsibility within a cloak of good intentions. For Taylor, history is deceptively simple. Tell it how it is and why, exposition and not judgment. But if it is exposition left unmeasured against any realistic yardstick of probabilities and "what ifs", it may also be exposition for which the historian cannot be held responsible. Unchecked from this quarter, and quite inspired by a sense of one's own impartiality, it becomes easy to fudge the difference between explanation and judgment. And so Taylor is intent on "explaining", sometimes magnanimously, where the British and French went wrong, how they misread Hitler and completely misunderstood him, thought he was planning to do them in, when he was not. Hitler was only waiting; waiting for his chance to extract more concessions. Their mistake, Taylor explains, beyond their basic misreading, was to have resorted to concessions, whether from drift or deliberation.

Is that it? They should have seen that Hitler was an arch opportunist, not a planner, and then denied him his opportunities. That would have left the initiative to him, would have put pressure on him, but with what likely result? We do not know; Taylor does not know. All we know is that such a disobliging approach had been characteristic of French policy over reparations and disarmament, a policy that had drawn much criticism from London at the time and one which Taylor himself likes no better than the over-supple policy of concessions in the later 1930s. Indeed, one has the nagging impression that the French can never get things quite right. Their disarmament policy earlier in the decade was criticized for being too rigid and unbending which, for the most part, it probably was.[53] In 1938 their policy was similarly condemned, partly because it appeared tough, and partly because it proved weak. Flexible or unyielding, French policy just never seemed quite in time with the beat followed in Whitehall. That led to contemporary British criticism and complaints, a perspective which Taylor seems to find eminently justified. Moreover, it is not clear from Taylor how, when or why the French – had they understood Hitler the way he does – might have changed from hard to soft policy, or vice versa. Neither is it clear how the British – endowed with Taylor's vision – might have responded to a more perspicacious French policy. It is enough for him to know where they went wrong. It is not necessary to test or confirm it; no flicker of interest from him over what would or could have happened if they had known what he knows. This, it must be reckoned, is the behavior of a judge, one who is forever appraising negligence, if not culpability, and who recognizes no obligation to justify any judgment. If it is not ostensibly a verdict, it is ostensibly more than an explanation. This, however, does not much concern Taylor, a man who is really not given to second thoughts. Over the years he has surrendered little ground, made few concessions, lest it be the relatively recent decision to minimize brushes with academic colleagues. "My view is that they should get on with writing books in their way and I will get on with writing them in mine."[54] Who will not approve, or fail to wish him well?

NOTES

1   A. J. P. Taylor, *The Origins of the Second World War* (Penguin, 1964), p. 336. All references are to this edition, one which contains his supplementary essay entitled "Second Thoughts". References to this are made under the essay's title.

2   Taylor, *Origins*, p. 38.

3   Taylor, "Second Thoughts", p. 15.

4   Taylor, *Origins*, pp. 134–5.

5   ibid., pp. 134, 151, 306. See "Metternich" in A. J. P. Taylor, *Grandeur and Decline* (Pelican, 1967), p. 23.

6   Taylor, *Origins*, pp. 141, 194, 212.

7   ibid., pp. 228, 234, 235.

8   Taylor, "Second Thoughts", pp. 9, 7.

9   Taylor, *Origins*, pp. 234–5, 201, 225. There is some irony to this

criticism. Twenty-five years ago Taylor was criticized for having treated Hitler as some ordinary German, despite the enormity of the crimes committed by his regime. By so doing, Taylor was charged with abdicating his moral responsibility as an historian. Today he is being criticized for making too many moral judgments about the French, principally by means of implication and insinuation. For the earlier criticism, see C. Robert Cole, "Critics of the Taylor view of history", in *The Origins of the Second World War*, ed. E. M. Robertson (London, 1971), pp. 142–57. See also the articles by Oswald Hauser and John W. Boyer in the special issue of *Journal of Modern History*, vol. 49, no. 1 (March 1977), pp. 34–9, 40–72.

10   R. J. Young, *In Command of France: French Foreign Policy and Military Planning, 1933–1940* (Cambridge, Mass., 1978), p. 1.

11   A. J. P. Taylor, "Accident prone, or what happened next", *Journal of Modern History*, vol. 49, no. 1 (March 1977), p. 18.

12   Taylor, *Origins*, pp. 161, 167, 204, 222.

13   ibid., p. 233.

14   ibid., pp. 149, 158.

15   ibid., pp. 203, 233.

16   ibid., p. 37.

17   These and other materials are surveyed in R. J. Young, *French Foreign Policy, 1918–1945. A Guide to Research and Research Materials* (Wilmington, Del., 1981).

18   Taylor, *Origins*, p. 72.

19   ibid., pp. 107, 197, 209.

20   ibid., pp. 216, 219, 225, 322, 233.

21   ibid., p. 236.

22   ibid., pp. 126, 130–8, 175–87, 264–336.

23   Taylor, "Second Thoughts", p. 10.

24   Taylor, *Origins*, p. 109.

25   ibid., pp. 246, 202.

26   ibid., p. 132.

27   ibid., p. 148.

28   ibid., pp. 225–6, 228.

29   ibid., pp. 219–20.

30   In 1938 the British Chiefs of Staff admitted their uncertainty as to whether the Germans were capable of delivering a knockout blow against England from the air. For his part, the prime minister warned his cabinet in August that the country could not face the prospect of war with much confidence. See R. A. C. Parker, "Perceptions de la puissance par les décideurs britanniques 1938–1939: le Cabinet", in *La Puissance en Europe, 1938–1940*, eds René Girault and Robert Frank (Paris, 1984), p. 48.

31   Taylor, *Origins*, pp. 202, 246.

32   Conference paper by Philippe Masson, "La marine française et la stratégie alliée 1938–39", presented to the Colloque Franco-Allemand, Bonn, 1978. See also Eleanor M. Gates, *End of the Affair:*

The Collapse of the Anglo-French Alliance, 1939–1940 (Berkeley, 1980), pp. 3–17; and R. J. Young, "La Guerre de Longue Durée: some reflections on French strategy and diplomacy in the 1930s", in *General Staffs and Diplomacy before the Second World War*, ed. Adrian Preston (London, 1974), pp. 41–64.

33 See the two fine papers by René Girault and Robert Frankenstein, respectively entitled, "The impact of the economic situation on the foreign policy of France, 1936–1939". and "The decline of France and French appeasement policies, 1936–1939", in *The Fascist Challenge and the Policy of Appeasement*, eds Wolfgang J. Mommsen and Lothar Kettenacker (London 1983), pp. 209–26, 236–45.

34 Taylor, *Origins*, p. 129.

35 D. C. Watt, "Some aspects of A. J. P. Taylor's work as diplomatic Historian", *Journal of Modern History*, vol. 49, no. 1 (March 1977, p. 33.

36 J.-B. Duroselle, *La Décadence, 1932–1939* (Paris, 1979), pp. 11–27.

37 René Girault, "Les décideurs français et la puissance française en 1938–1939", in *La Puissance en Europe*, p. 39.

38 Taylor, *Origins*, p. 322.

39 Duroselle, *Décadence*, pp. 355–6. See also his *L'Abîme, 1939–1945* (Paris, 1982), pp. 17–18. This conclusion has been questioned by the remarkable, not to say extraordinary, construction advanced by a psychohistorian who perceives a "suicidal group fantasy" at work on the inexorable road to 1940. See Stephen Ryan, "Reflections on the psychohistory of France, 1919–1940", *Journal of Psychohistory*, vol. 11, no. 2 (Fall 1983), pp. 225–41.

40 Duroselle, *Décadence*, pp. 444, 457.

41 Jean Bouvier and Robert Frank, "Sur la perception de la 'puissance' économique en France pendant les années 1930", in *La Puissance en Europe*, pp. 182–3. For the contribution of the Comité des Forges and the Conféderation du Patronat to this new mood, see H. Coutau-Bégarie, "Comment les Français se sont préparés à la guerre". *Revue d'Histoire Diplomatique*, vol. 97, nos 3/4 (1983), p. 347.

42 Général J. Delmas, "La perception de la puissance militaire française", in *La Puissance en Europe*, pp. 127–40. This paper is the work of a military study group which included Elisabeth du Réau, Lt.-Col. Henry Dutailly, Marc Nouschi, Patrick Facon, Maurice Vaïsse, Antoine Marès, and Lt.-Col. Turlotte. On the subject of French rearmament, see the work by Robert Frankenstein, *Le prix du réarmement français, 1935–1939* (Paris, 1982).

43 Jeffery A. Gunsburg, *Divided and Conquered: The French High Command and the Defeat of the West, 1940* (Westport, Conn., 1979). For a dissenting, if familiar, view of the French army, see the peculiarly self-possessed work by Williamson Murray, *The Change in the European Balance of Power, 1938–1939* (Princeton, NJ, 1984).

44 Martin S. Alexander, "Maurice Gamelin and the defence of

France: French military policy, the UK land contribution and strategy towards Germany, 1935–1939", unpublished doctoral thesis, (Oxford University, 1982), p. 325.

45   Conference paper by Lt.-Col. Robert Doughty, "French mechanized forces: the tank as an infantry-support weapon", presented to the Northern Great Plains History Conference, September 1983, p. 1.

46   Taylor, "Second Thoughts", p. 19.

47   Serge Berstein, "La perception de la puissance par les partis politiques français en 1938–1939", in *La Puissance en Europe*, pp. 294–6.

48   The following articles appear in a single issue of *Relations Internationales*, no. 33 (Spring 1983) addressed to "Images de la France en 1938–1939": Christine Sellin, "Les manuels scholaires et la puissance française", pp. 103–11; Rémy Pithon, "Opinions publiques et représentations culturelles face aux problèmes de la puissance. Le témoignage du cinéma français 1938–1939", pp. 91–101; Antoine Marès, "Puissance et présence culturelle de la France. L'example du Service des Oeuvres françaises à l'Etranger dans les années 30", pp. 65–80.

49   Robert Frank, "Les attachés financiers et la perception de la puissance en 1938–1939", ibid., pp. 23–42; Claude Lèvy, "L'image de la puissance française dans un hebdomadaire dépolitisé: *Marianne*", ibid., pp. 113–21.

50   See Elisabeth du Réau, "Enjeux stratégiques et redéploiement diplomatique français: novembre 1938–septembre 1939", *Relations Internationales*, no. 35, (Autumn 1983), pp. 319–35.

51   Duroselle, *Décadence*, chs 12–15. In recent years Professor A. P. Adamthwaite has developed one of the most intriguing interpretive possibilities, one which combines a renewed assertion of French independence and initiative with a perceived goal of appeasement rather than resistance. See his "France and the coming of war", in *The Fascist Challenge and the Policy of Appeasement*, pp. 246–56; his "War origins again", *Journal of Modern History*, vol. 56, no. 1 (March 1984), pp. 100–115; and his earlier book, *France and the Coming of the Second World War* (London, 1977).

52   Taylor, "Second Thoughts", p. 26.

53   See the fine study of Maurice Vaisse, *Sécurité d'Abord. La politique française en matière de désarmement, 9 décembre 1930–17 avril 1934* (Paris, 1981). See also his "Against appeasement: French advocates of firmness, 1933–1938", in *The Fascist Challenge and the Policy of Appeasement*.

54   Taylor, "Accident prone", p. 17.

5

Hitler's Foreign Policy

NORMAN RICH

The very fact that the present volume of essays has been prepared to mark the twenty-fifth anniversary of the publication of A. J. P. Taylor's *The Origins of the Second World War* attests to the impact of the book on historical thinking and its importance for all subsequent considerations of the subject. One may disagree with those admirers of Taylor who regard him as England's greatest living historian, but there can be no argument that he is one of the most provocative and controversial. And in none of his many works did he set forth more provocative ideas than in the book under discussion.

It is a brilliant book, filled with astute observations and insights, with challenges to conventional wisdom in almost every line. It is also a very readable book, in part because it is so controversial, for it constantly prods the assumptions of its readers, stirring up annoyance, argument – and upon occasion, admiration. It has compelled every student of the Nazi era to re-examine his own views about the subject, and over the years some of the ideas once considered controversial have become part of the conventional wisdom.

Taylor professes to be unhappy with his acceptance into the realm of conventional wisdom. In his memoirs he observes that *Origins* "despite its defects, has now become the new orthodoxy, much to my alarm". He denies, however, that his book has the qualities I have described above and which most of his colleagues have attributed to it. "Where others see it as original and provocative, I find it simply a careful scholarly work, surprising only to those who had never been faced with the truth before."[1] Taylor's work may be scholarly, but it is not careful, and much of it remains surprising to other historians, many of them as scholarly as Taylor and considerably more careful, who have arrived at very different interpretations of the "truth". For, contrary to what Taylor may think, much of *Origins* has not become part of the new orthodoxy, and the parts of the book which continue to be most vigorously contested are those which aroused most controversy in the first place, namely his theories about the subject of the present essay, Hitler's foreign policy.

In *Origins*, Taylor challenges the interpretation of other historians who based their views about Hitler's foreign policy, at least in part, on documents presented in evidence at the Nuremberg trials. He points out, quite correctly, that these documents were "loaded" and he maintains, without bothering to prove his point, that scholars who relied on them had found it impossible to escape from the load with which they were charged.[2] Taylor's method of escaping from that load was to ignore these documents altogether, and at the same time he cavalierly disregarded a great deal of other evidence which did not happen to fit with his own theories. Every historian, of course, is compelled to be selective in his use of evidence. The great weakness of Taylor's book, especially his treatment of Hitler's foreign policy, is the perverse nature of his selectivity and his deliberate rejection of much of the thoroughly reliable evidence on which the theories of many of his colleagues are based. An even graver weakness is that Taylor's own theories are frequently inconsistent and contradictory.

He rejects the Nazi claim that the formation of a Hitler government in January 1933 was a seizure of power, but he challenges the views of other historians as to why and how Hitler came to power. "Whatever ingenious speculators, liberal or Marxist, might say, Hitler was not made Chancellor because he would help the German capitalists to destroy the trade unions, nor because he would give the German generals a great army, still less a great war . . . He was not expected to carry through revolutionary changes in either home or foreign affairs. On the contrary the conservative politicians . . . who recommended him to Hindenburg kept the key posts for themselves and expected Hitler to be a tame figurehead." These expectations were confounded, Taylor says, for Hitler proved to be the most radical of revolutionaries. He made himself all-powerful dictator, destroyed political freedom and the rule of law, transformed German economics and finance, abolished the individual German states, and made Germany for the first time a united country.

In one sphere alone, Taylor says, Hitler changed nothing. "His foreign policy was that of his predecessors, of the professional diplomats at the foreign ministry, and indeed of virtually all Germans. Hitler, too, wanted to free Germany from the restrictions of the [Versailles] peace treaty; to restore a great German army; and then to make Germany the greatest power in Europe from her natural weight." The only difference between Hitler and "virtually all Germans" were occasional differences in emphasis. Two paragraphs later, however, Taylor informs us that Hitler's foreign policy did in fact differ from that of at least some of his predecessors, for Hitler did not attempt to revive the "world policy" which Germany had pursued before 1914, he made no plans for a great German battle fleet, he did not parade a grievance about lost colonies except to embarrass the British, and he was not at all interested in the Middle East. Taylor concludes that "the primary purpose of his policy, if not the only one" was expansion into eastern Europe.

With that Taylor is saying that the differences between Hitler's foreign policy and that of his predecessors were in fact far more significant than mere matters of emphasis. He then goes on to describe precisely that quality which distinguished Hitler most radically not only from his predecessors but from all other ordinary statesmen. "The unique quality in Hitler was the gift of translating commonplace thoughts into action . . . The driving force in him was a terrifying literalism." There was nothing new about denunciations of democracy; it took Hitler to create a totalitarian dictatorship. There was nothing new about anti-Semitism; it took Hitler to push anti-Semitism to the gas chambers. "It was the same with foreign policy. Not many Germans really cared passionately and persistently whether Germany again dominated Europe. But they talked as if they did. Hitler took them at their word. He made the Germans live up to their professions, or down to them – much to their regret."

More careful scholars may deplore Taylor's tendency to assume a knowledge of what "not many Germans" cared for, and with what intensity, and his own frequent inconsistencies on that subject, but many historians share his views about the importance of Hitler's terrifying literalism and many had drawn attention to this quality long before the appearance of *Origins*. Taylor, however, always unwilling to be thought in agreement with generally accepted opinions, pours scorn on colleagues who have purported to discover in Hitler's writings and policy statements an exposition of the ideas which he proposed to translate into action. *Mein Kampf,* Hitler's table talk, the records of his top-secret conferences with his senior aides and officers in which he described his future plans in minute detail – all these revelations of Hitler's thinking are dismissed by Taylor as irrelevant flights of fancy, not to be taken seriously as indications of his true intentions. Writers of great authority, Taylor says, have seen in Hitler a system-maker who from the first deliberately prepared a great war that would make him master of the world. Taylor rejects such theories with some contempt. In his opinion, statesmen are too absorbed by events to follow a preconceived plan; such plans are in reality the creation of historians, and the systems attributed to Hitler are really those of Trevor-Roper, Elizabeth Wiskemann, and Alan Bullock. Taylor concludes that Hitler did indeed create systems, but these were no more than day-dreams concocted in his spare time.

Taylor attributes much of the success of Hitler's foreign policy to his very lack of preconceptions and prejudices, and cites as examples his willingness to conclude a non-aggression pact with Poland and his disregard of German nationalist sentiment in conceding the South Tyrol to Mussolini to secure Italian friendship. Apart from that, Taylor attributes Hitler's success primarily to his ability to play a waiting game, to take advantage of the offers and opportunities presented to him by his adversaries. Even then Taylor is not sure whether this technique was at first either conscious or deliberate. "The greatest masters of statecraft are those who do not know what they are doing," he says, thereby suggesting that Hitler was both a great master of statecraft and that he did not know what he was doing.[3] Yet Taylor has already stated, on the preceding page, that the primary purpose of Hitler's foreign policy was expansion into eastern Europe, and only a few pages later he says that the mainspring of Hitler's immediate policy had been the destruction of the Versailles treaty, although once this objective had been attained he was at a loss of what to do next. As for any long-range plans, Taylor considers it "doubtful whether he had any".[4]

Taylor's inconsistencies continue. Although he states (p. 72) that the primary purpose of Hitler's policy was eastward expansion (which for Hitler meant the acquisition of living space or *Lebensraum*), he then denies (p. 105) that Hitler's desire for *Lebensraum* or economic motives in general were a cause of the Second World War. *Lebensraum* did not drive Germany to war, he says. Rather war, or a warlike policy, produced the demand for *Lebens-*

raum. Hitler and Mussolini were not driven by economic motives. Like most statesmen, they had an appetite for successes. They differed from others only in that their appetite was greater and that they fed it by more unscrupulous means. *Lebensraum* in its crudest sense meant a demand for empty space where Germans could settle but, Taylor argues, Germany was not over-populated in comparison with most European countries and there was no empty space in Europe. "When Hitler lamented: 'If only we had a Ukraine . . .', he seemed to suppose that there were no Ukrainians. Did he propose to exploit, or to exterminate them? Apparently he never considered the question one way or the other."[5]

These statements glaringly expose the disastrous consequences of Taylor's refusal to acknowledge the significance of those sources in which Hitler set forth his ideological preconceptions and revealed his long-range plans based upon them. For Hitler *had* considered the question of what to do about the Ukrainians; he *did* propose to exploit or exterminate them – and all other non-Aryan peoples in eastern Europe besides. These plans were set forth in detail in *Mein Kampf*, and Hitler continued to expound them in almost identical terms in subsequent policy statements before and during the war. In rejecting the evidence of such policy statements, Taylor misses the absolutely fundamental point of Hitler's foreign policy – the nature of the literalism which he proposed to translate into practice.

Taylor recognizes that when Germany actually conquered the Ukraine in 1941, Hitler and his henchmen tried both methods, exploitation and extermination, but he comments that neither method brought them any economic advantages.[6] Here again Taylor completely misses the point. Hitler was not primarily concerned with any immediate economic advantage – in 1941 he still thought Russia could be conquered within weeks, and when it became obvious that this would not be possible it was too late to reverse his policies even if he wanted to do so, which he did not. The primary purpose of Hitler's foreign policy and his fundamental aim in the Second World War was the realization of his long-range plan for the acquisition of *Lebensraum* in eastern Europe which was to ensure the security and well-being of the German people for all time. As he specifically declared in *Mein Kampf* and subsequent policy statements, this conquest of territory should not include the conquest of people and the absorption of non-Aryans into the Germanic empire, for such absorption would dilute the purity of Germanic blood and thereby weaken the Germanic peoples. It was for this reason that the non-Aryans would have to be eliminated. This was the policy Hitler and his henchmen actually introduced in Russia after 1941, a policy which, as Taylor correctly says, brought them no economic advantage. On the contrary, the economic consequences of that policy, not to mention the moral, political and military consequences, were disastrous and contributed significantly to Germany's ultimate defeat. This policy, like the extermination of the Jews, cannot be equated with that of other statesmen with a mere appetite for success. It was the policy of a fanatic idealogue who ignored sober calculations of national interest in order to put his manic ideas into practice.

Taylor's belief that Hitler was simply a political opportunist without long-range purposes remains a central theme of his chronicle and analysis of the actual course of Hitler's foreign policy, in which he continues to present us with inconsistencies and contradictions. In his discussion of the annexation of Austria, for example, Taylor concedes that Hitler "certainly meant to establish control over Austria", but he believes that the way in which this came about was for him a tiresome accident, "an interruption of his long-term policy" (whereby Taylor seems to admit that there was in fact a long-term policy.) At the same time he dismisses as a myth the theory that Hitler's seizure of Austria was a deliberate plot, devised long in advance. "By the *Anschluss* – or rather by the way in which it was accomplished – Hitler took the first step in the policy which was to brand him as the greatest of war criminals. Yet he took this step unintentionally. Indeed he did not know that he had taken it."[7]

Taylor is absolutely correct in saying that the *way* the *Anschluss* took place was to a large extent accidental and improvised, and that it was not carried out in accordance with a strategy prepared long in advance. In the *Anschluss* crisis, Hitler's hand was forced by the actions of others and he took the final step of actually incorporating Austria into the Reich only when the events of the *Anschluss* convinced him he could afford to do so. But to say that he took this step unintentionally, or did not know he had taken it, is nonsense. On the first page of *Mein Kampf* and in numerous subsequent policy statements, Hitler declared that the incorporation of Austria into the Reich was the primary immediate objective of his policy, and the documentary evidence leaves no doubt whatever that the annexation of Austria was indeed a deliberate plot, prepared long in advance, and that it was conceived as the first step in the domination of eastern Europe.

In his analysis of the *Anschluss* and all other episodes in Hitler's foreign policy, Taylor challenges the theory that Hitler was operating according to a carefully prepared blueprint and time-table. Taylor's emphasis on the accidental and improvised qual-ity in Hitler's actual execution of his policies is valid, but in tilting against the blueprint or timetable theories he seems to be setting up straw men in order to knock them down. It is true that some historians have written about blueprints and timetables, but even the most extreme champions of blueprint–timetable theories never suggested that Hitler had precisely conceived plans for every step of his expansionist policy and a precise timetable for carrying them out. Obviously he had to improvise, to take into account the constant fluctuations in the political scene, and to adjust to the moves of his opponents. All the blueprint–timetables people were saying was that Hitler had precisely defined war aims, primarily the conquest of *Lebensraum* in eastern Europe, that he had detailed plans for carrying them out, and that there was an uncanny consistency between the ideas expressed in his prewar policy statements and the policies he actually put into effect.

When *Origins* was first published, much of the critical wrath directed against the book (and in certain quarters, much of the critical approval it received) was aroused by the belief that Taylor was defending Hitler. Nothing could have been further from the truth. In saying that in foreign policy alone Hitler changed nothing, that his foreign policy was that of his pre-decessors "and indeed of virtually all Germans", he is not defending Hitler. Instead he is equating Hitler with "virtually all Germans", as he makes clear in a later edition of *Origins*. "Most of all, [Hitler] was the creation of German history and of the German present. He would have counted for nothing without the support and cooperation of the German people . . . Hitler was a sounding-board for the German nation. Thousands, many hundred thousand, Germans carried out his evil orders without qualm or question." And he concludes: "In international affairs there was nothing wrong with Hitler except that he was a German."[8]

With that Taylor reverts to the line adopted in his wartime book, *The Course of German History*, which some of his admirers have excused as a regrettable wartime polemic but which Tay-lor himself stoutly defended in a new preface to that book when it was republished in 1962, the year after the publication of *Origins*. In this preface he explains that his book had proved unacceptable to its original sponsors because it failed to show that Hitler was a bit of bad luck in German history and that all Germans, apart from a few wicked men, were bubbling over with enthusiasm for democracy, Christianity, or some other noble cause which would turn them into acceptable allies once we had liberated them from their tyrants. Not so, says Taylor. The entire course of German history "shows that it was no more a mistake for the German people to end up with Hitler than it is an accident when a river flows into the sea . . . Nothing, it seems to me, has happened since [i.e., between 1945 and 1962] to disturb the conclusions at which I then arrived." According to Taylor, the 70–80 million Germans have always feared the Slavs, and this fear underlay the Germans' plans for their conquest and extermination. "No German of political consequence thought of accepting the Slavs as equals and living at peace with them" – and Taylor believes the Germans have not changed in this respect.[9] The Third Reich, he writes in *The Course of German History*, represented the deepest wishes of the German people. "Every German desired the achievement which only total war could give. By no other means could the Reich be held together. It had been made by conquest and for conquest; if it ever gave up its career of conquest it would dissolve." In contrast to the Germans there were the Slavic peoples "with their deep sense of equality, their love of freedom, and their devotion to humanity", under whose auspices, Taylor believes, conditions in eastern Europe have improved immensely since the dark days of German and Magyar domination.[10]

Taylor continued to adhere to this interpretation of Germany and the Germans. In a discussion of the German problem as it emerged from the First World War, he writes that there has been an almost universal misunderstanding about the nature of that problem, "a misunderstanding perhaps even shared by Hitler". The Germans desired equality with the victor states, they wanted to cast off restrictions on their national soveriegnty imposed by the Versailles treaty, and many non-Germans sympathized with what they regarded as these perfectly legitimate aspirations. But the inevitable consequences of fulfilling those German desires, Taylor says, was that Germany would become the dominant state in Europe. And what this would have meant for Europe can be seen from the German plans for the rearrangement of Europe if they had won the First World War, plans exposed in detail in 1961 and after in the publications of the German historian Fritz Fischer and his school. "It was a

Europe indistinguishable from Hitler's empire at its greatest extent, including even a Poland and a Ukraine cleared of their native inhabitants. Hitler was treading, rather cautiously, in Bethmann's footsteps. There was nothing new or unusual in his aims or outlook."[11] Taylor thus endorses the most extreme interpretations of Fischer and his followers who, with virtually unrestricted access to German archival records following Germany's defeat in the Second World War, put together a monumental collection of policy statements and speculations about German diplomatic and military goals drawn up by German leaders from every walk of life before and during the First World War.

Taylor and the more extreme representatives of the Fischer school may be right in assuming that a German government victorious in the First World War would have behaved exactly as Hitler did in the Second World War, or worse. The only record we have of a German government's actual treatment of Slavs, however, is that of Prusso-German rule over those segments of Poland taken by Prussia in the eighteenth-century partitions of Poland, at which time, it will be recalled, Slavic Russia took the lion's share. The Prusso-German treatment of the Poles has often been criticized, and with good reason, but during the entire period of German rule over the Poles there was never any suggestion of an attempt to exterminate them. What the Germans were trying to do was to Germanize them, and with notable lack of success.[12] It was Hitler, and only Hitler, who attempted to rectify what he regarded as this mistaken policy of Germanization through extermination – and not at all cautiously, either.

In the years since the Second World War, the United States seems to have replaced Germany as Taylor's principal political bugbear, and although he is not uncritical of the Soviet Union, he has complacently accepted that state's assumption of the role of protector and spokesman of the Slavic peoples and all other nationalities of Eastern Europe. "I had not the slightest illusion about the tyranny and brutality of Stalin's regime," Taylor writes in his memoirs. "But I had been convinced throughout the nineteen thirties that Soviet predominance in eastern Europe was the only alternative to Germany's and I preferred the Soviet one. Moreover I believed that East European states, even when under Soviet control, would be preferable to what they had been between the wars, as has proved to be the case. Hence Soviet ascendency of eastern Europe had no perils for me." Taylor defends the communist takeover in Czechoslovakia and the

Russian suppression of the Hungarian revolution. "Better a Communist regime supported by Soviet Russia . . . than an anti-Communist regime led by Cardinal Mindszenty. Hence my conscience was not troubled by the Soviet intervention." Taylor's conscience was similarly untroubled when it was learned that the British art historian Anthony Blunt had spied for the Russians, and he successfully opposed Blunt's expulsion from the British Academy.[13] In notable contrast to this attitude towards the Russians, Taylor has condemned almost every act of American foreign policy. At the time of the Korean war, Taylor, who claims to have been a staunch opponent of appeasement in the 1930s, declared appeasement to be "the noblest word in the diplomat's language".[14] "Even now," he wrote in 1956, "which of us on the Left could say, hand on heart, that in a conflict between the United States and the Soviet Union our individual sympathies would be with the United States?"[15]

Such comments aroused consternation among many Americans and their British friends, and they were clearly intended to do so. For in his most recent books, as in *Origins* and indeed all his works, Taylor continues to play the role of gadfly, often striking out wildly and unfairly but often telling us unpalatable truths which other commentators lack the imagination to perceive or the audacity to express. In this essay I have not been sparing of my criticism of Taylor. I find many of his ideas ridiculous and his prejudices downright shameful for a historian, and I am irritated by his persistent efforts to surprise and confound his readers. Yet he has always been and he remains one of the most stimulating and readable of historians, whose great contribution is not his own scholarship but his challenges to the values and assumptions of his audience. In response to critics of *Origins* who accused him, quite mistakenly, of failing to condemn Hitler's criminality with sufficient vigor, Taylor confessed that he himself could not get it out of his head that Hitler was an indescribably wicked man. "But this is because I belonged to his generation. He was as wicked as he could be. But he was only a beginner. The rulers of the United States and of Soviet Russia are now cheerfully contemplating a hideous death for seventy million people or perhaps a hundred and fifty million people in the first week of the next war. What has Hitler to show in comparison with this? I think we had better leave Hitler's immorality alone as long as we go clanking around with nuclear weapons."[16]

As the preparation of the present volume reminds us, the publication of *The Origins of the Second World War* aroused enormous furor in the historical profession and provoked a reconsideration of the policies of all the major powers involved. So far as Hitler's foreign policy was concerned, the principal historical debate set off by Taylor's book was whether, as the Nuremberg prosecution and numerous historians maintained, his policy was dedicated to the achievement of long-range objectives, his strategy and tactics worked out long in advance; or whether, as Taylor contended, Hitler was an opportunist and improviser who took advantage of the accidental shifts in the international situation and the mistakes of his opponents. Taylor says that this debate is now sterile, but in stirring it up in the first place he compelled many historians to revise or modify their views and to recognize how much of Hitler's foreign policy was in fact improvised and opportunistic. Moreover, although the debate as originally formulated may be sterile, it remains central to controversies over Hitler's policies in general despite changes in the terminology employed, differences in emphasis, and the introduction of new varieties of evidence.

Because of the sheer amount of historical literature dealing with Hitler's foreign policy that has been produced during the past quarter century, it is manifestly impossible to provide an adequate evaluation of the individual works representing the various schools of thought on the subject in the scope of a a brief essay – a mere list of such works would fill a substantial volume. I have therefore confined myself to a short survey of what appear to me to be the principal lines of interpretation and controversy.[17]

Let me dispose at once of the small group of writers who seek to defend Hitler, who represent him as a man of peace who sought only justice and equality for Germany, as the hapless victim of the implacable hostility of Germany's enemies and of Bolshevik–Jewish–Capitalist conspiracies. Taylor describes one of these apologies as a "perfectly plausible book," which it is not.[18] Moreover, all such works are characterized by flagrant misrepresentations or outright falsifications of the evidence and do not deserve to be considered in a discussion of serious historical scholarship.

Apart from the old and neo-Nazis, those writers bearing the heaviest and most obvious ideological burden are the members of the Soviet and East European school of thought, which has been joined by a number of Marxists and other left-wing intellectuals in the West. This group represents Hitler, Nazism, and fascism in general as the products and instruments of capitalist-imperialist society, and the Second World War as a Western-capitalist conspiracy to destroy the Soviet Union. From this school we hear nothing about the Anglo-French guarantees to Poland in 1939 or the Hitler–Stalin pact, but much about appeasement which is generally interpreted as a diplomatic maneuver to direct Nazi aggression against Russia. Proceeding from these assumptions, the members of this school have no trouble finding and intepreting evidence which proves their case.

Theoretically akin to the East Europeans and their adherents, but on the whole far more honest in their use of evidence and imaginative in the questions they raise, are the members of what might be called the "fundamental forces" school of thought. These scholars regard Hitler and the Nazi movement as the products of fundamental forces in German political, economic, and social life, and of the institutions, modes of thought, and behavioral patterns developed in the course of the German historical experience. In their basic assumptions, the members of this school are thus in general agreement with Taylor, especially his *Course of German History*, but they have gone far beyond his simplistic explanations and generalizations. In their own search for explanations of the Hitler phenomenon, they have produced many profound and original studies of German life and society, and altogether they have enormously enriched our understanding of German history and institutions. There is nevertheless a certain uniformity and even sterility about their work. In proceeding from the assumption that Hitlerism was a product of fundamental forces in German history, they tend to search for and focus on those aspects of the German past which can be intepreted as being precursors of the Nazi movement. In the process they frequently ignore the contemporary circumstances in which those policies were conceived and conducted, or fail to take adequate account of the differences in values and attitudes of earlier epochs. And because their research is dedicated to discovering those qualities in German life that produced Hitler, the lines of their research as well as their conclusions are to a large extent predetermined.

Inseparable from the "fundamental forces" school, but requiring special mention because of its importance in contemporary German historiography, is the "continuity" school of German history. The members of this group differ from the "fundamental forces" scholars in their special emphasis on the consistency in the aims and methods of German leaders, and in their efforts to demonstrate that the policies of Hitler were a continuation of policies already pursued or planned by the rulers of Austria, Prussia, Imperial Germany, and Weimar. They too are thus in basic agreement with the Taylor thesis about German history, and in their research they have discovered an enormous quantity of evidence to substantiate that thesis. But, as in the case of the "fundamental forces" school, the results of that research is to a large extent predetermined, and as one recent critic has commented, "with the exercise of a little ingenuity almost anything can be fitted into this concept".[19]

To be fair to the "fundamental forces–continuity" historians, they do not all share the view that the Germans are invested with a particularly heavy dose of original sin. A number of them stress the importance of the peculiar nature of the German historical experience, the devastating effects of the Thirty Years War, and the more lasting effects of the treaties of Westphalia ending that war which sanctioned permanent French and Swedish interference in German affairs and for over two centuries halted German national development. Others have drawn attention to the importance of geographical factors, the position of the Germans in central Europe between the French in the west and the Slavs in the east, the Germans' lack of readily defensible or even definable frontiers and their consequent emphasis on the need for a strong army.

Opposed to both the "fundamental forces" and "continuity" schools are historians who refuse to accept the theory that Hitler was an inevitable product of German history or that his policies were simply the continuation of policies of earlier German leaders. Instead they regard him as a unique phenomenon in the German historical experience, and his regime and its bestial policies as a disastrous deviation from the main lines of German history. Members of this "discontinuity" school are of course unable to deny the existence of continuity, for all history is a continuous process, but they contend that both Hitler's domestic and foreign policies represented departures from previous German political and diplomatic traditions. This was particularly true of his foreign policy which, unlike all previous German foreign policies, was consciously based on racist ideology, conducted with revolutionary methods and dedicated to the realization of unlimited aims. "Discontinuity" historians concede that other German leaders and many ordinary Germans were anti-Semitic (as were the leaders and peoples of many other nations), but they insist that only Hitler advocated and actually attempted to carry out the total extermination of the Jews; other German leaders may have desired the acquisition of additional territories in Europe or overseas, but only Hitler conducted a war of conquest which involved the removal or extermination of the indigenous population.

Members of the "discontinuity" school, with their interpretation of Hitler as a unique phenomenon in German history, have been accused of attempting to exonerate the German people as a whole from blame for the Nazi experience, and the arguments of some of them are certainly intended to achieve this purpose. Whatever their motives, the members of the "discontinuity" school cannot avoid dealing with the question of how the German people as a whole accepted Hitler, how so many Germans were able to condone his bestial policies, and how so many were willing to put these policies into effect. Their attempts at explanation often bring them close to the "fundamental forces" school, but with notable differences in emphasis. Whereas the "fundamental forces" historians regard the Nazi experience as the inevitable product of the German past, their opponents contend that it required the demonic genius of a Hitler to mobilize all the most depraved features of German thought and behavior, that his propaganda successfully deceived the German people about his true intentions (as it deceived foreign governments with far better access to information), and that his totalitarian government successfully repressed all movements of dissent.

Into the controversies among the "fundamental forces", "continuity" and "discontinuity" schools fits the debate over the primacy of foreign politics versus the primacy of domestic politics. Is a country's foreign policy based in large measure on foreign political considerations and conducted quasi-independently of domestic affairs? Or is foreign policy conducted primarily in response to domestic problems and pressures? In dealing with Hitler's foreign policy, scholars who argue in favor of the primacy of foreign policy believe that his domestic program was designed to serve the purposes of his foreign policy; whereas their opponents believe his foreign policy was the product of domestic necessities.

Closely linked with this debate, and more specifically related to the Third Reich, is the controversy between what have been called the "functionalists" and the "intentionalists" (terms which seem to me only to add confusion to the argument.) The "functionalists" agree fundamentally with the primacy of domestic politics viewpoint. They contend that Nazi foreign policy was far more the outcome (function) of domestic dynamisms and crises within Hitler's Germany than the result of rational planning, that it was the result of the frantic but completely uncoordinated activity of competing power groups which produced a progressive radicalization of their measures. The "functionalists" emphasize the polycentric nature of the Nazi government and argue that Hitler, far from being an all-powerful dictator and decision-maker, was on the contrary a weak leader who pursued radical programs to ward off the rivalry of his associates and to escape from the realities of his own weakness. The "intentionalists", on the other hand, believe that Hitler himself made the major foreign policy decisions of the Nazi state, that he pursued politically intelligible goals, and that the best way to understand the foreign policy of the Third Reich is to understand the personality of Hitler and his ideology.

In their theoretical conceptions at any rate, the "fundamental forces" school and the "functionalist" historians deny the importance of the personal qualities of Hitler and in effect they are saying that if Hitler had not appeared on the German political scene, his place would have been filled by a Müller or a Schmidt. Their arguments are ingenious and they have contributed much to our understanding of the internal dynamics of the Third Reich, but they have obviously not convinced most scholars dealing with the Nazi question if one is to judge by the volume of research devoted to the background, personality and ideas of Hitler, or by the central position Hitler continues to occupy in virtually all studies of the Nazi state.

What is surprising, in view of the controversy aroused by Taylor's book and the immense amount of research devoted to the Nazi question since its publication, is how little the fundamental lines of interpretation and argument have in fact changed, and to what extent historians are still at a loss to explain the Nazi phenomenon. This situation may be observed in numerous works that have been published analyzing or reviewing interpretations of the Nazi question.[20] The most recent of these is by the German scholar Eberhard Jäckel. His *Hitler in History* summarizes the results of the latest research and comes to conclusions with which I agree on the whole and which I would like to use as a vehicle for conveying my own views.[21]

Jäckel makes the same point as Taylor that Hitler was not the pawn of big business, the Junkers, the army, or other established vested interests in Germany. Representatives of these interests recommended his appointment to Hindenburg in order to make use of the popular support he enjoyed, confident that they could control and manipulate him. Instead Hitler used the power conferred upon him to establish his totalitarian state. Those vested interests that did not seem a threat to his authority and which co-operated with his policies were absorbed into his political and social system, but he disregarded them completely in making all major policy decisions.[22]

It is over the question of Hitler's policies and their implementation that Jäckel, and I believe most historians who have worked through the evidence, would disagree with one of Taylor's most provocative points, namely that Hitler did not know what he was doing and merely took advantage of the opportunities presented to him by his opponents (although as mentioned earlier, Taylor himself is not altogether consistent on this point). Jäckel, who has written one of the most authoritative books on Hitler's ideology, says about this question: "Perhaps never in history did a ruler write down before he came to power what he was to do afterward as precisely as did Adolf Hitler. Hitler set himself two goals: a war of conquest and the elimination of the Jews." Jäckel goes on to review Hitler's war plans, the fundamental points of which he had already formulated in the 1920s, and comments:[23]

> Without knowing his war plans we cannot evaluate how he prepared for, initiated and conducted the war . . . Hitler's ultimate goal was the establishment of a greater Germany than had ever existed before in history. The way to this greater Germany was a war of conquest fought mainly at the expense of Soviet Russia. It was in the east of the European continent that the German nation was to gain living space (*Lebensraum*) for generations to come. This expansion would in turn provide the foundation for Germany's renewed position as a world power. Militarily the war would be easy because Germany would be opposed only by a disorganized country of Jewish Bolsheviks and incompetent Slavs.

Before launching his war of conquest in the east, however, Hitler had to meet certain fundamental preconditions. The first was the consolidation of his authority in Germany and rearmament. The second was to put an end to the possibility of a stab in the back in the west while Germany was at war in the east, for a successful attack on the Rhine-Ruhr industrial areas would deal a mortal blow to Germany's ability to wage war of any kind. France was the only power capable of striking such a blow;

France, therefore, had to be eliminated as a military power before Germany could launch its campaign in the east. To counter the power of France, Hitler hoped to win alliances with Britain, which was to be offered German support to retain its global empire, and with Italy, which was to be offered supremacy in the Mediterranean and assurances of continued control over the South Tyrol, despite that region's large German population. Hitler gained his alliance with Italy but by 1937 he had despaired of winning an alliance with Britain, although at least until 1941 he continued to hope that such an alliance might yet be possible. "Even a cursory glance at the diplomatic and military history of the Third Reich demonstrates that this program served as an outline of those German policies that were defined by Hitler himself," Jäckel says, "and there is ample documentary evidence to prove that he always kept this outline in mind. It was, of course, not a timetable or even a detailed prospectus, but a definite and structured 'list of objectives, priorities and conditions."[24]

Jäckel believes that the controversy between the "functionalists" and the "intentionalists" is based on a profound misunderstanding on both sides. "There is abundant evidence", he says, "that all major decisions in the Third Reich were made by Hitler, and there is equally abundant evidence that the regime was largely anarchic and can thus be described as a polycracy. The misunderstanding is to suppose that the two observations are contradictory and that only one of them can be true." Jäckel himself sees no contradiction here. "The monocrat comes to power on a polycratic basis, supported by conflicting groups that paralyze each other, and he maintains his power by ruling polycratically – that is, by playing the conflicting groups against each other. It is precisely this method that permits him to make the major decisions alone."[25] The ideas, too, were Hitler's. "He undoubtedly developed a program of his own, individually and alone", Jäckel says, but he goes on to observe that "his program must have coincided with the deeper tendencies and ambitions of his country and of his time. We may not be able to explain this, and yet we have to recognize it. Was he an author or an executor, a producer or a product?"[26]

In dealing with this question, Jäckel confesses his inability to provide definite answers, and refuses to take refuge in simplistic explanations. "What the fact-bound researcher can state and perhaps explain is only that the governments of the Weimar Republic did not seriously prepare for war, whereas Hitler did."[27] He points out that both the Japanese and Italians preceded the Germans in going to war for imperial reasons in the 1930s, and he might have added that the Poles and Hungarians were happy to join Hitler in the final spoliation of Czechoslovakia in 1939, that the Russians joined in the spoliation of Poland later in that same year and that they went on to take over the Baltic states, Northern Bukovina (at the expense of Romania) and to go to war against Finland. He might have added further that so-called democratic societies have not been altogether pacific in the past, that Britain and France, having acquired the world's largest overseas empires, were hardly in a moral position to point a finger of guilt at peoples (or regimes) which attempted to acquire similar empires, that the Soviet Union continues to control with an iron hand the multitude of national minorities conquered by the regimes of the tsars, and that the United States policy of westward expansion, in the course of which the white man ruthlessly thrust aside the "inferior" indigenous population, served as the model for Hitler's entire concept of *Lebensraum*.

Jäckel makes no attempt to exonerate the Germans. He stresses that they supported Hitler and carried out his criminal orders, and that their support and obedience was voluntary and not the result of terror and repression. Yet he believes "this pessimistic view cannot and should not lead to a blanket moral condemnation of the Germans living at that time, for they were as a whole no worse and no better than the generations before and after them. But they were subjected to ordeals and to temptations that others escaped." Again Jäckel attempts to avoid facile explanations. He is obviously uncomfortable with many of the schools of historical thought discussed earlier in this essay, especially attempts to explain the origins of National Socialism through polemical allusions to one's own political or ideological adversaries. "Such biased efforts are not only unscholarly but in most cases thoroughly contemptible." Jäckel believes it is vital to remember that the vast majority of Germans were denied the kind of information that ordinarily build the foundation of public opinion and that, although we now know that Hitler intended to implement the program presented in such detail in *Mein Kampf*, it is "beyond doubt that the Germans did not grant him power in order to implement that program".[28]

But then Jäckel plunges into a simplistic explanation of his own and seems to fall squarely into the "fundamental forces" school of thought. Hitler's foreign policy followed a rigid plan, he says, but that plan "was not wholly incongruent with general developments and its realization was therefore ensured". Later imperialistic territorial conquest was presaged in the development of Germany, just as it was in the development of Japan and Italy. "Thus Hitler, notwithstanding his own great personal responsibility in shaping events, was no more than the executor of a longstanding tendency."[29]

Here I part company with Jäckel, with whose views I am in almost complete agreement up to this point. All events, of course, are conditioned by the past, but to say that Hitler was no more than the executor of a longstanding tendency, thereby implying that the man and his policies were an inevitable product of German history, seems to me to place a dangerous emphasis on the principle of historical determinism and suggests that there is nothing an individual or nation can do to escape the fate dictated by its heritage.[30] To me there is something profoundly unhistorical about the "fundamental forces" school of thought for, by concentrating on problems that apparently foreshadow future developments, the historian may neglect or underestimate the importance of other aspects of a nation's past that may have been far more significant in an earlier age, or at least appeared so to perceptive contemporary observers. Such an approach in effect denies the importance of human beings in history, the role of thinkers, artists, leaders in a people's development, nor does it make sufficient allowance for the many accidents which befall a people (plagues, famines, foreign conquest) which are not necessarily the product of their heritage.

For the study of German history, the inevitability thesis has had the unfortunate result of requiring an emphasis on those features of the German past which seem to have produced the Third Reich and which made Germany different from, and by implication inferior to, more modern, moral and democratic societies. Such an attitude has led to a certain smugness if not to outright racism on the part of many non-Germans (vide Taylor), and to an exaggerated moral self-flagellation on the part of the Germans themselves. It has also contributed to a curiously myopic quality in many works on German history, which by focusing exclusively and obsessively on the problems of Germany and the Germans tend to ignore comparable problems in other societies and fail to take sufficient account of the terrifying universality of the German historical experience. If German history has anything to teach, it is that the veneer of civilization in all societies is perilously thin, and that the qualities we most admire in Western societies are in no way guaranteed by Western traditions, institutions, or national character, but must be safeguarded by eternal vigilance.

NOTES

1 A. J. P. Taylor, *A Personal History* (New York, 1983), p. 235.
2 A. J. P. Taylor, *The Origins of the Second World War*, first published in 1961. My references are to the American paperback Premier edition (Greenwich, Conn., 1963), p. 19.
3 ibid., pp. 69–73.
4 ibid., p. 107.
5 ibid., p. 105.
6 ibid., p. 105.
7 ibid., p. 146.
8 Foreword to a new edition of the *Origins*, "Second Thoughts"; Penguin paperback edition (Harmondsworth, 1964), pp. 26–7.
9 A. J. P. Taylor, *The Course of German History*, first published in 1945. My references are to the American paperback Capricorn edition (New York, 1962), pp. 7–8.
10 *Course of German History*, pp. 213–14, 222.
11 A. J. P. Taylor, "War origins again", reprinted from *Past and Present* (April 1965) in E. M. Robertson (ed.), *The Origins of the Second World War: Historical Interpretations* (London, 1971), pp. 139–40. Bethmann was German chancellor at the beginning of the First World War.
12 Taylor takes it for granted that Habsburg rule was German, but the Habsburgs made no efforts comparable to those of Prussia to Germanize the Slavs, and Hitler certainly never regarded their policies as a model for his own.
13 *Personal History*, pp. 181, 214, 270–1.
14 ibid., p. 182.
15 *New Statesman*, Vol. 52 (1956), pp. 523–4, quoted by John W. Boyer, "A. J. P. Taylor and the art of modern history", *Journal of Modern History*, vol. 49 (March 1977), p. 56.
16 "War origins again", p. 138.
17 All references to schools of thought must be qualified by observing that there are sharp differences of opinion among scholars who adopt the same general approach to historical problems. For a more detailed survey–analysis of major historical interpretations, see the recent intelligent and level-headed study by John Hiden and John Farquharson, *Explaining Hitler's Germany. Historians and the Third Reich* (Totowa, NJ, 1983).
18 "War origins again", p. 138.
19 Hiden and Farquharson, *Explaining Hitler's Germany*, p. 56.
20 The French scholar Pierre Ayçoberry, for example, concludes:

"One cannot say for certain whether the Third Reich was a radical departure from, or a continuation of preceding regimes. The question remains open, like a gaping hole in the historical consciousness. We still have not settled with the past." (*The Nazi Question. An Essay on the Interpretations of National Socialism, 1922–1975* (New York, 1981), p. 225.) Anthony Adamthwaite, writing in 1984, takes a parallel line. Many interesting questions remain unanswered he says, "but in the last analysis Hitler and Nazism can be understood, interpreted, or used as each generation wishes" ("War origins again", *Journal of Modern History*, vol. 56 (March 1984), p. 114).

21 Eberhard Jäckel, *Hitler in History* (Hanover, NH, 1984). My own interpretations may be found in "Die Deutsche Frage und der nationalsozialistische Imperialismus: Rückblick und Ausblick", in Josef Becker and Andreas Hillgruber (eds), *Die Deutsche Frage im 19. und 20. Jahrhundert* (Munich, 1983), pp. 373–92, and in the introductions and conclusions to my two volumes, *Hitler's War Aims*. Vol. 1, *Ideology, the Nazi State and the Course of Expansion*; Vol. 2, *The Establishment of the New Order* (New York, 1973–4).

22 Jäckel, *Hitler in History*, ch. 1.

23 ibid., pp. 23–5.

24 ibid., pp. 25–6.

25 ibid., p. 30.

26 ibid., p. 43.

27 ibid., p. 40.

28 ibid., pp. 90, 94, 96.

29 ibid., p. 104.

30 In an earlier draft of his book, which his publisher kindly sent me for purposes of writing this review article, Jäckel had emphasized the quality of inevitability more specifically. In this draft version he wrote that the realization of Hitler's foreign policy plan was ensured because it "derived from and conformed to" general developments, and that Hitler "was no more than the executor of the inevitable" (rather than merely the executor of a longstanding tendency).

6

Appeasement

PAUL KENNEDY

It is all too easy to comment upon the deficiencies contained in a book published twenty-five years ago[1] on the basis of the then available evidence, and to list the changes which would be needed to bring that volume up to date with more recent scholarship. Both the questions asked by historians, and the materials open to them (especially in respect of twentieth-century sources) change significantly from one decade to the next. If historians are, in E. H. Carr's phrase, part of a vast caravan winding through time, it is hardly surprising that perspectives about "appeasement" have altered between 1961 and 1986 – a more considerable period of years than that between the end of the Second World War and the publication of A. J. P. Taylor's book. Since the past two decades have also seen the opening up of the vast trove of British official records[2] on the interwar years, it is inconceivable that *The Origins of the Second World War* would not be "dated" in many respects – as its author has recently acknowledged.[3] What may perhaps be more surprising is the extent to which many of Taylor's judgments and (for want of a better word) "hunches" have stood the test of time.

A greater difficulty in an essay such as this is to deal with one strand – that of British appeasement policy – in isolation. It is difficult not merely because British attitudes and actions were, in Taylor's book, integrated into the overall story of why the Second World War occurred; but also because our own judgments of the validity of, say, Whitehall's worries about the size of the *Luftwaffe* will be affected by new researches on German aerial rearmament. Similarly our assessments of British policy towards Poland or the USA in the 1930s can be placed in a different light by newly released archival materials from those countries. Above all, the issue of how well, or how poorly, the British understood Hitler's real intentions can only be fully analyzed by reference to scholarship on

German policy, which is outside the bounds of this particular essay.[4] Students of British appeasement, if they desire to comprehend that topic, will always need to peer over the other side of the hill.

The enormous literature on "the meaning of appeasement"[5] can be dealt with briefly here, since its significance for our purposes lies chiefly in the way Taylor's revisionist work challenged a well-established orthodoxy. Although appeasement originally was a positive concept – as in the "appeasing" of one's appetite – the failure of Neville Chamberlain's policies turned it into a pejorative term by 1939, a tendency which grew ever stronger as the costs of the war mounted and the full horrors of Nazi policy were gradually revealed. Since Hitler was by then regarded as the Devil incarnate, it followed that Chamberlain and Daladier's diplomacy in the late 1930s had been hopelessly misconceived and morally wrong.[6] Instead of standing up to the Führer's manic ambitions, they had weakly appeased them.

Taylor's revisionism assaulted this orthodoxy on both the intellectual and the moral fronts. In his view, the restoration of Germany as a leading power, if not *the* leading power in Europe was natural and inevitable. The Versailles settlement was an artificial, spatchcocked one, leaving ethnic minorities on the wrong side of hastily-drawn boundaries; and it was seen as inadequate and unfair not only by all Germans but also by most enlightened Britons once their wartime anger had subsided. Changes were therefore fairly inevitable. "The only question was whether the settlement would be revised and Germany become again the greatest Power in Europe, *peacefully or by war.*"[7] Far from being a madman, Hitler was merely in a line of German statesmen – like Stresemann, for example – who thought that he could get revisions by negotiation, since the British in particular were making sympathetic noises. The Führer's distinctiveness lay not in what he wanted but in the fact that, when negotiations for border rectifications became tense, he had better nerves than anyone else and possessed the gambler's instinct for knowing when he could get away with a risky deal, and what his opponent's weaknesses were.

Because the German case for revision was a sensible one, and because Hitler had strong nerves while the appeasers did not, he could always rely upon other governments to rush forward and offer an improved settlement to satisfy German claims. This was particularly true after May 1937, when Neville Chamberlain assumed the premiership in Britain. He, Taylor writes,[8] was determined to start something. Of course he resolved on action in order to prevent war, not to bring it on; but he did not believe that war could be prevented by doing nothing . . . He believed, too, that the dissatisfied Powers – and Germany in particular – had legitimate grievances and that these grievances should be met . . . he had no difficulty in recognising where this injustice lay. There were six million Germans in Austria, to whom national reunification was still forbidden by the peace treaties of 1919; three million Germans in Czechoslovakia whose wishes had never been consulted; three hundred and fifty thousand people in Danzig who were notoriously German . . . Here was a programme for the pacification of Europe. It was devised by Chamberlain, not thrust upon him by Hitler.

While this policy of revision worked successfully in the two crises of 1938 – that is, concerning the incorporation of Austria and the Sudeten Germans into the Reich – it broke down over the Polish issue in the year following. By that time, and especially after the German acquisition of the rump state of Czechoslovakia in March 1939, British public opinion wanted Chamberlain and his Cabinet colleagues to take measures to "stop Hitler". In a tragi-comedy of good intentions going astray, the British government – with France in its wake – found itself tied into binding military commitments to a stubborn and reckless Polish regime under Beck. Since Chamberlain was still determined to settle things peacefully and was sending messages to that effect to Berlin, Hitler felt that he could proceed to solve the Danzig dispute by hints of action but without serious risk of war with the west; indeed, with the very strong chance that Chamberlain would arrange things in just the same way as he had done at Munich. It was only because the Poles declined to be as conciliatory as the Czechs that both Hilter's expectations, and Chamberlain's went awry. Although none of them planned to be at war with each other, by 3 September that very state of affairs existed. Far from being a maniac, Hitler had acted in a rational (if calculated) manner. But the appeasers, having willingly undermined the European status quo on numerous occasions in the 1930s, had now bungled things and gone to war "for that part of the [1919] peace settlement which they had long regarded as least defensible".[9]

The cries of outrage which greeted the publication of such views twenty-five years ago are easily understandable. On the one hand, there was Taylor's refusal to make moral judgments, or to give much weight to the significance of Nazi ideology, domestic politics, and racial doctrines. Then there were the critics who were alarmed at the possible implications of Taylor's suggestion that German hegemony in Europe was "natural" and ought not to have been resisted; if that applied to Hitler's Germany in the 1930s, might it not also apply to Krushchev's Russia in 1961, the year of the Berlin crisis as well as of the publication of Taylor's book? Above all, there were those infuriated by his flippant, throwaway style and sweeping remarks: e.g., that Hitler had no "preconceived plan" (p. 98); or that the Hoare–Laval scheme was "perfectly sensible" (p. 128); or that Munich was "a triumph for all that was best and most enlightened in British life" (p. 235); or that "it seems from the record that [Hitler] became involved in war through launching on 29 August a diplomatic manoeuvre which he ought to have launched on 28 August" (p. 336). All this was strong stuff.

The greatest indignation was, of course, reserved for Taylor's implicit (and sometimes explicit) "de-demonization" of Hitler, an interpretation which many critics thought untenable on both moral *and* factual grounds.[10] By contrast, Taylor's view of the British appeasers appeared less controversial, if only because the prevailing image of Neville Chamberlain was already a negative one. *The Origins of the Second World War* may have portrayed Britain's appeasement policy in a more dynamic and purposeful way than was hitherto imagined, but it still seemed unflattering by showing how eager London was to comply with, or even anticipate, the Führer's wishes. Consequently, the notion that that policy was both unwise and immoral was scarcely shaken, as could be seen in Gilbert and Gott's swingeing indictment, *The Appeasers*, published two years later.[11] Taylor himself might not wish to draw moral judgments about Chamberlain, or Sir Samuel Hoare, or Sir Horace Wilson, but many other historians were very willing to do so.

Apart from his general argument upon how British appeasement policy unwittingly contributed to the outbreak of the Second World War, Taylor offered detailed remarks upon the leading British personalities in this story, the arguments they deployed, and the phases they went through. All of this was based upon published British and German diplomatic documents for the interwar years, and upon older memoirs and biographies. Within another decade, however, virtually the entire official records for the 1930s (not to mention more and more private collections) were opened to historians – giving them the unexpected opportunity to measure Taylor's book, and other works, against the government's own documents. (By an act of 1967 the Labour government reduced the period of time in which public records were kept confidential from 50 years to 30 years (with some exceptions). Had that not happened, historians today would still be waiting to examine the Cabinet files on the Rhineland question of 1936, and much of what follows in this essay would have been impossible to write.) For the past sixteen or so years, therefore, a vast flood of scholarly books and articles dealing with British appeasement policy has appeared, and shows no sign of ceasing to date.

Many of Taylor's observations, it ought to be said at once, have stood the test of time rather well. His somewhat cynical view of statesmen, strengthened no doubt by his years of studying Bismarckian diplomacy, put him in good stead in describing the role of people such as Simon, MacDonald and Hoare. His coverage of Sir Nevile Henderson's debilitating functions as British ambassador in Berlin – constantly toning down the firmness of the Foreign Office's messages, and making deprecating noises to his German listeners about the Jews or the Czechs or the Poles – have required no amendments now that the files are open.[12] Above all, Taylor's observations upon Halifax, although brief, ring very true: the Foreign Secretary's aloofness, his sense of conscience (occasionally fostered by his Foreign Office staff), his sensitivity to what the Conservative Party and the country at large would think "fair", made him one of the few people – perhaps the only one – who could influence the prime minister during the Munich and Prague crises.[13]

By contrast, the portrait of Chamberlain in these pages seems one-dimensional. Taylor well captures the prime minister's personal decisiveness and sense of purpose, the businessman-turned-politician who knew how to run an organization on efficient, utilitarian lines; and many a later book, benefiting from the Cabinet papers, has shown how *dirigiste* an administration Chamberlain controlled.[14] On the other hand, historians who have gained access to the prime minister's private letters, especially those to his sisters, have shown Chamberlain to be increasingly uncertain about Hitler as 1938 turned into 1939. Expressions of confidence one week that all was going well and that the likelihood of war was fading, mingle with much more gloomy assessments in the week following.[15] No doubt these shifts of mood can partly be explained by the fluctuating reports of happenings on the continent, but Chamberlain's letters suggest a more complex figure than Taylor presents: sometimes briskly efficient, sometimes proud and privately boasting of his successes, sometimes worried and even bewildered at the turn of events. We still await Professor Dilks's second volume of his biography of Chamberlain[16] before we have the full picture, but the image which is emerging has already shown how difficult it is to assess the prime minister's character in a few, swift sentences.

On the internal politics of Great Britain in the interwar years, and their effect upon foreign policy, Taylor has not much to say, although the remarks he makes are usually accurate enough. For example, he shrewdly notes that Baldwin's pro-League statements in 1935 were intended to outwit the Labour Party just as a general election was pending. Similarly, Taylor's discussion of the spring 1939 considerations of an Anglo-Russian alliance to assist Poland nicely captures the dilemma in which Chamberlain found himself: if London negotiated with Moscow (which the prime minister and his colleagues greatly disliked), and was successful, it would be seen as vindicating the arguments of such varied critics of the government as Churchill, Lloyd George, and the Labour Party; if London refused to negotiate, or did so and failed to reach a settlement with Stalin, it would be blamed – by the British public, by a suspicious Hitler, and by posterity (as indeed it was). While Taylor does not provide Maurice Cowling's full picture of the internal-political dynamics of appeasement diplomacy – that is, of a Chamberlain needing a successful "deal" with Germany not only to preserve peace but also to secure his own political position and confound his critics to the left and right[17] – he does hint at this domestic dimension.

The newer researches upon the internal-political aspects of British policy have therefore tended to *supplement* Taylor's version rather than replace it. Cowling, for example, has gone even further in his argumentation, suggesting that Chamberlain's deeper concern was that another great war (with its total mobilization of national resources) would lead to significant advances by Labour and the trade union movement – just as the First World War had done. The preservation of peace was, therefore, intricately linked with the fate of the Conservative Party, a fact which (Chamberlain felt) the more reckless or "irregular" Tories like Churchill did not comprehend.[18] Just as such an account does not contradict Taylor, so also do the recent writings upon the "anti-appeasers" scarcely affect his picture: for the message of such works has generally been that Chamberlain's opponents, too, were uncertain of how to respond to the unprecedented circumstances of the late 1930s. There were all sorts of divisions among the ranks of the Conservative critics. Some of them disliked the appeasement of Germany, but strongly urged the appeasement of Italy; most of them – even Churchill – softened their attacks when the prospect of being invited to join the government seemed closer; the "Eden group" tried to keep its distance from the "Churchill camp", and so on. In the same way, the Labour Party was neither as forthright nor as consistent in its criticism of appeasement as it later liked to think. Attlee and his colleagues were very wary of being portrayed as warmongers, and warier still of co-operation with the old imperialist war-horses on the right of the Conservative Party. The revelation of such uncertainties gives us a better idea nowadays of how Chamberlain was able to preserve his commanding position in British politics for so long.[19]

British public opinion – the press, varied pressure-groups and the legendary "man in the street" – is not a key feature in *The Origins of the Second World War*. To be sure, Taylor refers to that general mood of pacifism, non-interventionism and dislike of "foreign politics" which conditioned the entire interwar period and made every administration from Lloyd George's coalition onwards reluctant to accept commitments in Europe and eager to see an amicable settlement of all international disputes. Over the past two decades, the study of British public opinion – especially the ideas and movements associated with pacifism, the Peace Ballot and the League of Nations Union, but also strands of opinion on the Right[20] – has become a major growth industry. The press's views of Germany, the Left Book Club, the public's attitude towards the Abyssinian crisis or the Spanish civil war, have all found their historians.[21] Here again, we are talking about additions to Taylor's version of events, and not challenges to it.

The two most significant disruptions of public opinion into the official policy of appeasing the dictators occurred, first, in late 1935, when the news of the Hoare–Laval pact provoked an explosion of discontent against this undermining of League of Nations principles; and secondly and more importantly, in the spring of 1939, when large segments of British public opinion, including many former supporters of Chamberlain's appeasement policies, decided that Hitler had to be stopped and urged all sorts of embarrassing proposals upon the government – guarantees to east European states, an alliance with Russia, further rearmament, closer ties with the French, and so on. While *The Origins of the Second World War* is good in showing how

Chamberlain became increasingly trapped between two uncontrollable forces – the exogenous force of Hitler, moving to further actions or threats of action, and the endogenous force of a resentful British public – much more might have been said about the vital change in mood and circumstances. There is little or nothing in Taylor's account, for example, of the anger and disgust produced in Britain by news of the *Kristallnacht* (9 November 1938), or of Hitler's rabid speeches of late 1938 in which he denounced Chamberlain's interfering diplomacy and proclaimed the Munich settlement as a victory for brute force – exactly the opposite of what the prime minister was saying.[22]

Where Taylor seems less correct is in his assumption (which he has repeated on many later occasions in the 1960s and 1970s), that the Munich agreement was overwhelmingly supported by the British press, with only *Reynolds' News* in opposition. In actual fact, both left-of-centre papers like the *Manchester Guardian, Daily Herald* and *News Chronicle,* and the distinctly right-wing *Daily Telegraph* wanted a firmer line taken towards Nazi Germany, and were joined in this by many individuals.[23] What is even more significant, and until recently less well known, were the persistent and very determined efforts made by Chamberlain and his colleagues to control the media – by influencing the press lords and editors, by getting critical talks suppressed on BBC Radio, by censoring the contents of the newsreels shown at the enormously popular cinemas – so as to give the impression to the world that the nation was behind the prime minister and his policies.[24] In view of this fascinating recent evidence, the older idea of a general consensus in British public opinion in favor of appeasement which only broke with the news of the German entry into Prague in March 1939 now looks distinctly wrong. The much more likely position was that opinion was already divided during the Czech drama, although this was obscured by the combination of the government's censorship efforts, the reluctance of Chamberlain's critics to appear as warmongers, and the caution produced by natural apprehension at the prospect of a major war. As soon as the shudders of relief at the avoidance of hostilities were over, however, the sense of unease returned – reinforced by one of shame at the fate of the Czechs, and anger at Hitler's speeches and programs. Seen in this light, the uproar over the Prague crisis was but one step (even if the most important one) in the dramatic switch of British public opinion against appeasement.[25]

Appeasement – if, by which, we mean the older sense of an

attempt to settle differences by negotiation and concession – was not a new feature in British diplomacy; as historians have pointed out, many aspects of it went back to Gladstone's time or even further.[26] What *was* quite new, and altogether more difficult for the British government to handle, was the unprecedented state of the international system after 1919. By that time, the USA was by far the most powerful financial and industrial (and, if wanted, military) state in the world – yet it rapidly abandoned most of its diplomatic responsibilities, even while the ups and downs of its enormous economy continued to affect trade, investment and prosperity across the globe. The other great continent-wide power, Russia, had been shattered by the First World War and was now ruled by the mysterious, threatening Bolsheviks. The Austro-Hungarian empire had dissolved into a cluster of rivalling, intensely-jealous small states. By contrast, Germany's territories (despite reductions in size, especially in the east) remained basically intact; and its power potential, as measured in terms of population, industrial capacity and national efficiency, was great – greater than France's in the long run. If and when the Germans organized themselves to assert their claims for a revision of the 1919 treaty, they would be inherently in a very strong position. Neither the "successor-states" of eastern Europe, nor a nervous, politically fragmented and economically weaker France, would be able to resist for more than a relatively short period – unless aided by another Great Power. Yet with the USA excluding itself, and the USSR in partly enforced, partly self-chosen isolation, only Britain remained; and it found it less easy to escape into isolation, much as it wanted to.

This fundamental change in the international balances as compared with the pre–1914 era Taylor captured very well, illuminating basic trends to which he had already drawn attention in his important earlier work *The Struggle for Mastery in Europe 1848–1918*.[27] The First World War, then, had not "solved" the German question: if anything, it had made it "ultimately more acute". "If events followed their course in the old 'free' way", Taylor suggested, "nothing could prevent the Germans from overshadowing Europe, even if they did not plan to do so."[28] To be sure, Britain could have carried out her traditional balance-of-power policy, but many things conspired to make that seem less useful than ever before. In the first place, for the entire 1920s it was Germany's weaknesses and France's (and even Poland's) strengths which caught the eye. Secondly, as noted above, the British public in the post-Versailles era did not want any further commitments in Europe; and, like most British ministers, soon came to feel that the 1919 boundaries ought to be revised – by peaceful means, of course, and under the aegis of the newly-created instrument of the League of Nations. The fact that Japan now appeared as a potential threat in the Far East, where Britain had much more substantial interests than any other European country, also made it easy "to understand why the British felt distinct from the Powers of Europe and why they often wanted to withdraw from European politics".[29] After the Abyssinian crisis and the Spanish civil war had revealed not only a new potential enemy in the form of Mussolini's Italy but also the complete ineffectiveness of the League of Nations, the international reasons for settling German grievances seemed more pressing than ever before – or so it appeared to the firm-minded Chamberlain when he took over in 1937.

In discussing the general external structure in which the British government now had to carry out its diplomacy, Taylor's book is very lucid. It is also essentially correct in its portrayal of British policy towards potential allies among the other Great Powers. Thus, London's dismay at the difficulties of persuading the United States government to do anything substantial either in Europe or in the Far East, and Neville Chamberlain's personal suspicion that the Americans were "all words, and no actions", have been amply confirmed in the excellent new studies by David Reynolds and Callum MacDonald.[30] In the same way, Taylor's picture of the far greater dislike shown by Chamberlain and his colleagues towards the Soviet Union – as a general threat to the Western order of things and, more specifically, in the context of a possible Anglo-Russian alliance to support Poland in 1939 – has not been shaken by the newer literature. And, since Taylor distinguishes between this general mistrust of Russia on the one hand, and a (non-existent) policy of trying to provoke a German-Russian war on the other, his portrayal is much more balanced than those strained pro-Moscow writings which seek to explain appeasement as fundamentally an anti-Marxist device.[31] Finally, *The Origins of the Second World War* nicely captures the ambivalent British feelings towards France: resenting it for being the "disturber of the peace" and so para-noically anti-German in the 1920s, disliking the fact that its very existence (not to mention its unwise obligations in eastern Europe) made British isolation from the continent possible, and yet also fearful, at least by late 1938/early 1939, that the French government was suffering such a crisis of morale that it might agree to everything demanded of it in Berlin unless it were given firmer British backing. In this latter sense, too, the six months following Munich were therefore a watershed in British policy and strategy: for the "continental commitment", avoided by Whitehall for some twenty years, could not in the last resort be repudiated.[32]

The individual phases of British appeasement policy in the interwar years are dealt with by Taylor in a less balanced way – even if one readily concedes that the importance which historians attach to individual episodes must, to some degree, be a matter of choice as well as of existing documentary evidence. (Note that only 47 pages are devoted to the 1920s; while the period from the Manchurian crisis to the *Anschluss* gets 100 pages; and the Czech and Polish crises of 1938/9 command nearly 150 pages. It is chiefly for this reason that my own comments have focused heavily upon the late 1930s as well.) There is a fair-sized coverage of such topics as the Locarno pact of 1925 (pp. 81–6), the disarmament conference of 1932–3 (pp. 93–107), and the Abyssinian crisis of 1935–6 (chapter 5); and while the very substantial recent literature has added many further details to our knowledge of those negotiations, the differences which have emerged are more ones of morality and ideology – for example, in Frank Hardie's strongly disapproving account of *The Abyssinian Crisis*[33] – than of historical accuracy. Taylor's remarks upon the role of pessimistic Admiralty opinion in influencing British policy in 1935 is, for example, amply confirmed in the late A. J. Marder's article on that point.[34] But it is curious that there are only two pages (pp. 90–2) on the very important Manchurian crisis of 1931–3,[35] and less than half a page (p. 118) on the Anglo-German naval treaty of 1935, towards which the British government attached such importance and which has, in consequence, attracted the attention of a number of scholars.[36] There is also very little in *The Origins of the Second World War* about the various schemes for "colonial appeasement", that is, the satisfying of German grievances by the return of some of her former colonies. In actual fact, this was not especially important to a dictator intent in the first place upon revising the *European* order; but it did obsess many Germans, consume the attention of many Britons (both for and against such a colonial deal), and was a major strand in British appeasement policy for some time – as recent works show.[37]

In a clever, wide-ranging article on appeasement published in 1965, after the appearance of Taylor's book but *before* the opening of the official records, Professor Donald Watt presciently suggested that, when further evidence was available, it was probably going to be difficult to maintain the simplistic older line that the appeasers merely "lacked guts". Watt felt that a future investigation of the files might reveal, *inter alia*,[38]

> the fears of Britain's Conservative leaders of the unrealism of current British opinion, and the existence of a degree of military weakness in 1935–36 which paralysed Britain's military planners, giving them years of sick apprehension as their daily companion. It may reveal three services so unable to agree on a common strategy that one was imposed on all three of them by the Treasury, obsessed not with Britain's economic strength at home, but with the state of her gold and dollar balances, her foreign investments, and her earning power abroad. It may reveal a Commonwealth divided on everything else but its dislike of Versailles and its wish for non-involvement in European affairs.

Some of these aspects are indeed referred to in *The Origins of the Second World War*, but only briefly (such as defence weaknesses, or the influence of the Treasury); and the role of the dominions, or the empire as a whole, is not mentioned at all. Yet if one feature of the historiography of appeasement since the opening of the official records stands out, it is the massive attention which has been paid to the evidence of Britain's frightening economic and strategical-global weaknesses in the 1930s.

Taylor is brief but reasonably good in referring to "economic appeasement", presumably since the published German and British documents detailed at least some of the efforts made by Whitehall to soften German resentments by offers of trade credits, access to raw materials, exchange arrangements, and outright loans; but his remarks upon the baneful influence of the Treasury upon British rearmament now look very dated. As a flood of newer works has shown, it was simply not true that a nice burst of Keynesian "pump-priming" by means of higher armaments spending would have solved Britain's problems, reducing unemployment *and* strengthening the armed services. It is of course likely that in the early 1930s some extra expenditure on the forces would have had beneficial effects in strategic and industrial and employment terms; but the amount of cash that was needed to rebuild a two-ocean navy, to provide the Royal Air Force with both its fighter defenses and its long-range bombers, and to equip the army for a European field role – all of which the Chiefs of Staff desired – was well beyond the industrial and financial capacity of the country. The long economic decline, exacerbated by the world slump after 1929, had eroded the British industrial base to an alarming extent. There were incredibly few skilled workers, especially in the vital engineering trades. There were insufficient machine-tools. There were few modern factories, and no modern shipyards. What was more, simply throwing money at these problems could never produce easy and fast solutions; it might, indeed, weaken the British economy still further by provoking inflation, hurting the balance of payments, and producing bottlenecks. For such an ailing patient, only a gentle stimulus seemed proper.

By the late 1930s, the Treasury's arguments were proven to be correct, even when – or, rather, *especially* when – it had lost its battle to keep defense spending down to levels which it judged to be economically safe. The great increases in government expenditures by that time, and the large defense loans, did cause inflation; the many orders abroad for the machine-tools, steel, aircraft, and instruments which a weak British industry could not produce itself, drastically raised the amount of imports; yet the transition of the economy from a peacetime to a wartime basis meant that the proportion of manufactures devoted to exports was falling rapidly. The balance of payments was worsening, the standard rate of income-tax was higher than at any time since 1919, and the floating of government loans to pay for defense was weakening Britain's credit and leading to a run on sterling. With the Treasury warning in early 1939 that the continuation of defense spending at the present rate "may well result in a situation in which the completion of our material preparations against attack is frustrated by a weakening of our economic stability, which renders us incapable of standing the strain of war or even of maintaining those defences in peace",[39] it was perhaps not surprising that Chamberlain still strove for a compromise settlement of the Danzig issue.

But if the Treasury's words were gloomy, they were nothing like as dark as those of the Chiefs of Staff, the "Cassandras in gold braid", as Corelli Barnett has described them.[40] Years of under-funding, together with the constraints imposed by the Ten Year Rule, had left Britain and its empire in a dreadfully weak position militarily – as the service chiefs were eager to explain after 1932, when the first attempts to assess the defense requirements of the empire were made. A whole series of reports were then laid before a worried Cabinet for the next six years, always with the same depressing message. The Royal Navy had been run down far below Washington treaty standards, and was incapable of sending a "main fleet to Singapore" *and* of maintaining a one-power standard in European waters (hence the Admiralty's concern to restrain German naval rearmament by the 1935 treaty).[41] There was not one adequately defended base throughout the entire empire. A miniscule army could not possibly play a role in preserving the European equilibrium – which is why the Chiefs of Staff frowned upon talks with the French military in 1938, and repeatedly warned the Cabinet that Britain could not do much to help Czechoslovakia.[42] Above all, perhaps, there was the weakness in the air: far from the British being in a position to deter Germany by means of a long-range bomber force, it seemed much more vulnerable to aerial attack from the imposing *Luftwaffe*.[43] Going to war against one of the dictator states would be difficult enough; fighting all three was impossible. Appeasement was the only solution. Or, as the Chiefs of Staff pointed out in December 1937:[44]

> we cannot foresee the time when our defence forces will be strong enough to safeguard our trade, territory and vital interests against Germany, Italy and Japan at the same time . . . [we cannot] exaggerate the importance from the point of view of Imperial Defence of any political or international action which could be taken to reduce the number of our potential enemies and to gain the support of potential allies.

Here was an argument for appeasement which at first sight was utterly compelling. Yet apart from a brief mention of Britain's supposed vulnerability to aerial attack – which Chamberlain used in order to cow Cabinet critics during the Munich crisis – the reader gains little sense from Taylor's account of the significant role of defense weaknesses in influencing appeasement policy. This is not a charge of negligence on his part: the mass evidence was simply not available to scholars in the late 1950s.

As if this catalogue of gloom was not enough, the global international crisis of the 1930s threatened to split the British empire apart. Ever since 1919 Afrikaners and French-Canadians – not to mention, after 1921, the fiercely independent Irish Free-Staters – had bitterly opposed any idea of "imperial defense" and expressed even more hostility to the notion of being dragged into a war in consequence of European quarrels. And while Australia and New Zealand were more willing to co-operate with Britain, they too were worried that European issues would divert resources from the more immediate danger of Japanese aggression in the Pacific. In addition, the dependent empire was much less tractable than in the days of Disraeli or

Salisbury. A widespread Indian nationalist movement, Egyptian discontents, a near-civil-war situation in Palestine by the late 1930s, were all pinning down British troops and resources and, last but not least, reinforcing Whitehall's arguments for not being committed in Europe.[45] Moreover, these fissiparous movements *within* the empire could not be completely separated from the *external* threats to the Mediterranean route and especially to the British possessions in the Far East – a region whose significance, were one to measure it in terms of new books published on that aspect of British policy alone, overshadowed everything else![46]

Not only did the Chiefs of Staff and the Treasury have contradictory ideas of the British government's existing priorities – with one side pressing for more defense spending, and the other pressing for financial stability – but their prognostications for a *future* conflict, should one actually come, were also at odds. From the armed services' viewpoint, Britain had a chance of successfully fighting Germany and Italy only if the war was a long one, during which the population and *materiel* resources of the empire could steadily be mobilized. In the Treasury's opinion, Britain could only afford to fight a short war, since it would very swiftly run out of gold and dollar holdings.[47] Impaled on the horns of this dilemma, was it surprising that Cabinet ministers should endeavour to avoid a conflict of any kind?

Because the official archives have revealed this catalogue of industrial, financial, strategic and imperial weaknesses with which successive British governments grappled in vain during the interwar years, the tendency of recent writings has been much more emphatic (and even sympathetic) towards the appeasers. In consequence, the "guilty men" interpretation of the 1940s and 1950s looks unbalanced and unfair. Far from finding Chamberlain's policy in the late 1930s inexplicable, it now seems quite understandable to many historians. As one of them has put it,[48]

> If one begins to tot up all the plausible motivations for appeasement . . . one sees that these are far more than enough to explain it. It was massively over-determined; any other policy in 1938 would have been an astounding, almost inexplicable divergence from the norm.

All of this newer evidence upon Britain's weaknesses affects Taylor's arguments only indirectly. To the extent that many of the recent writings have suggested, implicitly if not explicitly, that appeasement was unavoidable and predetermined, they do place Chamberlain and his colleagues in a more favorable light than appeared in *The Origins of the Second World War*. But such materials would probably not have centrally affected his main thesis, that the coming of war in September 1939 was an accident, and one caused more by the erratic moves of the appeasers and the stubbornness of the Poles than by Hitler's own calculations. Nor, one suspects, would they have altered his own sceptical view that the politicians rarely consulted "their military experts in a detached way before deciding on policy. They decided policy first; and then asked the experts for technical arguments with which this policy could be justified."[49] It was because of that habit, Taylor writes elsewhere, that even when British leaders used such "practical arguments" as aerial weaknesses during the Czech crisis, it was to *reinforce* their own conviction that appeasement was morally right.[50]

Given the weight of this newer evidence, few historians today will be as cynical and cavalier as Taylor was then about the role of military advice (or Treasury advice) on British policy. None the less, his remarks may be useful in reminding us that strategic memoranda are not the "be-all and end-all" of historical causation, and that we still have the task of properly integrating the newer evidence into our larger understanding of what appeasement meant.

As noted above, the weakness of the older "guilty men" literature upon appeasement appeared to be that it denounced Chamberlain and his colleagues for a failure of morality and willpower *without* much appreciation (or knowledge) of the difficulties under which British governments of the 1920s and 1930s labored. By contrast, most of the later works have focused upon the seemingly compelling strategic, economic and political motives behind British policy at that time, but *without* much concern for the moral and ideological aspects of it. That is to say, the mass of cool Treasury memoranda and the well-honed strategic assessments of the Chiefs of Staff, available for everyone to see in the Public Record Office, now occupy such a prominent position in the story that they are in danger of overshadowing those very important personal feelings behind appeasement: the contempt and indifference felt by many leading Englishmen towards east-central Europe, the half-fear/half-admiration with which Nazi Germany and fascist Italy were viewed, the detestation of communism, the apprehensions about future war.

Of course the warnings of the Treasury and the Chiefs of Staff about Britain's impending financial and strategical bankruptcy were important; but the fact is that such statements were not infallible, and that they *were* sometimes used by Chamberlain to justify policies he already wanted to pursue. For example, as Correlli Barnett and Williamson Murray have pointed out, both the Chiefs of Staff and the Cabinet were making some excessively gloomy predictions during the Czech crisis. Germany's own weaknesses were not considered. The value of the Czech army was ignored. Britain's vulnerability to aerial attack was repeatedly stressed, but without consideration of whether the *Luftwaffe* would or could throw itself against London whilst Germany was engaged in a central European war. Furthermore, the Cabinet minutes reveal that when some ministers (Duff Cooper, Stanley) actually wanted to take a stronger stand against Hitler despite the risks to Britain and its empire, they were swiftly overwhelmed by counter-arguments from Chamberlain and his friends:[51] objectors within the Cabinet had to be silenced, just as the press and BBC had to be controlled. Even when, by early-to-mid 1939, British public opinion was moving strongly against appeasement, when Britain's aerial defenses were much improved, and when the dominions were more supportive of a firm line, Chamberlain and his fellow-appeasers were still seeking, in secret rather than in the open, to buy off Hitler. After Prague, making concessions to Germany was neither as logical nor as "natural" as it might have been in 1936 and 1926; on the contrary, it seemed to many a policy lacking both in practical wisdom *and* moral idealism. Yet it was still being attempted by Downing Street, which suggests that individual convictions – in this case, Chamberlain's – must play a central part in our explanation of British policy, and that it cannot be fully understood simply in terms of "objective" strategical and economic realities.

Appeasement, then, is not a simple phenomenon which can be defined in a few, sharp words. Older histories tend to see it as a shameful and bankrupt policy of surrender to the dictator-states. Taylor has portrayed it as a well-meaning series of bungles which eventually embroiled both Hitler and the West in a war neither of them desired. Some scholars have seen it as a natural and rational strategy in the light of Britain's weaknesses in the world by the 1930s. Others have pointed out that it was, albeit in a more intensified form, a normal continuation of the British diplomatic tradition of attempting to settle disputes peacefully.

Appeasement was, in fact, all of the above and needs to be understood as such. It also needs to be investigated at different levels of causality, so that distinctions can be made between the nebulous, sometimes confused mentality of the appeasers on the one hand, and the cluster of military or economic or imperial or domestic-political motives which justified (or seemed to justify) concessions to the dictators on the other. Only when it is approached in such a way will the historians rise above the simplistic, one-dimensional descriptions, and deal with appeasement as the complex, variegated, shifting phenomenon which it really was.

NOTES

1 This essay is concerned with the text of the original (1961) edition of Taylor's *The Origins of the Second World War*, and not with the "Second Thoughts" Foreword (1963), nor "War origins again", *Past and Present* (April 1965), nor "1939 revisited" (the 1981 Annual Lecture of the German Historical Institute, London).

2 There are some exceptions, like the Intelligence records, which historians have to trace by roundabout means: see D. Dilks, "Appeasement and intelligence", in D. Dilks (ed.), *Retreat from Power*, 2 vols (London, 1981), Vol. 1, pp. 139–69.

3 Taylor, "1939 revisited", *passim*.

4 See Chapter 5, "Hitler's Foreign Policy", in this collection of essays. G. L. Weinberg, *The Foreign Policy of Hitler's Germany*, 2 vols to date (Chicago, Ill., 1970 and 1980); N. Rich, *Hitler's War Aims*, Vol. 1 (New York, 1973); W. Carr, *Arms, Autarky and Aggression* (London, 1972); E. Jäckel, *Hitler's World View* (Cambridge, Mass., 1981); K. Hildebrand, *The Foreign Policy of the Third Reich* (London, 1973), are all helpful here.

5 The general survey literature is now so large as to be almost out of control; but recent historiographical pieces to note are D. C. Watt, "The historiography of appeasement", in A. Sked and C. Cook (eds), *Crisis and Controversy* (London, 1976); D. Dilks, "Appeasement revisited", *University of Leeds Review* (1972); D. Carlton, "Against the grain – in defence of appeasement", *Policy Review* (1980); P. Kennedy, "Reading history: appeasement", *History Today* (October 1982). There are also very important analyses by German scholars such as B.-J. Wendt, G. Schmidt, G. Niedhart, W. Gruner, R. Meyers and others – some flavor of which can be gleaned from the important collection, edited by W. J. Mommsen and L. Kettenacker, *The Fascist Challenge and the Policy of Appeasement* (London and Boston, 1983), and summarized in part in P. Kennedy, "The logic of appeasement", *Times Literary Supplement*, 28 May 1982.

6 The works by Wheeler Bennett, Namier, and Churchill are very much in this tone, as are pro-Moscow books and articles.

7 *Origins* (Penguin edn, 1964), p. 79 (italics added).

8 ibid., p. 172.

9 ibid., p. 335.

10 Some sense of this outrage can be gleaned from contributions in E. M. Robertson (ed.), *The Origins of the Second World War* (London, 1971), and W. R. Louis (ed.), *The Origins of the Second World War: A. J. P. Taylor and His Critics* (New York, 1972). The most sustained repudiation of the Taylor line is in volume two of Weinberg's *Foreign Policy of Hitler's Germany*, which is meaningfully sub-titled *Starting World War II, 1937–1939*.

11 M. Gilbert and R. Gott, *The Appeasers* (London, 1963).

12 Compare Taylor's remarks on Henderson with A. L. Goldman, "Two views of Germany: Nevile Henderson vs. Vansittart and the Foreign Office, 1937–39", *British Journal of International Studies*, vol. 6 (October 1980).

13 *Origins*, pp. 198–9 *et seq.* Compare M. Cowling, *The Impact of Hitler* (Cambridge, 1975), pp. 271ff.

14 Cowling, *Impact of Hitler*, *passim*; I. Colvin, *The Chamberlain Cabinet* (London, 1971), *passim*; K. Middlemas, *Diplomacy of Illusion* (London, 1972), *passim*; C. Barnett, *The Collapse of British Power* (London and New York, 1972), *passim*.

15 Some of these ups-and-downs are covered in L. W. Fuchser, *Neville Chamberlain and Appeasement* (New York, 1982). See also D. C. Watt's perceptive essay, "Misfortune, misconception, mistrust: episodes in British policy and the approach of war, 1938–1939", in M. Bentley and J. Stevenson (ed), *High and Low Politics in Modern Britain* (Oxford, 1983).

16 D. Dilks, *Neville Chamberlain*, Vol. 1 (Cambridge, 1984), only goes to the year 1929.

17 Cowling, *Impact of Hitler*, *passim*.

18 ibid., *passim*.

19 N. Thompson, *The Anti-Appeasers* (Oxford, 1971), confirms Cowling's descriptions of these divisions, as does D. Carlton in his critical biography of *Anthony Eden* (London, 1981). See also, J. F. Naylor, *Labour's International Policy* (London, 1969), pp. 252ff.

20 The literature is now too extensive to be listed in its entirety, but readers can consult M. Ceadel, *Pacifism in Britain 1914–45* (Oxford, 1980); D. S. Birn, *The League of Nations Union 1918–1945* (London, 1981); D. O. Lukowitz, "British pacifists and appeasement", *Journal of Contemporary History*, vol. 9 (1974). For the Right, see (apart from the works on fascism in Britain) R. Griffiths, *Fellow-Travellers of the Right* (London, 1980).

21 F. R. Gannon, *The British Press and Germany 1936–39* (Oxford, 1971); J. Lewis, *The Left Book Club* (London, 1970); D. Waley, *British Public Opinion and the Abyssinian War, 1935–36* (London, 1975); K. W. Wat-

kins, *Britain Divided: The Effect of the Spanish Civil War on British Public Opinion* (London, 1963).

22 On which, see Weinberg, *Foreign Policy of Hitler's Germany*, Vol. 1, pp. 516ff.; T. Taylor, *Munich: The Price of Peace* (London, 1979), pp. 937ff. See also the excellent analysis of the erosion of pro-appeasement feelings during late 1938/early 1939 in L. Kette-nacker, "Die Diplomatie der Ohnmacht", in W. Benz and H. Graml (eds), *Sommer 1939. Die Grossmächte und der Europäische Krieg* (Stuttgart, 1979), esp. pp. 239, 247ff.

23 This is not to say that the *Telegraph* or *Guardian* did not share, to some extent, the relief that war had been avoided in 1938, but their line was altogether much firmer than the government's. See Gan-non, *British Press and Germany, passim*; Thompson, *The Anti-Appeasers*, pp. 165ff.; P. Kennedy, "Idealists and realists: British views of Germany, 1864–1939", *Transactions of the Royal Historical Society*, fifth series, vol. 25 (1975), pp. 154ff.

24 A. Adamthwaite, "The British government and the media", *Journal of Contemporary History*, vol. 18 (1983), pp. 281–97.

25 Kettenacker, "Die Diplomatie der Ohnmacht".

26 P. Kennedy, "The tradition of appeasement in British foreign policy, 1865–1939", *British Journal of International Studies*, vol. 2 (1976); W. D. Gruner, "The British political, social and economic system and the decision for peace and war: reflections on Anglo-German relations 1800–1939", *British Journal of International Studies*, vol. 6 (1980); M. Gilbert, *The Roots of Appeasement* (London, 1966).

27 A. J. P. Taylor, *The Struggle for Mastery in Europe 1848–1918* (Oxford, 1954).

28 *Origins*, p. 48.

29 ibid., p. 68.

30 D. Reynolds, *The Creation of the Anglo-American Alliance 1937–41* (London, 1981); C. A. MacDonald, *The United States, Britain and Appeasement* (London, 1981).

31 See Taylor, *Origins*, pp. 256, 279ff. Compare G. Niedhart, *Grossbri-tannien und die Sowjetunion 1934–1939* (Munich, 1972), as well as the two very good articles by Niedhart and Herndon, in Mommsen and Kettenacker (eds), *The Fascist Challenge and the Policy of Appeasement*. The pro-Moscow versions are briskly (perhaps too briskly?) dealt with in D. N. Lammers, *Explaining Munich: The Search for Motive in British Policy* (Stanford, Calif., 1966).

32 For the military aspects, see especially M. Howard, *The Continental Commitment* (London, 1972), chs. 4–6; for the general political and cultural side, see *inter alia* A. Wolfers, *Britain and France between Two Wars* (New York, 1966; first published 1940), and J. C. Cairns, "A nation of shopkeepers in search of a suitable France, 1919–1940", *American Historical Review*, vol. 79 (1974), and the brief but pertinent comments in E. M. Gates, *End of the Affair* (London, 1981), pp. 8ff.

33   F. M. Hardie, *The Abyssinian Crisis* (London, 1974), whose definition
      of appeasement (p. 4) is "not mere failure to resist an act of
      aggression but connivance at it". Locarno and its results are
      covered in J. Jacobson, *Locarno Diplomacy: Germany and the West,
      1925–1929* (Princeton, NJ, 1972); A. Orde, *Britain and International
      Security, 1920–1926* (London, 1978). The 1932–3 Disarmament con-
      ference is covered in the excellent book by E. W. Bennett, *German
      Rearmament and the West 1932–1933* (Princeton, 1979).

34   A. J. Marder, "The Royal Navy and the Ethiopian crisis of
      1935–36", *American Historical Review*, vol. 75 (1970).

35   On which, see the important study by C. Thorne, *The Limits of
      Foreign Policy: The West, the League and the Far Eastern Crisis of 1931–1933*
      (London, 1972).

36   E. H. Haraszti, *Treaty-Breakers or Realpolitiker? The Anglo-German Naval
      Agreement of June 1935* (Boppard, 1973); D. C. Watt, "The Anglo-
      German naval agreement of 1935", *Journal of Modern History*, vol. 28
      (1956); J. Dülffer, "Das deutsch-englische Flottenabkommen vom
      18. Juni 1935", in W. Michalka (ed.), *Nationalsozialistische Aussenpoli-
      tik* (Darmstadt, 1978).

37   On the German side, see W. W. Schmokel, *Dream of Empire: German
      Colonialism 1919–1945* (New Haven, 1964), and K. Hildebrand, *Vom
      Reich zum Weltreich* (Munich, 1969). There is no full book on British
      policy (until Dr Andrew Crozier's appears), but see Crozier's
      "Imperial decline and the colonial question in Anglo-German
      relations 1919–39", *European Studies Review*, vol. 11 (1981), and the
      coverage in Gilbert and Gott's *The Appeasers*.

38   D. C. Watt, "Appeasement, the rise of a revisionist school?",
      Political Quarterly (April–June 1965).

39   Cited in R. P. Shay, Jr., *British Rearmament in the Thirties: Politics and
      Profits* (Princeton, 1977), p. 243. Also very important is G. C. Peden,
      British Rearmament and the Treasury 1932–1939 (Edinburgh, 1979).
      Many of these points are summarized in P. Kennedy, "Strategy
      versus diplomacy in twentieth-century Britain" *International History
      Review*, vol. 3, (1981).

40   Barnett, *Collapse of British Power*, ch. 5, analyzes the role of the strategic
      advisers; but see also N. Gibbs, *Grand Strategy*, Vol. 1 (London, 1976),
      and R. Meyers, *Britische Sicherheitspolitik 1934–1938* (Düsseldorf, 1976).
      The general findings of these newer works are reviewed in P. Kennedy,
      "Appeasement and British defence policy in the inter-war years",
      British Journal of International Studies, vol. 4 (1978).

41   British naval policy is covered in S. Roskill, *Naval Policy between the
      Wars*, 2 vols (London, 1968 and 1976). The strategical "juggling-
      act" is covered nicely in L. R. Pratt, *East of Malta, West of Suez:
      Britain's Mediterranean Crisis, 1936–1939* (Cambridge, 1975).

42   Howard's *Continental Commitment* covers the army's dilemma well
      but the most thorough study now is B. Bond, *British Military Policy
      between the Two World Wars* (Oxford, 1980).

43 Among the innumerable studies on air policy and aerial defense, see U. Bialer, *The Shadow of the Bomber: The Fear of Air Attack and British Politics 1932–1939* (London, 1980); H. Montgomery Hyde, *British Air Policy between the Wars* (London, 1976), and now M. Smith, *British Air Strategy between the Wars* (Oxford, 1984).

44 Cited in Howard, *Continental Commitment*, pp. 120–1.

45 Barnett, *Collapse of British Power* is best here; but see also R. Ovendale, *Appeasement and the English-Speaking World* (Cardiff, 1975); R. Meyers, "Britain, Europe and the Dominions in the 1930s", *Australian Journal of Politics and History* (1976).

46 W. R. Louis, *British Strategy in the Far East 1919–1929* (Oxford, 1971); C. Thorne, *Allies of a Kind* (Oxford, 1978); S. L. Endicott, *Diplomacy and Enterprise: British China Policy 1933–1937* (Vancouver, 1975); A. Trotter, *Britain and East Asia 1933–1937* (Cambridge, 1975); B. A. Lee, *Britain and the Sino-Japanese War, 1937–1939* (Stanford, 1973); W. D. McIntyre, *The Rise and Fall of the Singapore Naval Base* (London, 1979); J. Neidpath, *The Singapore Naval Base and the Defence of Britain's Eastern Empire 1919–1941* (Oxford, 1981); A. J. Marder, *Old Friends, New Enemies: the Royal Navy and the Imperial Japanese Navy* (Oxford, 1981); P. Haggie, *Brittania at Bay: The Defence of the British Empire against Japan* (Oxford, 1981); P. Lowe, *Great Britain and the Origins of the Pacific War, 1937–1941* (Oxford, 1977); A. Shai, *Origins of the War in the East: Britain, China, and Japan, 1937–41* (London, 1976).

47 See again, Kennedy, "Strategy versus diplomacy", *passim*.

48 P. W. Schroeder, "Munich and the British tradition", *Historical Journal*, vol. 19 (1976), p. 242.

49 *Origins*, p. 155.

50 ibid., p. 234.

51 Barnett, *Collapse of British Power*, pp. 505–20. For fresh assessments of the balance, see W. Murray, *The Change in the European Balance of Power 1938–1939* (Princeton, NJ, 1984), especially ch. 7.

7

A. J. P. Taylor
and the Russians

TEDDY J. ULDRICKS

Late in the night of 23 August 1939 Soviet Foreign Commissar
Viacheslav Molotov and German Foreign Minister Joachim von
Ribbentrop signed their names to a treaty of non-aggression
which signaled the beginning of the Second World War. Significantly, this pact lacked the usual escape clause which invali-
dates such agreements if either party were to be the aggressor in
a war against some third country. The omission was deliberate, since the Soviet leaders realized that the Germans intended
to attack Poland within a week. Moreover, the treaty was supplemented by a highly secret protocol which divided all of eastern
Europe into Soviet and German spheres of interest. In addition,
four days earlier Moscow and Berlin had also concluded an
extensive commercial agreement. The trade treaty and the non-
aggression pact, with its secret protocol, together constituted a
quasi-alliance between Stalin and Hitler.[1]

These cynical agreements, which neither side saw as more
than temporary expedients, were accompanied by an equally
hypocritical scene. The same Ribbentrop who had nodded
approvingly when Hitler had previously unfolded his plans for
invading the Soviet Ukraine now assured the Russians of the
German people's deep feeling for them. In response, Joseph
Stalin, the self-proclaimed defender of the toiling masses and
sworn enemy of fascist oppressors, raised his glass and declared,
"I know how much the German nation loves its Führer; I should
therefore like to drink to his health".

Ever since the signing of the Nazi-Soviet pact, the motives of
the Kremlin for entering into the agreement, as well as the
broader purposes of Soviet foreign policy throughout the 1930s,
have been the subject of intense, and often acrimonious, debate.

A. J. P. Taylor's widely-read book, *The Origins of the Second World War*, has played a significant role in this controversy. Before assessing Taylor's contribution to the debate, however, it is necessary to outline briefly the course of Soviet diplomacy in the 1930s.

The Soviet Union did not assume a position of hostility toward the Nazi regime when it first came to power in Germany. The Moscow-dominated Communist International and the German Communist Party deluded themselves that the Nazi phenomenon embodied a last, desperate stage of German capitalism, a prelude to its imminent demise. National Socialism would undermine bourgeois democracy and thereby prepare the ground for revolution. The executive committee of the International resolved in April 1933 that "The establishment of an open fascist dictatorship destroys all illusions of the masses and liberates the masses from the influence of Social Democracy".[2] The Kremlin leaders also hoped that, despite Hitler's radical anti-communist rhetoric and talk of *Lebensraum*, Germany would not renounce the Rapallo tradition of friendship with the USSR. On that assumption, the Russians renewed their 1926 commercial treaty with Germany just four months after Hitler became chancellor of the Reich. Ideologically, dealing with a fascist regime was no more repugnant than dealing with the liberal-democratic states. On a more practical level, the Russians still regarded Britain as their chief enemy. They needed Germany, just as they had during the 1920s, as a counterweight to the presumed British threat.

Hitler soon demonstrated, however, that he had no interest in continuing the Rapallo relationship with the USSR. The Nazis butchered the German Communist Party, Germany negotiated a non-aggression pact with Poland, the traditional enemy of both Moscow and Berlin, and the Führer refused to sign a mutual guarantee of frontiers with the Soviet Union. Stalin was forced to reassess his policy toward the Reich. He had to face the grim possibility that the responsibilities of power might not tame the Nazis, as so many Western statesmen expected, and that the blood-curdling rantings of *Mein Kampf* might indeed be the foreign policy of the Third Reich. Soviet policy in Europe, therefore, altered dramatically in 1934 by espousing the concept of collective security. The Soviets attempted to build a solid front of anti-fascist nations encircling Germany, the combined strength of which might deter Hitler from aggression or decisively defeat the Reich if war could not be avoided. To this end Russia threw its weight behind the League of Nations, Soviet diplomats sought treaties of mutual assistance with the Western powers, and the Comintern tried to construct a united front against fascism of all the "progressive" political forces in Europe.

The Soviet Union had always been hostile to the League, regarding it as an imperialist, counter-revolutionary bastion. Yet in 1934 the USSR joined the League and the Soviet Commissar of Foreign Affairs, Maxim Litvinov, emerged as the most eloquent tribune at Geneva for collective security against aggression. "Germany", Litvinov warned, "is striving not only for the restoration of the rights trampled underfoot by the Versailles treaty, not only for the restoration of its prewar boundaries, but is building its foreign policy on unlimited aggression, even going so far as to talk of subjecting to the so-called German race all other races and peoples."[3] The Soviet commissar had discerned the essence of Nazi intentions. Denouncing appeasement as a suicidal policy, Litvinov told the League delegates at Geneva:[4]

> They [the aggressor states] are now still weaker than a possible bloc of peace-loving states, but the policy of non-resistance to evil and bartering with aggressors, which the opponents of sanctions propose to us, can have no other result than further strengthening and increasing the forces of aggression, a further expansion of their field of action. And the moment might really arrive when their power has grown to such an extent that the League of Nations or what remains of it, will be in no condition to cope with them, even if it wants to . . . With the slightest attempt at actual perpetration of aggression, collective action as envisioned in article 16 must be brought into effect progressively in accordance with the possibilities of each League member. In other words, the program envisioned in the Covenant of the League of Nations must be carried out against the aggressor, but decisively, resolutely and without any wavering.

Despite setbacks to the League's ability to thwart aggression in Manchuria and Abyssinia, the Russians still hoped to revitalize the international organization as an effective instrument of collective security.

Supplementing multilateral diplomacy in Geneva, the USSR wished to negotiate mutual defense treaties with its neighbors in eastern Europe and, more importantly, with Britain and France. In 1935 the Soviet Union signed mutual defense pacts with France and Czechoslovakia, though in the latter case the Russians were not obligated to come to Prague's aid unless France did so first.

Another aspect of the Soviet collective security drive was

embodied in the Popular Front line which the Third International inaugurated in 1935. After years of vilifying the non-communist left as the working man's worst enemy, the Comintern executed a complete reversal, now urging communists everywhere to join together with socialists, trade unionists, and even liberals in anti-fascist electoral coalitions. The twofold objective was to prevent the seizure of power by fascist movements in any other country and to elect governments that would pursue an anti-German, pro-Soviet foreign policy. Supporting rearmament and a strong defense of their homelands was also a radical about-face for western communists. Not long before, Maurice Thorez, head of the French Communist Party, had proclaimed that he and his comrades would not fight even if their country were invaded. All this changed when word came through from Moscow that party members in the western democracies were to spare no effort in rallying national political and military resistance to Hitler.

Although Soviet diplomats and foreign communists labored tirelessly on behalf of collective security, they failed to weld a powerful alliance capable of deterring or defeating Nazi aggression. Litvinov's entreaties could not transform the League from the powerless debating society that it had become, into a mighty anti-German rampart. Nor was the Foreign Commissar any more successful in directly approaching London and Paris for alliances with the USSR. France had signed a mutual defense pact with Soviet Russia in 1935, but British opposition, internal frictions within the Popular Front, and French army doubts about the military effectiveness of Russian aid combined to vitiate that agreement. French commanders were never willing to hold the detailed staff talks with their Red Army counterparts essential to implementing the pact. Actually, the French wanted only a political tie with Moscow which might intimidate Berlin but would not require them to perform any specific military action. With Britain and Poland the Soviets were even less successful. Neither country would seriously consider an alliance with the USSR. The Comintern's Popular Front strategy was equally barren of results. Leftist coalitions managed to form governments in only two countries – Spain and France. In the former case, the *Frente Popular* regime in Madrid provided an excuse for a right-wing insurrection with Italian and German participation. Both the radicalism of the Spanish civil war and the potential danger of widening the conflict frightened people in the western democracies and made them even more inclined to appease the dictators. In the latter case, Blum's cabinet was able neither to aid the Spanish republic nor to effect military co-operation with the USSR.

Munich fully exposed the fruitlessness of the Soviet campaign for collective security. Without firing a shot, Hitler had undermined the most important bulwark of the Versailles system in eastern Europe – the Czech republic. And Moscow could do nothing about it. Chamberlain and Daladier had readily agreed to Hitler's demand to exclude Soviet Russia from the Munich conference. The Munich débâcle precipitated a change in Soviet foreign policy. Deputy Foreign Commissar Vladimir Potemkin forecast the shift when he lamented to the French ambassador in Moscow, "My poor friend, what have you done? As for us I do not see any other outcome than a fourth partition of Poland."[5] There were also hints of a change in course when Stalin spoke to the eighteenth congress of the Communist Party of the Soviet Union on 10 March 1939. For the first time in years the Germans and Italians were not singled out as aggressors. Instead Stalin pictured the current world situation as virtually a state of war among the imperialist powers in which the fascist regimes were trying to get a larger share of the capitalists' plunder from Britain, France and the United States. He openly charged that the appeasement policy of the western countries was calculated to divert the main thrust of the aggressors toward the USSR. Stalin warned that the democracies were playing a dangerous game – one which might very well backfire on them.[6]

Even during the heyday of the collective security campaign from 1935 through 1938, the Soviet Union had occasionally made tentative secret approaches to Berlin for a normalization of relations. The Nazis had rebuffed each of these probes. Now in the spring of 1939 the Soviets once again signaled the Germans that a *rapprochement* was possible while, at the same time, warning the British and French to act quickly if they wanted an alliance with Russia. Those messages were also implicit in the dismissal of Litvinov from his post as Commissar of Foreign Affairs at the beginning of May 1939, and his replacement by Viacheslav Molotov. Unencumbered by his predecessor's Jewish background or image as a champion of collective security, Molotov could deal with Chamberlain or Hitler. Stalin had not entirely given up hope for an alliance with the Western powers against Germany, but his patience was running out. Moreover, the outbreak of hostilities with Japan on the Soviet–Manchurian border in the summer of 1938 raised the possibility of an imminent conflict in the Far East. If a disastrous two-front war were to be avoided, the Soviet Union needed to reach agreement with either the democracies or Nazi Germany as soon as possible. The Soviets, therefore, mounted a dual campaign. On the one hand they continued their open, noisy, high-pressure attempts to come to terms with London and Paris. On the other hand they began, rather delicately and secretly, to probe German intentions. In April 1939 the Soviet ambassador in Berlin, Aleksei Merekalov, told a German diplomat, "there exists for Russia no reason why she should not live with [Germany] on a normal footing. And from normal, the relations might become better and better."[7] Soon thereafter, previously interrupted Russo-German economic negotiations were resumed which, in turn, led to discussions of political co-operation between the USSR and the Reich.

At the same time the Western powers were finally beginning to show some interest in a coalition with Soviet Russia to check Nazi aggression. Hitler's destruction of Czechoslovakia in March had convinced most Frenchmen that war with Germany was inevitable. Despite their previously negative assessments of Soviet military capability, the French were now anxious for an alliance with Moscow. By May the British Cabinet had also, if reluctantly, concluded that some kind of co-operation with the USSR was desirable. What the Anglo-French and Soviet sides could not agree on, however, was what form their prospective collaboration should take. After debating various possibilities all summer without resolution, military talks opened on 12 August in Moscow. The British made a poor impression from the beginning, belatedly sending a low-ranking delegation which was not actually empowered to conclude an agreement. The conference bogged down immediately over the same issues that had prevented agreement in the previous months. If the USSR were to go to war with Germany in support of the Allied effort to stop Hitler, the Soviets insisted that their military might be brought directly to bear on the enemy. That entailed massive Soviet troop movements through Poland and Romania. The Russians would not consent to function merely as a vast arsenal and warehouse for the Polish army. The Soviet delegation also demanded highly detailed and firm commitments from the Western powers. They wanted precise definitions of what circumstances would precipitate war and what forces Britain and France would immediately commit to the struggle. Finally, Moscow wanted the proposed alliance to respond against "indirect aggression" in eastern Europe, as well as to overt military attacks. In undermining Austria and Czechoslovakia Hitler had employed techniques of internal subversion so effectively that a violent assault had not been necessary. The Soviets intended to prevent that sort of bloodless Nazi conquest from occurring in the states along their western border.

The British opposed the Soviet position on each of these issues. To begin with, they were not at all sure that the USSR was worth having as an active military ally. The Great Purges had devastated the Red Army officer corps in 1937–8. Almost 80 percent of Soviet officers above the rank of captain had been executed or sent to concentration camps. The British General Staff told the Cabinet that, because of the purges and the danger of precipitating Japanese involvement, Russian intervention in a European war would more than likely be "an embarrassment rather than a help". The purges also raised a larger political question for the West. Thousands of top Soviet government, party, industrial, scientific and military leaders had been publicly accused and found guilty of spying for Germany or Japan. If the charges were true, it meant that the whole Soviet elite was riddled with treason. If they were false, the implications were even more horrifying. In either case, the purges diminished the value of Soviet Russia as an alliance partner.

Another obstacle to Soviet–Western co-operation concerned the problem of getting the Red Army to the potential battlefield. Since the USSR and the Reich had no common border, Soviet troops would have to be transported across Poland or Romania in order to confront the *Wehrmacht*. Both of those states were adamantly opposed to any Russian military presence within their borders. Each of them had taken territory from a devastated Russia in 1918–20 (part of Belorussia for Poland and Bessarabia for Romania). Beyond the fear of losing these districts, Warsaw and Bucharest were afraid that if Soviet armies entered their territory, they might never leave. Britain refused to put pressure on Poland or Romania over the issue of Red Army units crossing their lands. As the British Foreign Secretary, Lord Halifax, put it, "we must not risk offending Colonel Beck . . . if we had to make a choice between Poland and Russia, it seemed clear that Poland would give the greater value".[8]

Prime Minister Chamberlain was reluctant to meet Soviet demands for transit rights in eastern Europe and for a full-blown, ironclad military alliance because his view of the international situation was fundamentally different from Stalin's. The

British leader still held out hope that a general European war could be prevented. In fact, he feared that pursuit of an aggressively anti-German policy by Britain might precipitate a conflict. "Our policy", he told Parliament, in 1938, "is not one of dividing Europe into two opposing *blocs* of countries, each arming against the other amidst a growing flood of ill will on both sides, which can only lead to war."[9] The prime minister was determined not to re-establish the system of mutually hostile alliances which, he felt, had led to war in 1914. Beyond that consideration, Chamberlain and many of his fellow Conservatives suspected that the Soviet Union actually wanted to see a war break out in Europe which would devastate Germany and the Western democracies, leaving them ripe for communist revolution. Under these circumstances the British could never bring themselves to offer the sort of binding, comprehensive alliance terms which the Russians sought.

Hitler suffered from no such qualms. In late May 1939 he told his generals that Poland would be destroyed "at the first suitable opportunity", but the Franco-British guarantee to Poland and the possibility of an alliance between the USSR and the democracies upset his calculations. He still believed that Britain and France, despite their guarantee, either would not fight at all or, at most, would make some feeble gestures in defense of Poland. Still, it was essential to prevent the formation of a new Triple Entente linking Moscow, London and Paris. That was the one development which could have forestalled Hitler's design for achieving European hegemony piecemeal. German diplomats, therefore, began to press their Soviet colleagues for an agreement in the summer of 1939. As one German official put it to the Soviet chargé d'affaires in Berlin:[10]

> What could England offer Russia? At best participation in a European war and the hostility of Germany, but not a single desirable end for Russia. What could we [Germany] offer, on the other hand? Neutrality and staying out of a possible European conflict and, if Moscow wished, a German-Russian understanding on mutual interests which, just as in former times, would work to the advantage of both countries.

The Nazis were anxious to reach agreement, whereas the Western powers were hesitant. The Germans had no compunctions about offering Russia political and territorial concessions at the expense of other countries, while Britain would not exert the slightest pressure on Warsaw to come to terms with the USSR.

Stalin, always an extremely suspicious man, misread Western timidity and caution as a plot. If Britain and France permitted German aggression, he reasoned, it could not be because of their shortsightedness or weakness, but because they wished to encourage Hitler's ambitions in the east. Appeasement, in the Kremlin's view, was a cynical method of deflecting Nazi aggression toward the Soviet Union. After all, as recently as December 1938 Paris and Berlin had signed a declaration of friendship and goodwill. Even more menacing, Goehting's representative, Helmuth Wohlthat was in London during June and July 1939 ostensibly negotiating trade matters, but in fact discussing with high government officials the terms on which Britain might support Germany's claims against Poland. Perhaps, the Russians feared, the Anglo-French military negotiations with the USSR were only a ruse to entice Hitler into the Western camp.

By August, with their projected invasion of Poland just a few weeks away, the Germans were desperate for an agreement with the USSR which would isolate Poland and probably convince the British and French to dishonor their guarantees to Warsaw. Stalin, moreover, had recently learned from his intelligence sources that the Soviet Union was in less immediate danger of a Nazi attack than he had feared. Soviet spies at the German embassies in Warsaw and Tokyo had reported that after the destruction of Poland, Britain and France were to be Hitler's next victims. The assault on the USSR would come later. Therefore, when Hitler personally pressed the Soviets to receive his Foreign Minister, Joachim von Ribbentrop, to conclude a non-aggression pact by 23 August at the latest, the Kremlin agreed.

The central characters in A. J. P. Taylor's *The Origins of the Second World War* are Hitler and a succession of British and French statesmen. Soviet Russia is ascribed a lesser role, as earlier critics have pointed out.[11] For Taylor, the really important action takes place in Berlin, London and Paris, not Moscow. This is a serious weakness because, by "tilting" his analysis to the West, Taylor limits himself to an incomplete and interpretively distorted account of Europe's descent into war. Ironically, this Western orientation leads Taylor seriously to underestimate the influence of anti-communism and Russophobia within the British leadership.

The Soviet state is largely absent from the early chapters of the book. In Taylor's view Russia had fallen from the ranks of the

Great Powers by 1918. He even goes so far as to refer in several places to the "disappearance" of Russia.[12] It is certainly true that the Bolshevik regime did not at first enjoy the same material base of military strength relative to the other European powers that its imperial predecessor had possessed, and that this shift in the balance of power benefited Germany. Yet, contrary to Taylor, the USSR had not disappeared. In fact, the Western nations – mesmerized by the threat of revolution – may well have accorded more attention to communist Russia than they ever had paid to the Romanov empire. This oversight, fostered by Taylor's disinclination to give weight to ideological factors in international relations, causes him to misinterpret Western policy in a number of important ways. For example, he criticizes the Allies for leaving Germany united and, thus, still potentially the strongest country on the continent. But this judgment misses the critical point that the victors, for all their hatred for the defeated enemy, felt that they needed Germany intact as an anti-communist rampart in central Europe.[13]

Similarly, Taylor's aversion to the ideological factor causes him to write of the Bosheviks' "sense of security" during the decade after the First World War.[14] He assumes that the Soviet leaders must not have felt threatened, because he knows in hindsight, that no other power attacked or even seriously planned to strike the USSR after the end of foreign intervention in the Russian civil war. Bolshevik perceptions were, in fact, quite different. The belief that the imperialist powers intended to renew their bloody assault on the homeland of socialism was an article of faith in the Kremlin. The Dawes Plan, Locarno, German membership in the League of Nations and the Young Plan were each interpreted in Moscow as parts of a concerted imperialist strategy to undo the October revolution. These fears may not have been realistic, but they were real.[15] Having dismissed these fears as either rhetorical or manipulative devices, Taylor underrates the tremendous importance the Rapallo treaty had for the Russians.[16] Both emotionally and ideologically, it was the centerpiece of the Soviet diplomatic system. It gave the Bosheviks some minimal reassurance that a united phalanx of capitalist powers was not yet poised to crush the Soviet experiment.

Taylor's treatment of Soviet foreign policy, and also of the USSR as a factor in the diplomacy of other powers, is somewhat better for the 1930s than for the previous decade. His self-proclaimed historical "intuition" seems to serve him better in this period.[17] There is for the 1930s somewhat more extensive coverage of Moscow's significance in European affairs, though the amount of attention accorded Soviet Russia is still not proportional to its actual role in the origins of the Second World War. The Soviet Union still did not fully re-emerge, in his view, as a European Great Power until the signing of the Nazi-Soviet pact in August 1939.[18] Taylor is also willing to give Soviet anxieties more credence in the Hitler era. He sees that the Kremlin perceived every diplomatic combination which excluded them (Mussolini's projected Four Power Pact, the Munich conference, etc.) as a conspiracy against the USSR. He recognises that the defensive pacts which the USSR signed with France and Czechoslovakia did not allay those fears and suspicions. Because the French refused to give it substantive military content, the Franco-Soviet agreement, remained an "empty" gesture.[19] That, in turn, vitiated the alliance with Prague, which was dependent on relations between Paris and Moscow.

The subject of British views of and policy toward the USSR is, on the whole, perceptively handled in *The Origins of the Second World War*. Taylor demonstrates that the British government constantly rebuffed the attempts of the Kremlin to draw it and France into a system of collective security against the menace of Nazi aggression. Far from alliance, excluding the Soviet Union from European affairs was a consistent British objective. Chamberlain did not trust the Kremlin, nor did he respect its strength. Moreover, he assumed that an alliance with Russia would provoke Hitler, thus making war more, rather than less, likely. The only really significant gap in Taylor's description of British policy towards the USSR is, once again, the omission of its ideological underpinnings. He seriously underestimates the strength of anti-communism as a motive force in British foreign policy, not only toward Soviet Russia, but in regard to Germany as well.[20] Thus, Taylor notes, the Great Purges (especially the destruction of the Soviet officer corps) reinforced the prime minister's belief that the USSR was scarcely worth having as an ally, but he misses the more important point that Chamberlain was doctrinally opposed to any real alliance with the communist state – even if Stalin had been a benevolent ruler instead of a bloody tyrant.[21]

French foreign policy and diplomacy is treated in much less detail. Taylor follows the traditional interpretation of France as a self-imposed captive of British policy. The French, as he notes, grew more anxious for a binding military convention with the

USSR as the German threat continually mounted in the late 1930s. A powerful Franco-Soviet alliance never emerged, however, due to British opposition. Instead of recreating the Triple Entente, Paris had to choose between two alternative dual alliances – London or Moscow.

The steady progression of German advances from the announcement of rearmament to the absorption of Czechoslovakia finally caused a partial reassessment of British appeasement. After the German seizure of Prague, London responded more positively to the Soviet collective security campaign. Yet even at this juncture Taylor suggests, "the British government, in fact, were not interested in solid military co-operation with Soviet Russia; they merely wanted to chalk a Red bogey on the wall, in the hope that this would keep Hitler quiet".[22] Opening talks with Moscow was also a strategy for keeping their French ally in line. The British reluctantly took the lead in negotiations with the Soviets during 1939, Taylor suspects, because they feared that if they did not do so, France might make binding military commitments with the USSR which could subsequently drag Britain into war as well.[23]

The negotiations between the Western powers and the Soviet Union in the spring and summer of 1939 never had much chance of success. The two sides came to the talks with divergent goals and expectations. The British still hoped that war could be avoided. If it could not be prevented, they thought that Western forces, together with those of Poland, would bear the brunt of the fighting. Given the purge-ravaged condition of the Red Army, they looked to Russia only as a supply base, not as the main striking force of the prospective alliance. In addition, Western strategy anticipated a long war of attrition, much like the First World War, in which Germany would be worn down by a prolonged blockade. The Soviet role in such a conflict would be limited to supplying and supporting a static eastern front in Poland and Romania. The Soviets saw things differently. They had little faith that war could be avoided and even less confidence in the Polish army. They sought an alliance with Britain and France that included iron-clad military commitments, in which the Soviet army would play an aggressive and leading role from the onset of hostilities. They were convinced that only a great Franco-Soviet offensive on two fronts could prevent German victory. Differing forecasts of war or peace as well as divergent expectations of the nature of a possible conflict thus erected further barriers to co-operation between the Western democracies and the USSR.[24] Chamberlain doubted the value of a defense pact with the Soviet Union, but he was sure that, if such a treaty were signed, the presence of the Red Army in east-central Europe would be neither necessary nor desirable. Therefore, he saw no need to force the Poles or the Romanians to grant transit rights to large Soviet military formations. The Polish regime's refusal to permit the passage of Soviet troops was allowed to stand as the apparent barrier to an Anglo-Russian alliance which the British government did not want in the first place.[25]

In contrast to his relatively thorough and insightful treatment of British relations with the USSR, Taylor's characterization of Nazi policy toward Bolshevik Russia is completely inadequate. The source of this problem – the fundamental error which runs throughout the book – is the author's failure to take Hitler's ideas seriously. Taylor cannot believe that anyone would make the insane (and ultimately suicidal) National Socialist racist doctrines the basis for national policy. Instead, he treats Hitler as if the Nazi dictator were a rational and practical, if rather wicked, English statesman. Having dismissed Hitler's racist ideology as meaningless rhetoric with no bearing on the operative goals of the Reich, Taylor has lost touch with the well-springs of Nazi behavior. Refusing to admit the racist core of the *Lebensraum* doctrine, he must try to explain it as an "economic" idea. That, in turn, leads him to waste time refuting the economic explanation of Germany's entry into the war.[26] Taylor notes that Hitler was gravely concerned about the explosive growth of Soviet economic power, but denies that he had any long-range plans to attack the USSR. Hitler could not have harbored any aggressive intent toward Russia because, in Taylor's judgment, he did not adequately prepare for a major war.[27] That might be a valid assumption in regard to a Bismarck or a Palmerston, but not for Hitler. In reality, his conception of *Lebensraum* necessitated the conquest of the Ukraine and the extermination of its population.

As noted above, Taylor does not devote as much attention to the motives and actions of Soviet diplomacy as he does to those of Germany, Britain or even France. The primary motives of Stalin's foreign policy during the 1930s, in his view, were fear of attack by one or more of the imperialist powers and the desire to stay out of a European war. Taylor argues that the principal objective of Soviet diplomacy from the beginning of the collective security campaign in 1934 to its bankruptcy in 1939 was the construction of a solid military barrier to Nazi aggression, in co-operation with the Western democracies. The USSR, like Britain, occasionally entertained the possibility of closer ties with Germany, but he dismisses these gambits as mere "soundings", unrepresentative of the overall thrust of Soviet policy. Throughout the period, a defensive pact with London and Paris, not an offensive alliance with Berlin, remained Moscow's primary goal.[28] This is a controversial interpretation (though one with which this writer agrees) which will be discussed in detail in the historiographical section below.

Taylor is considerably less critical of Soviet diplomacy during the 1930s than many other Western historians. He considers the collective security strategy to have been rational and appropriate to Russian national interest. He assumes the Kremlin pursued this course straightforwardly until finally deflected from it in 1939 by continual Western rejection. Decreasing Soviet aid to the republican forces in Spain is, therefore, seen as a reaction to the growing Japanese menace in the Far East, rather than as an early sign of Moscow's disenchantment with the West.[29] On the hotly debated issue of whether the Soviets would have come to the aid of Czechoslovakia during the Munich crisis, if the Czechs and the Western powers had stood their ground, Taylor suspects that they would have.[30] In the matter of transit rights for the Red Army through eastern Europe, however, he admits the possibility that Stalin may have had designs on his neighbors' territory, but he still criticizes the Western statesmen for rationalizing the rejection of an alliance with the USSR on such hypothetical grounds. He is willing to accept the Soviet contention that a major Russian offensive through Poland and Romania was necessary to defeat Germany.[31] Taylor also believes that the Kremlin was reluctant to abandon its collective security campaign as late as August 1939. He even suggests that Molotov may have deliberately stalled negotiations with Germany in order to give the democracies one more chance.[32] When the Soviets finally chose to deal with Hitler, Taylor contends that "the Russians, in fact, did only what Western statesmen had hoped to do".[33] Finally, he argues that the Nazi–Soviet pact should not be considered an aggressive alliance (a conclusion difficult to support in view of Soviet territorial gains and the degree to which the Soviet economy functioned as the primary supplier of several otherwise unobtainable resources for the German war machine from September 1939 to June 1941).

The Nazi–Soviet pact and, more broadly, the nature and aims of Soviet foreign policy throughout the 1930s has been the subject of intense debate. The controversy encompasses two extreme, opposing poles and a wide spectrum of opinion between them. At one extreme is the official Soviet interpretation, according to which the USSR pursued a clear, unambiguous and even noble policy of building a European-wide shield of collective security against Nazi aggression. This diplomatic course was based, not on cynical self-interest or the desire for aggrandizement, but on high principle, since the Soviet Union represents the forces of historical progress and was, therefore, bound to take the lead in opposing the barbarous and retrogressive schemes of Nazi Germany. If collective security ultimately failed, it was not for the lack of unstinting and sincere Soviet effort, but rather because of the treacherous failure of the Western democracies to oppose Hitler's murderous plans. In the words of the authoritative *History of Soviet Foreign Policy*, co-edited by Foreign Minister Andrei Gromyko:[34]

> When the nazis seized power in Germany, the threat of another world war became very real in Europe. However, at the time it was still possible to avert fascist aggression through the concerted efforts of countries desiring peace. Had the Soviet proposals for collective security been put into effect it would have been possible to erect a powerful barrier to any aggressor . . . But this project was wrecked by the joint efforts of the fascist states and Poland with British encouragement . . . In this atmosphere the Soviet Union never for a moment relinquished its efforts to create a system of collective security.

Soviet commentators also minimize the significance of the Russo-German non-aggression treaty and rationalize it as necessitated by the grave threat of German and Japanese attacks on the USSR, combined with the betrayal of the cause of collective security by Britain and France. They contend that the pact cannot be considered an alliance with Nazi Germany in any sense, while they ignore, and sometimes even deny the existence of, the secret protocol that divided all of eastern Europe between Hitler and Stalin.[35]

At the opposite extreme is the allegation that collective security against aggression was never the Kremlin's real objective, but only a front behind which Stalin sought throughout the decade to woo a reluctant Hitler into an aggressive alliance.[36] Robert Tucker has advanced an especially radical version of this interpretation. He contends that, as far back as 1928, Stalin determined to divide the capitalist states against each other and maneuver them into a mutually destructive inter-imperialist war, from which the USSR would emerge unscathed and in a strong position to expand territorially all along its borders. To bring about this war Stalin allegedly aided Hitler's rise by deliberately steering the policy of the Comintern and the German Communist Party on a suicidal course. The Nazi–Soviet pact was, in this view, always implicit in Stalin's plans, while the collective security line was never anything more than a mask for his designs and a bait to attract Hitler.[37]

There is very little evidence to support his theory. Lacking any direct evidence, Tucker must rely on a painstaking (and often strained) exegesis of certain portions of Stalin's published writings. Yet the Soviet dictator's statements were sometimes ambiguous and often ran counter to the thesis Tucker is trying to sustain.[38] The ambitious and aggressive policy of collusion with Germany, which Tucker ascribes to Stalin, is not a continuation of the Rapallo orientation (as he claims). The Rapallo policy, though certainly designed to split the imperialist camp by courting Weimar Germany, was a defensive strategy aimed at preventing the outbreak of a war in central Europe that could easily draw in the USSR. The course of action which Tucker describes is a reckless, high risk strategy. Hitler was that sort of desperate gambler; Stalin was not. Tucker has also suggested that the purges were necessary to clear away the opposition within the Bolshevik elite to an opportunistic deal with Hitler. Thus the Great Purges provide evidence, he argues, for his theory that collective security was always a ruse.[39] The problem with this argument is that Stalin had the wrong people killed. Among Soviet diplomats, for example, numerous senior officials with a strongly pro-Rapallo orientation, such as Krestinskii and Karakhan, were purged, while many of their pro-Western colleagues, like Litvinov, Maiskii and Kollontai, were spared.[40]

A less extreme version of the theory that Stalin always preferred co-operation with Germany (whether Weimar or Nazi) to a defensive alliance with the Western powers is advanced by Gerhard Weinberg. Although his major two-volume study concentrates on German foreign policy, Moscow's policy toward Berlin is an important sub-theme which is explored in some detail. He is especially interested in contacts between David Kandelaki, head of the Soviet trade mission in Berlin, and Hjalmar Schacht.[41] Although their tentative discussions did not lead to a Russo-German *rapprochement*, Weinberg is convinced that

Stalin only tolerated the collective security line as a poor second choice while repeated Nazi rejections of Soviet feelers kept his preferred alternative – an agreement with Hitler – out of reach. Weinberg's version of Stalin's alleged preference for Germany over the democracies is certainly more temperately argued and much more thoroughly researched than Tucker's, but it, too, lacks sufficient evidence to be convincing. It makes 98 per cent of all Soviet diplomatic activity in the 1930s a brittle cover for the remaining covert 2 per cent. Lacking conclusive evidence to the contrary, it is more reasonable to assume that Soviet representatives spent the majority of their time and effort trying to accomplish their real objectives.

When A. J. P. Taylor wrote *The Origins of the Second World War* there was very little Soviet documentary and memoir material available on which to build an interpretation of Soviet conduct. His bibliography lists, "Soviet Russia: Nothing." Since 1961 useful sources have appeared. The *Dokumenty vneshnei politiki SSSR* series is now available for the 1930s.[42] Although this official collection has been tendentiously edited to support the current party line, it still contains a great deal of valuable material. There are also several new documentary collections from other governments, most notably the French and the Italian, which contain important evidence of Soviet diplomatic activities.

An interesting new memoir, Evgenii Gnedin's *Katastrofa i vtoroe rozhdenie*, has also appeared.[43] Gnedin was First Secretary at the Soviet embassy in Berlin and then press spokesman at the Foreign commissariat in Moscow during the latter half of the 1930s. In 1962 he was asked to prepare a report on Russo-German relations in the 1930s, in connection with a Central Committee investigation into the past "miscalculations and errors" of Molotov. In other words, Gnedin was requested to help with the compilation of politically damaging material against the former foreign commissar now in disfavor. The anti-Molotov project was subsequently scrapped, however, and Gnedin's commission to prepare the report was withdrawn. Gnedin did not abandon his research, although his work could not be published in the increasingly conservative Kremlin atmosphere after the fall of Khrushchev. Finally, in 1977 his writings began to be published abroad.

Gnedin believes that Stalin permitted Molotov to pursue a foreign policy different from the official collective security campaign then being waged by Litvinov. Under Molotov's direction, Gnedin contends, various non-diplomatic personnel (Kandelaki, Sergei Bessonov and Karl Radek) surreptitiously attempted to weld a Russo-German alliance. These initiatives were kept hidden not only from the Western states, but were also carried out behind the backs of the Foreign Commissar and his diplomats. Gnedin angrily condemns Stalin and Molotov for undermining the anti-fascist and collective security policies. Gnedin's works contain a great deal of useful information about the Soviet system in the 1930s and the 1960s, but they are not an entirely reliable guide to Soviet diplomacy leading up to the Nazi–Soviet pact. The author did not have access to Soviet archives, not even when he was preparing a quasi-official report for the Central Committee, so his memoirs rely heavily on personal memory of events forty years old. The result is a number of obvious errors and discrepancies. Beyond that, as a relatively junior member of the Foreign Commissariat, Gnedin did not have access to Stalin or Molotov. Lacking either personal experience or uncensored documentary sources upon which to draw, his reconstruction of their activities is largely hypothetical. Moreover, Gnedin was discharged from the diplomatic service in May 1939, so he has no direct knowledge of the events leading up to the Russo-German pact. Also, Gnedin's judgment has been affected (quite understandably) by his experiences as a prisoner in the *GULAG* system. He knows that Stalin and Molotov are evil men, so he assumes that they must have conducted an evil foreign policy.[44] Though informative in a number of respects, Gnedin's writings are something less than the all-revealing "insider" memoirs that they at first appear to be.

Memoirs and collections of diplomatic documents now available have been utilized extensively in two recently published, major studies of Soviet foreign policy in the 1930s. Jiri Hochman elaborates (with considerably more scholarly apparatus) on Gnedin's thesis that Molotov, with Stalin's blessing, systematically undermined Litvinov's attempts to build an anti-Nazi alliance.[45] Hochman, a veteran of the "Prague spring" who emigrated to avoid further imprisonment after the Soviet crack down, is disillusioned that Stalinist foreign policy was not "principled". He argues vehemently that, despite Litvinov's high-sounding rhetoric, the Soviet Union worked assiduously to ensure the failure of collective security. He is eager to prove the Soviet Union ill-intentioned at every turn. The Soviets, Hochman claims, did not want to strengthen their pact with France, did not wish to solve the troop transit issue with their east European neighbors, never intended to come to the aid of

Czechoslovakia under any circumstances and, finally, used the purges to dissolve the (supposed) resolution of Britain and France to take a firm stand against German aggression.

Hochman simply has not understood the real nature of the collective security campaign. When it fails to live up to the altruistic and "principled" image created by communist propagandists, Hochman must reject it, root and branch, as a thoroughly unprincipled and devious strategem. Ironically, he commits the same error as apologists for the Soviet regime who claim that the responsibility for failing to stand up to Hitler in time to prevent a disastrous war can be attributed to only one side. In actuality, both the USSR and the Western democracies appeased Germany; both pursued short-sighted policies aimed at keeping themselves out of the war looming on the horizon, rather than at preventing or winning it. Hochman's work is also marred by his use of sources. He cites numerous documents from the Czech and Romanian archives, repositories that are generally closed to all except a few loyal to the regime, but does not discuss the provenance of these items. Worse still, he buttresses several points critical to his analysis with reference to a work entitled *Notes for a Journal*, which its publishers attribute to Maxim Litvinov.[46] Hochman does not seem to know that such knowledgeable Kremlinologists as Bertram Wolfe and Philip Mosely have denounced this work as a forgery. He makes no comment as to why he feels justified in employing this dubious source. He also follows the annoying practice, whenever he cannot find documents to prove his point, of assuming that such documents exist but are missing or have been suppressed. In fairness, it must also be said that even readers who reject the author's overall thesis will profit from reading this book. The discussion of negotiations with Romania for troop transit rights, for example, is more detailed than in any other study.

Jonathan Haslam's *The Soviet Union and the Struggle for Collective Security in Europe*, which appeared at about the same time as Hochman's book, is a much superior treatment of the subject.[47] Haslam has used the full range of available archival and published sources (except for a handful of east European archival documents cited by Hochman), and he has used them with great care. The most interesting aspect of Haslam's work is his ability to expose opposing factions within the Soviet foreign policy formulating process. In his view the principal opponents of Commissar Litvinov, and therefore of the collective security strategy as well, were Molotov and Andrei Zhdanov. Haslam calls their foreign policy orientation "isolationism", by which he means a combination of doubt about the possibility of achieving security in alliance with the democracies, nostalgia for the days of Rapallo-style co-operation with Germany, and a desire to insulate the USSR from the war about to burst over Europe by avoiding commitments to any of the imperialist powers. Stalin, he believes, did not take a resolute position on either side of the argument between Litvinov and the isolationists. Instead, the Soviet dictator followed the alternative that appeared most likely to protect his state from a disastrous war – which meant the collective security line for most of the 1930s, until he despaired of its success at the end of the decade. Given the fragmentary evidence available, delineating Kremlin factions is a perilous enterprise for any scholar, but Haslam's conclusions are carefully reasoned and suitably tentative.[48]

Haslam's book is the most realistic treatment now available of the evolution of Soviet foreign policy from collective security to the Nazi–Soviet pact. Not only does he attempt to demonstrate the diversity of opinion within the Kremlin leadership, he also gives full weight to the plethora of Soviet fears – fear of German aggression, fear of an anti-Soviet alliance between Germany and the Western powers, fear that the democracies would "buy off" the fascist regimes by encouraging them to move eastward, fear of a Japanese attack, etc. He avoids the trap of seeing Soviet policy as either sublimely "principled" or diabolically unprincipled. Instead, along with A. J. P. Taylor, Haslam assumes that the Kremlin elite was searching for whatever course would best protect the interests of the Soviet Union. Thus, Stalin's "preferred" policy is neither a defensive alliance with Britain and France nor a pact with Germany, but whatever policy would provide the greatest degree of security. Given the virtually unrelenting hostility of the Nazi regime, the only alternative (before August 1939) was the collective security line.[49]

Haslam's interpretation of two crucial periods, the Czech crisis of 1938 and the dual set of negotiations in the summer of 1939, are particularly well argued and based on thorough research. He demonstrates that Stalin followed Litvinov's collective security line throughout 1938, as opposed to the "isolationist" alternative, and that the Soviets would have aided the Czechs against a German attack (at least if France did so, too). The Kremlin was still convinced that a show of resolution by Britain, France and Russia together would have forced Hitler to back down, but the Western powers were determined to appease

Germany, so they undermined Soviet efforts for joint action.[50] Haslam places the blame for the breakdown of the collective security drive and for the signing of the Nazi–Soviet pact squarely on Britain. He believes that Stalin did not make the final decision for a deal with Hitler until August. Up to that point, Soviet diplomacy still sought an alliance with the democracies, but their mutual suspicions and vastly different reading of the international situation prevented such an agreement.[51] "Confronted with the evident unwillingness of the Entente to provide immediate, concrete and water-tight guarantees for Soviet security in Europe . . . the Russians were left with little alternative", Haslam contends, "but an agreement with Germany creating a condominium in Eastern Europe."[52]

The course of Soviet diplomacy in the 1930s will, doubtless, remain a controversial issue among historians, especially since there is no indication that Soviet archives will open at any time in the foreseeable future. Fortunately, however, the dedication to dispassionate and rigorous scholarship of investigators like Haslam and Weinberg has raised the level of Western analysis of Soviet foreign policy in this period. Cold War rhetoric and partisanship no longer dominate the scene as they once did. A. J. P. Taylor, similarly was striving to overcome the problems of doctrinal bias and political purpose when he wrote *Origins*, though he went too far in denying the influence of ideological conceptions on international affairs. Moreover, the recent outpouring of studies on Soviet diplomacy in the 1930s has demonstrated the important role of the USSR in Europe's drift toward the conflagration. Future historians of the origins of the Second World War will have to pay more attention to the Kremlin than Taylor did twenty-five years ago.

NOTES

1   The text of the Nazi–Soviet pact, together with captured German diplomatic documents pertaining to its negotiation, are in Raymond J. Sontag and James S. Beddie (eds), *Nazi-Soviet Relations* (Washington, 1948), pp. 1–78.

2   Jane Degras (ed.), *The Communist International, 1919–1943: Documents* (London, 1965), Vol. 3, p. 262.

3   Jane Degras (ed.), *Soviet Documents on Foreign Policy* (London, 1953), Vol. 3, pp. 282–94.

4   *Dokumenty vneshnei politiki SSSR* (Moscow, 1977), doc. 357.

5   Robert Coulondre, *De Staline à Hitler* (Paris, 1950), p. 165.

6   Stalin's speech was first published in *Pravda* on 11 March 1939.

7   Sontag and Beddie, *Nazi-Soviet Relations*, p. 2.

8   Quoted in Robert Manne, "The British decision for alliance with Russia, May 1939", *Journal of Contemporary History*, vol. 9 (1974), p. 12.

9   Quoted in Martin Gilbert, *The Roots of Appeasement* (New York, 1966), p. 169.

10 Sontag and Beddie, *Nazi-Soviet Relations*, p. 34.

11 See T. M. Mason, "Some origins of the Second World War", *Past and Present*, no. 29 (1964), pp. 67–87; and D. C. Watt, "Some aspects of A. J. P. Taylor's work as diplomatic historian", *Journal of Modern History*, vol. 49 (1977), pp. 19–33.

12 A. J. P. Taylor, *The Origins of the Second World War* (Greenwich, Conn., 1965), p. 25 and *passim*. The reference here and elsewhere in this chapter is to the American second edition which includes a new preface for American readers as well as a postscript in which the author defends himself against some of his early critics.

13 On the importance of anti-communism and counter-revolution in the foreign policy of the Western states, see Arno J. Mayer, *Politics and Diplomacy of Peacemaking: Containment and Counterrevolution at Versailles* (New York, 1967); and John M. Thompson, *Russia, Bolshevism and the Versailles Peace* (Princeton, 1966).

14 Taylor, *Origins*, pp. 40–1.

15 For evidence of the Soviet regime's fundamental insecurity in the international arena see Teddy J. Uldricks, "Russia and Europe: diplomacy, revolution, and economic development in the 1920s", *International History Review*, vol. 1 (1979), pp. 55–83; John P. Sontag, "The Soviet war scare of 1926–27", *Russian Review*, vol. 34 (1975), pp. 66–77; and Jonathan Haslam, *Soviet Foreign Policy, 1930–33: The Impact of the Depression* (New York, 1983). Cf. Karlheinz Niclauss, *Die Sowjetunion und Hitlers Machtergreifung* (Bonn, 1966).

16 Taylor, *Origins*, pp. 52–3. Cf. Carole Fink, *The Genoa Conference: European Diplomacy, 1921–1922* (Chapel Hill, NC, 1984).

17 A. J. P. Taylor, "Accident prone, or what happened next", *Journal of Modern History*, Vol. 49 (1977), p. 7. Borrowing a gardener's term from Sir Lewis Namier, Taylor refers to his historical "intuition" as "green fingers": "Some may say that I have relied on my green fingers too much. I think that I have relied on them too little."

18 Taylor, *Origins*, p. 216.

19 ibid., p. 85. Cf. John E. Dreifort, "The French Popular Front and the Franco-Soviet Pact, 1936–37: a dilemma in foreign policy", *Journal of Contemporary History*, vol. 11 (1976), pp. 217–36.

20 For a sophisticated discussion of the bases of British appeasement policy which takes the factor of anti-communism into account (though, perhaps, still not sufficiently) see Martin Gilbert, *Roots of Appeasement*. Cf. Gottfried Niedhart, "British attitudes and policies towards the Soviet Union and International Communism,

1933–9", in Wolfgang J. Mommsen and Lothar Kettenacker (eds), *The Fascist Challenge and the Policy of Appeasement* (London, 1983), pp. 286–96.

21 For Western perceptions of Soviet military strength (or weaknesses) see Ronald R. Rader, "Anglo-French estimates of the Red Army, 1936–1937", *Soviet Armed Forces Annual*, vol. 3 (1979), pp. 265–80; and James H. Herndon, "British perceptions of Soviet military capability, 1935–9", in Mommsen and Kettenacker, *The Fascist Challenge*, pp. 297–319.

22 Taylor, *Origins*, p. 246.

23 ibid., p. 226.

24 ibid., p. 247. Since Taylor developed this argument, the matter of Western expectations of the nature of future wars has been studied in much greater detail. See Adrian Preston (ed.), *General Staffs and Diplomacy before the Second World War* (London, 1978); and Robert J. Young, *In Command of France: French Foreign Policy and Military Planning, 1933–1940* (Cambridge, Mass., 1978). These more detailed studies tend to support Taylor's suggestion that differing strategic conceptions added to the gulf between London and Moscow.

25 Taylor, *Origins*, pp. 205–6, 247.

26 ibid., p. 105. For an alternate interpretation stressing the logical continuity of theory and practice in Nazi foreign policy see Gerhard L. Weinberg, *The Foreign Policy of Hitler's Germany*, Vol. 1, *Diplomatic Revolution in Europe, 1933–36* (Chicago, 1970), and Vol. 2, *Starting World War II, 1937–1939* (Chicago, 1980).

27 Taylor, *Origins*, pp. 211–12.

28 ibid., pp. 224–6, 232–3, 249.

29 ibid., pp. 158–9.

30 ibid., p. 167.

31 ibid., pp. 246–8.

32 ibid., p. 250.

33 ibid., p. 252.

34 B. Ponomaryov, A. Gromyko and V. Khvostov (eds), *History of Soviet Foreign Policy, 1917–1945* (Moscow, 1969), pp. 337–8. For the Soviet view also see I. K. Koblyakov, *USSR: For Peace, Against Aggression, 1933–1941* (Moscow, 1976); I. F. Maksimychev, *Diplomatii mira protiv diplomatii voiny* (Moscow, 1981); and A. L. Narochitskii (ed.), *SSSR v bor'be protiv fashistskoi agressi, 1933–1941* (Moscow, 1976).

35 Ponomaryov *et al.*, *History of Soviet Foreign Policy*, pp. 381–6.

36 Franz Borkenau, *European Communism* (New York, 1953), pp. 117, 132–5 and 234–5; Boris Nikolaevskii, "Stalin i ubiistvo Kirova", *Sotsialisticheskii vestnik*, no. 10 (1956), p. 186 and no. 12 (1956), pp. 239–40; W. G. Krivitsky, *I Was Stalin's Agent* (London, 1939), pp. 18–34, 37–40; and Vladimir Petrov, "A missing page in Soviet historiography: the Nazi-Soviet partnership", *Orbis*, vol. 11 (1968), pp. 1113–37.

37 Robert C. Tucker, "The emergence of Stalin's foreign policy",

Slavic Review, vol. 36 (1977), pp. 563–89, 604–7. A similar argument is made by Sven Allard, *Stalin und Hitler: Die sowjetrussische Aussenpolitik, 1930–1941* (Bern and Munich, 1974).

38 See Teddy J. Uldricks, "Stalin and Nazi Germany", *Slavic Review*, vol. 36 (1977), pp. 599–603 for a critique of the logic of Tucker's argument.

39 Robert C. Tucker, "Stalin, Bukharin and history as conspiracy", in Robert C. Tucker and Stephen F. Cohen (eds), *The Great Purge Trial* (New York, 1965), p. xxxvi. Also see George F. Kennan, *Russia and the West under Lenin and Stalin* (New York, 1961), pp. 288–91, 296.

40 Teddy J. Uldricks, "The impact of the Great Purges on the People's Commissariat of Foreign Affairs", *Slavic Review*, vol. 36 (1977), pp. 187–204.

41 Weinberg, *Diplomatic Revolution*, pp. 220–2, 310; and *Starting World War II*, p. 214. Cf. his earlier work, *Germany and the Soviet Union, 1939–1941* (Leyden, 1954). Weinberg's latest work, *World in the Balance* (Hanover, NH, 1981), p. 7, advances even more strongly the theory of Stalin's preference for an agreement with Germany over one with the democracies. Similar interpretations of Stalin's foreign policy can be found in Adam Ulam, *Expansion and Coexistence* (New York, 1974), pp. 183–279; and James E. McSherry, *Stalin, Hitler, and Europe* (Cleveland, Ohio, 1968), Vol. 1.

42 Also see V. M. Falin *et al.* (eds), *Soviet Peace Efforts on the Eve of World War II (September 1938–August 1939): Documents and Records* (Moscow, 1973), 2 vols.

43 Evgenii Gnedin, *Katastrofa i vtoroe rozhdenie: memuarnye zapiski* (Amsterdam, 1977). Gnedin's other writings which deal with Soviet foreign policy in the 1930s include *Iz istorii otnoshenii mezhdu SSSR i fashistskoi Germaniei: dokumenty i sovremennye komentarii* (New York, 1977); *Vykhod iz labirinta* (New York, 1982); and "V narkomindele, 1922–1933: Inter'viu s E.A. Gnedinym", *Pamiat (istoricheskii sbornik)*, no. 5 (1981), pp. 357–93.

44 Gnedin's indictment of Molotov for undermining the collective security drive is echoed by another Soviet dissident, Roy Medvedev, *All Stalin's Men* (Garden City, NY, 1984), pp. 89–90.

45 Jiri Hochman, *The Soviet Union and the Failure of Collective Security, 1934–1938* (Ithaca, NY, 1984).

46 Maxim Litvinov (pseud. for Grigorii Besedovskii?), *Notes for a Journal* (New York, 1955).

47 Jonathan Haslam, *The Soviet Union and the Struggle for Collective Security in Europe, 1933–39* (New York, 1984).

48 ibid., pp. 5, 7, 22–3, 30, 33, 154–6, 158, 201.

49 ibid., pp. 230–2.

50 ibid., pp. 158–94. Cf. Donald N. Lammers, "The May crisis of 1938: the Soviet view considered", *South Atlantic Quarterly*, vol. 69 (1970), pp. 480–503, who doubts Soviet resolution to support the Czechs; and Marcia Lynn Toepfer, "The Soviet role in the Munich

crisis: a historiographical debate", *Diplomatic History*, vol. 1 (1977), pp. 341–57, whose work tends to support Haslam's position. Also see Barry Mendel Cohen, "Moscow at Munich: did the Soviet Union offer unilateral aid to Czechoslovakia?", *East European Quarterly*, vol. 12 (1978), pp. 341–8.

51   Haslam, *Soviet Union and the Struggle for Collective Security*, pp. 195–229. Robert Manne reaches similar conclusions about the tragic failure of the Anglo-Soviet negotiations, though he is not as critical of the Chamberlain government as is Haslam. See Manne, "The British decision", pp. 3–26, and Manne, "Some British light on the Nazi-Soviet pact", *European Studies Review*, vol. 11 (1981), pp. 83–102.

52   Haslam, *Soviet Union and the Struggle for Collective Security*, p. 231.

8

Poland between
East and West

PIOTR S. WANDYCZ

The Polish theme in Taylor's book runs like a thin thread
through the European fabric during the 1920s and early 1930s.
In the last two years of peace, Poland moves to the center of the
diplomatic stage. Reading the detailed account of the moves and
countermoves in 1938–9 one regrets the superficial and the all
too brief presentation of the Polish background. True, many of
the more important works on Poland's relations with Germany
and Russia, on the French alliance, and other aspects of the
country's foreign policy appeared after the publication of *The
Origins of the Second World War*.[1] So did some of the documentary
collections.[2] Still, the memoirs of the French ambassador in
Warsaw, Jules Laroche, were presumably available to Taylor, as
was the pioneering study of Hans Roos on Poland and Europe.[3]
One looks in vain for an indication that they had been consulted.
The same seems true for the Polish White Book, *Les Relations
polono-allemandes et polono-soviétiques au cours de la période 1933: recueil
de documents officiels* (Paris, 1940), an admittedly fragmentary but
important collection.

Origins, as we know, met with a critical reception among
Western scholars and provoked a considerable and adverse
reaction in Poland. According to a Polish historian, Taylor was
invited to Warsaw for a discussion of his thesis but declined the
invitation, urging instead that his book appear in a Polish
translation.[4]

It is a banality to recall that Poland's international problems
were intimately connected both with Germany – which, as Taylor rightly insists, was *the* European issue between the wars – and
with the Soviet Union. The treatment of these two powers and
their leaders is therefore highly relevant from our point of view.

This is not the place to dwell once again on Taylor's eccentric characterization of Hitler. The straw man he erects – an alleged half-madman blindly adhering to a meticulously worked out timetable of conquest – is, of course, an easy object of Taylor's pen. Obviously, Hitler was capable of rational behavior and pursued elastic tactics. Otherwise no diplomatic intercourse with the Third Reich would have been possible. Poland's foreign minister, Colonel Józef Beck, was one of many who came to believe only as late as 1939 that the Führer had lost all sense of proportion. To say this, however, is not to accept the image of a patient gambler who had only to wait for all the aces to tumble his way. Nazi foreign policy, as Jacobsen rightly points out, "ist ohne die Rolle der Ideologie nicht hinreichend zu verstehen".[5] This of course is hardly a novel point.

Taylor's general statements about Russia strike even a non-specialist in Kremlinogy as "curiouser and curiouser": by 1930 all Soviet "dreams of world revolution had long vanished" (p. 78); their leaders' indifference toward international communism was marked (p. 125); Russia, the author tells us *ex cathedra*, "sought security in Europe, not conquests" (p. 241). Elsewhere we learn, however, that Russia was naturally opposed to the status quo in eastern Europe which "stemmed essentially from the two humiliating treaties of Brest-Litovsk and Riga" (p. 227). Thus Soviet designs on the Baltic countries, eastern Poland and Romanian Bessarabia do not qualify as conquests since these lands had once been part of the multinational Romanov empire. Even Lenin would have rejected this reasoning. The line between conquest and change of the status quo is indeed thin. One looks in vain in *Origins* for a characterization of Stalin. To invoke the inaccessibility of the Soviet archives is too easy, and when Taylor states: "From . . . Stalin . . . not a line, not a word" (p. 16), he conveniently overlooks the voluminous works of Stalin. Are they to be dismissed out of hand as a historical source?

The treatment of France – the third power with which Poland's fate was so closely bound – is less controversial as far as general interpretations go. Yet not all is plain sailing here, even though one can advance the excuse that *Origins* preceded the publication of *Documents diplomatiques français*, which is still incomplete. Taylor seems unaware of the existence of the Franco-Polish military convention of February 1921, even though its gist had been summarized by Gamelin in 1946.[6] Worse still, he twice asserts that none existed, and then proceeds to call the 1939 Franco-Polish military protocol a convention (p. 159 misquoting L. Noël, *L'agression allemande contre la Pologne*; and on p. 238). This is serious, for the Franco-Polish relationship turned around the axle of the 1921 military convention which Paris strenuously sought to weaken from the late 1920s on.

Interwar Polish foreign policy was shaped by Marshal Józef Pilsudski, with the exception of the brief period, 1923–6 when he was not in office. After his death, Beck, a faithful disciple, attempted to steer his country's diplomacy in accordance with Pilsudski's precepts, or at least what he understood them to be. Yet Pilsudski is mentioned only once (p. 80) in connection with the German–Polish declaration of non-aggression. No real attempt is ever made to appraise the marshal's thoughts and guidelines.[7] This seeming nonchalance may well stem from Taylor's condescending view of Poland and the Poles: Poland was part of this "No Man's land of small states" (p. 21); it belonged to these French "satellites and clients: inspired by national enthusiasm, but carried to independence by Allied victory and helped thereafter by French money and French military advisers. The French treaties of alliance with them made sense as treaties of protection, like those which Great Britain made with the new states in the Middle East" (p. 37). The term "satellite" will reappear later, although how satellites can detach themselves from their orbit or vary their course is not satisfactorily explained.

In discussing the Versailles settlement of Poland's borders, Taylor rightly notes the paradox that what was regarded as a compromise solution over Danzig aroused particular German ire, as did the drawing of the German–Polish borders with which even an impartial judge would find little fault (p. 47). The "corridor" was "inhabited predominantly by Poles" and the transit arrangements were satisfactory (see p. 26). This, of course, did not prevent the Germans from viewing the Diktat as iniquitous or the British from persuading themselves that "the frontier with Poland was wicked" (p. 46, 48). The author's assertion, however, that Poland was "treated generously" at Versailles, but not because of "considerations of strategy" is more dubious (p. 26). Surely the French support for Poland's western borders had a great deal to do with strategic considerations, and Silesia was viewed principally as an arsenal which should be denied to Germany. This point had already been made by Arnold Wolfers in his well-known book and developed by others.[8] The concept of

a "barrière de l'est", revived or reinterpreted, played a significant role in France's policy toward Poland at this early stage.
The drawing of the Polish–Soviet frontiers, a result of the
1919–20 war and the Treaty of Riga, receives virtually no attention. Riga is lumped together with Brest-Litovsk (pp. 227, 232)
which, to put it mildly, is an oversimplification.

As already noted, Taylor is inclined to give Russia, whenever
possible, the benefit of the doubt. Rapallo is presented as no
challenge to peace treaties, and Berlin and Moscow "asked no
more than to be left alone" (p. 49). Such a thesis was dubious
when *Origins* appeared and is even more so today. If Russia could
do little more than sound Germany in 1924 about driving Poland
back to its ethnic core (whatever that was), and Stresemann
emphasize revision only by peaceful means, this was more by
necessity than choice.[9] Taylor admits that much when he subsequently says that Germany could not contemplate war against
Poland "as late as 1934" (p. 42). If this was so, and the point
appears valid, how can he then accuse Paris of a "surprising
exaggeration" of Polish and Czech strength, at least before the
mid-1930s (p. 38)?

A penchant for sweeping generalizations often plays Taylor
false. Stressing the defensive posture of France and stating that
the French asked: "how can our Eastern alliances help us, and
never – how can we help them?", Taylor is right except for the
word "never". Up to the 1924 general elections in France, the
government and the army *did* give serious thought to co-
ordination of offensive strategies with their eastern allies, an
evolution, as marked by changing moblization plans, took
time.[10]

The few references to French–Polish military collaboration are
often inexact if not misleading. When Taylor says that under
Locarno "the French were still free to operate their eastern
alliances" (p. 55), he does not indicate that under the Franco-
Polish treaty of 1925 the alliance was partly subordinated to the
working of the League, Hence, France could provide aid only
under articles 15 al. 7 and 16, although it promised that this
would be immediate. Whether this was meant to be simultaneous with the decision of the League or following it was not clear.
Moreover, the new provisions were at variance with the still valid
military convention of 1921, and the French attempted to water
down the latter. The Poles naturally objected. This, as well as
the long story of Polish efforts to obtain new guarantees in
connection with the premature evacuation of the Rhineland, is

ignored, thereby making the understanding of subsequent
developments very difficult.

Although the German cabinet minister Treviranus hardly
"started an agitation against the Polish fronter" (p. 62) – it had
been systematically pursued for years – German revisionism did
become more stringent in the early 1930s. This was one of the
reasons why the Nazi take over appeared to the Poles as an
improvement over the Weimar Republic in so far as it meant a
certain subordination of the demands for revision of the
German–Polish border to a much vaster program of change.
Here the rearmament question, both before and after Hitler,
became vital to Poland. The opposition to the *Gleichberechtigung*
declaration, in which France acquiesced without consulting
Warsaw, was one of the elements of the subsequent direct Polish
overtures to Berlin.

An alternative to concessions was force, and Taylor mentions
Polish preventive war plans and speaks of "repeated, though
empty, calls [which] came from Poland" (p. 79). The story of the
"preventive war" is much more controversial than a reader of
Origins may assume. Those who believe in Polish proposals[11] are
confronted by critics who assert than none were made, and that
the rumors originated from Warsaw to "soften" Germany and
make it more amenable to a détente with Poland.[12] In view of the
well-known French abhorrence of the very idea of a preventive
war, one can almost rule out the likelihood of direct and explicit
proposals for a preventive war (in the strict sense of the word).
Pilsudski did let it be known that he would not hesitate to take
some forcible action, and the Westerplatte incident (a reinfor-
cement of the Polish garrison) may well be seen as a notice
served both on Paris and Berlin. It is true, however, that a good
deal of documentation which points this way was not readily
available to Taylor.

A growing disenchantment with France, which the Four
Power Pact accentuated, played an important role in Pilsudski's
effort to reach a direct understanding with Berlin. Besides,
Pilsudski had believed for years that Polish foreign policy ought
to be based on two "canons": a principle of balance between
Germany and Russia, and the principle of alliances with France
and Romania.[13] The treaty of non-aggression with the Soviet
Union of 1932 was thus to be completed by a declaration of
non-aggression with Germany in January 1934. Taylor's observations on the latter, which strictly speaking was not "a pact",
are neither novel nor profound. His opinion that the declaration

freed Hitler "from any threat of Polish support for France" (p. 81) could be downright misleading unless one clarifies the word "support". The non-aggression declaration expressly recognized all Poland's international obligations including the Franco-Polish alliance. But it deepened the differences in perception, by Warsaw and Paris, of the actual role of the alliance. For the French it was mainly a diplomatic instrument to be used as a deterrent, and it implied co-ordination of foreign policies of both countries. To the Poles it was mainly a military instrument to ensure that in case of war France and Poland would together fight a common enemy. But this did not necessarily entail Poland being in the tow of French diplomacy. It was one of the objects of the German–Polish "pact" to enhance Warsaw's international position by placing Poland on a footing of political equality with France.

The German–Polish declaration of non-aggression of 26 January 1934 created a certain equivocation between France and Poland – just as Locarno had done nine years earlier – in addition to an equivocation between Warsaw and Berlin. The latter, Taylor says, was to be expected "in an agreement between two such men as Hitler and Beck" (p. 81). The Polish foreign minister, according to Taylor, "always possessed complete self-confidence, though not much else" (p. 80). Having thus reduced the issue to personalities, Taylor seems to indicate his lack of awareness of the fact that the January declaration was Pilsudski's brain child. Beck acted as an executor but did not make the decisions. Whether the Polish foreign minister was "sure" that he could "tame the tiger" is something for which we have to take Taylor's word.

The equivocation of the January declaration did not stem from Hitler's assumption that "Poland had been detached from the French system which indeed she had" (p. 81) but rather from the long-range incompatibility of German and Polish objectives. To Hitler the "pact" with Warsaw made sense if it ultimately opened the gates to eastern expansion. Pilsudski and Beck knew very well that a joint German–Polish drive toward the Ukraine would reduce Poland to the status of Berlin's vassal. Warsaw was always determined to prevent this, and Taylor acknowledges that the Poles were resolved not to co-operate with Russia against Germany, and "almost equally resolved" not to co-operate with Germany against the Soviet Union. Hitler "never understood" this (p. 196). Why "almost"? In December 1933, Pilsudski told Rauschning that "Poland would never under any circumstances respond to any German attempts to turn Polish efforts toward the Russian Ukraine". Rauschning reported this to Berlin.[14] When Göring endeavored to reopen this subject with Pilsudski in 1935 he was cut short by the marshal.[15] The Polish position was thus unequivocal, and the Poles could assume that Hitler got the message. It was only in December 1938 that the undersecretary of state Jan Szembek remarked that "the whole attitude of Germany toward us is based on the thesis, subscribed to by the highest figures of the Third Reich, that in a future German–Russian conflict, Poland will be a natural ally of Germany. In such circumstances the result could be that the entire good neighbor policy stemming from the 1934 accord is really a fiction."[16]

If, after Pilsudski's death, Polish diplomacy tended to over-estimate the value of the declaration – although being "blindly confident" (p. 151) is an exaggeration – the marshal himself had regarded the arrangement mainly as a temporary device. He told his intimate collaborators on 7 March 1934 that he could not guarantee more than four years of peace with Germany (the declaration was valid for ten years), and expressed concern whether his successors would be able to deal with the developing situation.[17] Surely this remark, as well as Pilsudski's subsequent comment that Poland was sitting on two stools and was bound to fall off one or the other, the question being only when this would happen,[18] throws new light on the marshal's reasoning. Taylor could not know of it when he wrote his book. His observation that the Poles feared Russia more than Germany in the mid-1930s is generally correct, although new documentation shows that there was no unanimity in this respect.[19]

Poland's opposition to the eastern pact stemmed mainly from Warsaw's determination not to lose the status of being the principal ally of France in the east, and to avoid being reduced to the role of an "advance guard for a Franco-Russian alliance" (pp. 80, 84). But there was more to it.[20] The pact would have placed Poland in a state of dependency on Russia, wrecking the policy of equilibrium, and diminishing direct French obligations to Warsaw. In peace Warsaw would have lost all freedom of diplomatic maneuver, and in the event of war would become a German–Russian battleground. Remembering the lesson of partitions, the Poles did not care to be defended by Russia against Germany or vice versa.

Polish opposition to the eatern pact was therefore colored less by Pilsudski's aspiration "to play the part of a Great Power"

(p. 80), but more by the illusory hopes for a strengthening of Franco-Polish ties. In that sense the visit of Louis Barthou to Warsaw in the spring of 1934, followed by the mission of General Debeney, played an important part in Pilsudski's attitude. To ignore these events means depriving the reader of important background for later developments. The same can be said about Warsaw's reaction toward the Franco-Soviet pact of 1935. When Taylor blames Poland for the fact that the pact "never became a reality" (p. 194) he seems to contradict himself by writing correctly in another place that for France it "was a reinsurance, no more" (p. 79). The pact's "reality" was questionable from its very inception.

Poland's role during the Rhineland crisis is presented in *Origins* rather superficially.[21] While some Polish historians may have exaggerated Beck's offer to stand by France, and everything seems to indicate that Beck felt that Paris would not resort to force, the main object of his offer was to revive the Franco-Polish alliance. This was not such an absurd notion as Taylor's readers may assume. In fact, General Gamelin came to Warsaw for staff talks in July 1936, and on 30 August the Polish commander-in-chief General (later Marshal) Edward Rydz-Smigly arrived in Paris. The Rambouillet agreement which followed foresaw French armament credits to Poland of four yearly instalments of 500 million francs. True, only a fraction of that amount was actually delivered, and a French intrigue to tie the loan to Beck's dismissal (which failed) could hardly contribute to his cordial feelings toward Paris. Yet, the whole episode deserves at least a brief mention. Instead, Taylor engages in airing a paradoxical view that the remilitarization was hardly the right moment to oppose Hitler. There as "no sense in opposing Germany", he writes, "until there was something solid to oppose" (p. 101).

Polish policy during the *Anschluss* and the Czech crisis in 1938 has found few defenders. In the former case, Warsaw proved unable to obtain any real quid pro quo, even though its ultimatum to Kaunas, forcing Lithuania to establish regular diplomatic relations with Poland, somewhat strengthened the northern flank. This move came as a surprise to Germany and may be worth recalling, for it throws some light on the character and methods of Polish diplomacy.

One might agree that at this point Poland "stretched the Non-Aggression Pact far in Germany's interest" (p. 194), if that means that the principle of maintaining equal distance from

Berlin and Moscow was somewhat vitiated. Yet, Taylor seems unaware of the German–Polish friction during the Czech crisis which did affect subsequent developments. His harsh words to describe Poland's behavior – "a useful jackal to Germany" (p. 194) – are hardly in keeping with the assurance in the introduction that he intends neither to excuse nor to condemn but to explain. Did Warsaw's relentless pressure on Czechoslovakia, culminating in an ultimatum, contribute decisively to Benes's capitulation? Taylor tends to equivocate. Mentioning Benes's claim made in 1944 that "the Polish threat at Tesin had given him the final push to surrender", he comments: "if so, it was only a push in the direction which he had determined to go" (p. 185). At another place, however, we read that the Polish ultimatum "finally decided Benes, according to his own account, to abandon any idea of resisting the Munich settlement" (p. 194). No comment this time.

We read in *Origins* that Poland's attitude "ruled out any possibility of Soviet aid to Czechoslovakia" (p. 194), but was such aid seriously considered? There is no unanimity of views on that subject. That Munich was the "logical culmination of French [eastern] policy" (p. 188) is another sweeping assertion which is at best controversial – but an examination of these questions would transcend the limits of this essay.

With the autumn of 1938 we begin to enter the phase of direct German–Polish confrontation that constitutes the immediate origin of the Second World War. Understandably, Taylor devotes about one third of his book to this last stage, and the remainder of this essay will follow the same pattern.

The ostensible cause of the German–Polish controversy was Danzig, connected to some extent with the "corridor" question and the German minority in Poland. The latter, according to Taylor, amounted to one million and a half in "Silesia and the corridor" (p. 194). The figure is fictitious, and it is hard to tell how he arrived at it. Even the postwar German study on Poland indicates that this border area (including Poznania) was inhabited by about 585,000 Germans.[22] As far as Danzig is concerned, a recent work rightly differentiates between local problems in the Free City – ostensibly the cause of German–Polish difficulties – and the general issue of Danzig. It was on the latter that German propaganda successfully concentrated, obscuring the local roots; historians have fallen victim to this obfuscation.[23]

The first Nazi overtures to Poland for a comprehensive settlement – on 24 October 1938 and in early January 1939 – turned around the following proposals: a reunification of Danzig with the Reich, the building of an extra-territorial highway and railroad linking Germany with East Prussia, and Poland's access to the anti-Comintern pact signifying a joint policy toward Russia. In exchange the Germans hinted at the possibility of the extension of the January Declaration for another twenty-five years and a guarantee of Poland's borders. Relating, not always very accurately, these conversations (pp. 195–6), Taylor seems to suggest that a settlement along these lines would not have been unreasonable. The Führer was allegedly more friendly to the Poles than he ever was toward the Italians (p. 195), and while he "may may have been cheating the Poles over Danzig all along – demanding its return as the preliminary to their destruction", Danzig "seemed a triviality in comparison" (p. 196) with a possible satisfaction of Polish ambitions in the Ukraine. The Poles looked at that matter in an entirely different way. At a meeting in which the president, the premier, the vice-premier, the commander-in-chief and Beck participated, it was concluded that:[24]

> If the Germans would maintain pressure in matters that are so secondary for them as Danzig and the highway, one could not have any illusions that we are threatened with a large-scale conflict. These [German] objectives are only a pretext, and in view of that, a vacillating position on our side would lead us inevitably toward a slide, ending with loss of independence and the role of Germany's vassal.

Being unaware of the real Polish thinking, Taylor is downright misleading in writing that when Ribbentrop visited Warsaw on "February 1", Beck "made no secret of the fact that Poland had aspirations toward the Soviet Ukraine" (p. 196). Not only is the date wrong – Ribbentrop was in Warsaw from 25 to 27 January – but this is hardly a correct reading of Beck's remarks. In fact, Warsaw was as determined as ever not to co-operate with Germany in any Ukrainian venture, and Beck was alarmed by Berlin's machinations in eastern Galicia and the sub-Carpathian Ukraine. Both the Germans and the British knew at the time that there could be no common ground on which Berlin and Warsaw could meet.[25]

Were the Poles unyielding because they were "blindly confident in their own strength" and because they believed that this was the "only safe method of doing business with Hitler"

(p. 196)? There is some evidence for both assertions although the "blind confidence" is exaggerated, and meeting bluff with bluff did not exclude some elasticity on the tactical level. Army directives worked out in March 1939 were based on the assumption that in the event of German aggression the main task of the Polish army was to avoid immediate defeat and hold out until France could bring effective assistance.[26] Polish diplomacy played with the idea of some form of a bilateral German–Polish guarantee of Danzig that would have recognised full sovereignty of the Free City on the local level while avoiding its official transfer to Germany. Taylor briefly touches on this last issue without showing much comprehension of what was involved.

The Russian aspect is of significance at this point. In the winter of 1938–9 Soviet–Polish relations improved and a series of economic accords was signed. Warsaw was clearly interested in normalizing relations but not in a *rapprochement*. On the Russian side one can discern the later familiar features of a double game: hints to the French ambassador that Munich could only lead to a fourth partition of Poland, and Potiomkin's assurances to the Poles that Soviet policy "would always be guided by Lenin's principle of inviolability of Poland's independence and territorial integrity".[27] The Polish ambassador in Moscow could not help but suspect that the USSR was interested above all in a war among the capitalist states, and was taking a pro-Polish stance in order to bring about a conflict between Germany and Poland.[28] The Polish ambassador and the Romanian minister in Paris agreed that "if Hitler should be willing it would not take a half hour to form an alliance between Germany and the Soviet Union. Stalin was panting for such an agreement".[29] But this, it was generally assumed, was an unlikely development.

Taylor cuts the Gordian knot of the intricate Polish maneuvers at this point with a typically blunt statement: the Poles "forgot that they had gained their independence in 1918 only because both Russia and Germany had been defeated. Now they had to choose between Germany and Russia. They chose neither. Only Danzig prevented co-operation between Germany and Poland. For this reason, Hitler wanted to get it out of the way. For precisely the same reason, Beck kept it in the way. It did not cross his mind that this might cause a fatal breach" (p. 196). Almost every assertion here is questionable. The Poles did not forget 1918 but they could not choose between their two neighbors without committing political suicide. The term "co-operation" for the German–Polish relationship Hitler had in mind, and to which Taylor later returns, is singularly inappropriate. And several things did cross Beck's mind, in spite of Taylor's suggestion that he was brainless. Incidentally, even Beck's enemies never accused him of lacking intelligence.

Danzig, in Pilsudski's old saying, was a "barometer" of German–Polish relations, and it was perfectly obvious to Warsaw that Berlin wanted to "rivet Poland to the German side" (p. 210) rather than to "destroy her". But such riveting – "alliance" was an euphemism – was tantamount to Poland's loss of freedom. Taylor leaves out the dramatic confrontation between Beck and the German ambassador Moltke in the course of which the Pole declared that a seizure of Danzig would be treated as *casus belli*. The following exchange then took place: Moltke: "You want to negotiate on the point of the bayonet." Beck: "That is your own method."[30]

If Beck thought that Hitler was bluffing and should be answered with a counter-bluff, he was not impervious to the dangerous situation. By 23 March he had instructed the Polish ambassador in London to propose a secret bilateral Anglo–Polish arrangement on consultation. True to his disbelief in multilateral declarations – like the one proposed by the Soviet Union – he felt that a *secret* accord would significantly strengthen Warsaw without making a negotiated agreement with Germany (on Polish terms) impossible and without offending Russia.[31] All this provides a necessary background to the British guarantee to Poland of 31 March.

There is no need to repeat the familiar reasons that prompted Chamberlain to make his public declaration. Taylor's main point that this was not a guarantee for war but to make German–Polish negotiations more equitable and more likely to succeed is valid, and has been further developed by historians. The British wanted to strengthen Beck's bargaining position but an equivocation was bound to ensue, namely the difference between Warsaw and London on what was negotiable and what was not. Fears that Berlin might succeed in bringing Poland over to its side, which would enable Hitler to expand his base against the West, explain the surprise of British diplomacy at the swiftness with which Beck accepted the guarantee. Once again Taylor cannot refrain from exerting his wit at Beck's cost. Citing the alleged remark of the Polish foreign minister to an unknown friend, which was mentioned by Namier, that he (Beck) accepted the guarantee "between two flicks of the ash off his cigarette",[32]

Taylor writes: "Two flicks; and British grenadiers would die for Danzig. Two flicks; and the illusory great Poland, created in 1919 [?], signed her death warrant." No longer could the British "press for concessions over Danzig; equally they could no longer urge Poland to co-operate with Soviet Russia" (p. 211).

These phrases are meant to convey the impression of Beck's nonchalance, nay irresponsibility, as well as to condemn British diplomacy for tying its hands. Neither is quite accurate. Efforts to come closer to Britain had been evident for some time; since October 1938, the Polish ambassador in London was working in this direction. Nor were they confined to Beck and his entourage, for a prominent Polish diplomat, then retired and in opposition to Beck, Jan Ciechanowski, was urging Halifax to extend a guarantee to Poland.[33] The fact that Beck accepted the guarantee immediately was not dictated by a whim, but because he considered it the best available option at this point. His main concern was to avoid Poland's international isolation.[34] The Polish foreign minister was also aware that a guarantee did not bind the hands of the guarantor – the British would be the judge of when the guarantee would be applicable – and therefore sought to transform it into a bilateral engagement. Surely, even if additional documentation makes it clear, this was already fairly evident when *Origins* was published.

Taylor's appraisal is strongly colored by a dislike of Beck and seemingly of other Polish diplomats. He refers to Beck's "usual 'great power' arrogance", ironically calls his indubitably skilful handling of the April talks in London "a virtuoso performance", and bemoans the British acceptance of Beck's "every whim" regarding Russia (p. 212–13, 226). His favorite word to describe Polish iron nerves in dealing with Berlin is "obstinacy", and he virtually accuses Ambassador Lipski of indolence and sabotage of British efforts.[35]

There is no doubt that the March guarantee could and did, have many side effects. Taylor, as mentioned, stressed that the objective was to negotiate, even force the Poles to "give way over Danzig". Simon Newman in his book, *March 1939*, argues that it was given to "ensure a German–Polish deadlock". According to him, this was not a deterrence but a challenge to Hitler, and it was realized that it would "cause Polish intransigence".[36] Another historian has commented that the guarantee was undertaken with "a casual look at the strategic issues".[37] All these elements undoubtedly entered into the making of the guarantee, since Britain was unsure whether Beck might not succumb to Hitler's pressure, and wanted both to stiffen Polish resistance and not to close the door to negotiations. The risk of war was there, although at the moment it did not seem immediate. During his April visit to London, when Beck succeeded in turning the guarantee into a mutual assistance accord, the Polish foreign minister did not fully reveal the extent of the German–Polish deadlock over Danzig. Beck, comments Newman, "was misleading, though not actually mendacious".[38] But, if he did not show all his cards, the British did not really show theirs either. Chamberlain and Wilson were still inclined to stage another Munich, and as Thorne argues, if left to themselves they may have done so.[39] Small wonder that Beck, while still clinging to the hope of negotiations with Berlin, did not want to resurrect the specter of Runciman. It is to this stage then, that Taylor's earlier-cited opinion of Britain being no longer able to dictate concessions in Danzig and forcing Poland to collaborate with Russia is applicable.

Taylor bemoans the fact that the Anglo-Polish alliance pledged Britain to defend "a country far in Eastern Europe" – almost an echo of Chamberlain at the height of the Munich crisis – "which had not been deemed worth the bones of a British grenadier" (p. 215). Danzig became the "symbol of Polish independence". Indeed it became that and more, for it could be separated from other German demands only in the mind of the author of *Origins*, and of some contemporary diplomats such as Henderson.

Ivone Kirkpatrick commented on 5 May: "The [German] goal is the elimination of Poland from the number of independent states in Europe ... as a stage in the realization of vaster aims".[40] Sargent and Cadogan held similar views. Taylor states that Britain pledged itself to fight not only in defense of Poland but also "of Soviet Russia's frontiers" (p. 229). This para-doxically-sounding remark refers to a crucial point that must not be ignored. E. H. Carr had opined that the British guarantee virtually ended the isolation of the USSR, and as Murray puts it, "gave Stalin an excellent bargaining position".[41] Adam Ulam phrased this more dramatically when he wrote: "On its face, the British government's pledge guaranteed Poland; in fact, its *timing* and *circumstances* provided a guarantee to the USSR, and doomed the Polish state".[42]

Ulam argues persuasively that given the Soviet fear of facing Germany alone – with the West remaining neutral – Moscow's preferred option was Anglo-French struggle against Germany, the second best alternative being Western military commitment to the USSR. Hence, it mattered a great deal to Russia that the British guarantee to Poland be as strong and as unequivocal as possible to ensure Western military involvement. Ulam recalls Soviet hints to that effect in the spring of 1939 combined with remarks about Russia's "attitude bienveillante" and even understanding of Polish fears about the passage of the Red Army through Poland. A Western guarantee to the Poles thus meant to the Russians that even if Poland were defeated, the West would be embroiled in war and need Soviet Russia as an ally. In turn, it would be essential for Hitler to neutralize the Soviet Union; hence one could expect bids from both sides. Ulam contends that Ribbentrop overcame Hitler's repugnance to an alignment with the USSR by the argument that a Russo-German deal would result in the West abandoning Poland; hence Stalin would be doublecrossed, for a new Munich would be a disaster from Moscow's point of view. The Russians may well have seen through this game, and their double negotiations tended to ensure that the West could not back out.[43] In that sense, Erickson's statement that Soviet aims had "little to do with preservation of European peace" becomes perfectly clear.[44]

While Ulam agrees that the handling of the negotiations by the West only provided ammunition for subsequent criticism of Western fumblings, he stresses that it did not decisively influence the final outcome. The only thing, he writes, which would have made Stalin accept an alliance with France and Britain would have been Machiavellian Western tactics, namely making their defense of Poland *conditional* on Soviet participation. This, they obviously could not do. This line of argument is reinforced by the opinion of the noted sovietologist, Robert Tucker, that the Russo-German deal in August was more than a temporary device, being in fact a "fruition of Stalin's whole complex conception of the means of Soviet survival in a hostile world and emergence into a commanding international position".[45]

Compared with the above analysis, Taylor's discussion of the causes of the breakdown of Western–Soviet negotiations appears naive and superficial. To select Poland as an excuse for the collapse of the talks was a masterly Russian stroke. They knew perfectly well, and had said so in the spring, that Poland would oppose a passage of Russian armies. Taylor's attempts to give credence to the Soviet position on military grounds – they believed in an offensive across Poland – and to play down their territorial objectives, belong to the weakest passages in *Origins*.

Territorial objectives were already hinted at on 18 April when the Soviets demanded that Britain guarantee Poland only against Germany.[46] As for the offensive capabilities of the Red Army, even Voroshilov had to refer to the fact that the army was "not well disposed for offensive operations". Polish military leaders were not the only ones highly suspicious of the military reasons alleged by the Soviets: the British doubted the offensive capabilities of the Red Army as well.[47] Since the end of 1938, the Soviet armored divisions were being broken up, with tank detachments assigned to infantry divisions. Judging by the Red Army's shoddy performance in Poland in September 1939, the disastrous Finnish campaign and the series of defeats in 1941, a Soviet–German military confrontation in 1939 would have been a catastrophe. One must agree with Erickson that the Western–Soviet military conversations "did not collapse over Poland but over the absence from the very beginning of mutually compatible purposes".[48] By mid June 1939, the German bid was stronger than that of the West; all that Moscow still wanted was to make sure that the war would ensue, and it did.

Taylor's denial that the Ribbentrop–Molotov pact was an agreement for the partition of Poland cannot be taken seriously. He is not even correct in his assertion that the secret protocol affected only the area east of the Curzon Line "inhabited by Ukrainians and White Russians" (p. 262). Not only did this area include several million Poles, but the line of division of August – later corrected – comprised some purely Polish ethnic territory.[49]

Warsaw's wish to see genuine military assistance from the West was, of course, as real as Moscow's, though for different reasons. The response was not too encouraging. Paris placed a greater emphasis on a military alignment with the USSR than London did, largely because of the more exposed position of France, and also because it was more fearful of a Soviet–German deal at Poland's expense.[50] As far as direct assistance to Poland was concerned, staff conversations held in Paris led to a Franco-Polish protocol completed on 19 May, to become operative only after a political agreement which the French delayed until after the outbreak of the war.[51] The protocol was "very precise".[52] It promised immediate action by French aviation, almost immediate local offensive operations, and a major offensive "avec les gros de ses forces" on the sixteenth day of the war.[53] Gamelin's play on words – an alleged distinction between "le gros" [total] and "les gros" [partial effectives] – was a disinge-

nuous attempt to evade the obligations. Taylor wonders that
"the Poles were so easily satisfied" (p. 238), yet the minutes
show as persistent probings on their part as possible. Little can
be done against ill will.

Taylor's presentation of the feverish moves and countermoves
in the last days of August brings out Henderson's endeavors to
save peace even on Hitler's terms. The author's sympathies
seem to lie on the ambassador's side. The picture is somewhat
distorted, as Kennard's different views are given very little
attention. The Foreign Office was more judicious in its negative
appraisal of the "stream of hysterical telegrams and letters"
emanating from the ambassador in Berlin which it contrasted
with Kennard's reports.[54] Taylor's position is predicated on his
basic assumption that Hitler did not want war; evidence to the
contrary is systematically played down.[55] That Hitler would
have been happy to accept a Polish surrender without a fight
does not mean that he was not deliberately playing with fire.
Taylor concludes that the Poles "kept their nerve unbroken to
the last moment" (p. 276); perhaps a back-handed compliment
but a compliment all the same.

Did the British ever threaten to withdraw their guarantee to
Poland in order to force Warsaw to be more accommodating to
Berlin? Parker finds no evidence to suggest it.[56] Indeed, as
Gladwyn Jebb opined in June, to wriggle out of the guarantee
would have been a disaster: "the effects on our own position in
the world would be apparent to the meanest intelligence".[57]

Taylor does not raise the hypothetical question whether the
Poles left to their own devices would have fought in any case.
Newman feels that it cannot be predicted "how Polish policy
would have evolved" if the country had received no Western
guarantees.[58] Perhaps, but there is enough circumstantial evidence to suggest that they would have chosen an unequal fight
rather than surrender. The state of Polish public opinion was
such that a government that would have capitulated to Berlin
could not have survived. The largely unpopular Beck became a
hero overnight after his speech of 5 May. In it, the minister
declared that peace was most desirable but not at any price.
"There is only one thing in the life of men, nations and states
which is without price, and this is honor." A romantic notion,
one may say, but also an ingrained belief that had prevented
Poland from being "digested" during the century of partitions,
and one that was to sustain it during the darkest hours of Nazi
occupation and the Stalinist aftermath.

In sum, the Polish theme in *Origins* is not really as "revisionist" as the inconoclastic nature of Taylor's brilliant essay might make us believe. The Polish story is strongly colored by the author's interpretation of Hitler and the Soviet Union. Just as the Western powers had seldom treated Poland on its own merits but rather as a function of their own attitudes toward Germany and Russia, so Taylor sees Poland through the German–Russian prism. Many value judgments are stereotypes; there is little effort to probe deeper into Polish motivation. In that sense, *Origins* did not provide a sure guide to a study of Poland when it was published; with the appearance of new documentation its value is even less today.

NOTES

1   In this essay, page references are to the 1963 hardback edition of *The Origins of the Second World War*. Among the most important works available in Western languages which came out after its publication are: Kay Lundgreen–Nielsen, *The Polish Problem at the Paris Peace Conference: A Study of the Policies of the Great Powers and the Poles 1918–1919* (Odense, 1979); Piotr S. Wandycz, *Soviet–Polish Relations 1917–1921* (Cambridge, Mass., 1969); M. K. Dziewanowski, *Joseph Pilsudski: A European Federalist 1918–1922* (Stanford, 1969); Norman Davies, *White Eagle, Red Star: The Polish–Soviet War 1919–20* (New York, 1972); Anna M. Cienciala and Titus Komarnicki, *From Versailles to Locarno: Keys to Polish Foreign Policy 1919–1925* (Lawrence, Kans, 1984); Harald von Riekhoff, *German–Polish Relations 1918–1933* (Baltimore, 1971); Piotr S. Wandycz, *France and Her Eastern Allies: French-Czechoslovakia-Polish Relations from the Paris Peace Conference to Locarno* (Minneapolis, 1962); Josef Korbel, *Poland between East and West: Soviet and German Diplomacy toward Poland 1919–1933* (Princeton, 1963); "La Pologne entre Paris et Berlin de Locarno à Hitler, comprising three contributions by Piotr S. Wandycz, Peter Krüger and Georges-Henri Soutou, *Revue d'Histoire Diplomatique* (April–December 1981); Gaines Post, Jr., *The Civil-Military Fabric of Weimar Foreign Policy* (Princeton, 1983) which deserves to be included in view of its high relevance for Poland; and books more closely related chronologically to Taylor's *Origins*: Bohdan B. Budorowycz, *Polish-Soviet Relations 1932–1939* (New York, 1963); Marian Wojciechowski, *Die polnisch-deutsche Beziehungen 1933–1938* (Leiden, 1971); and Anna M. Cienciala, *Poland and the Western Powers 1938–1939: A Study in the Interdependence of Eastern and Western Europe* (Toronto, 1968). Articles by Z. J. Gasiorowski deserve attention. Major Polish works on the immediate origins include: Henryk Batowski, *Europa zmierza ku przepasci* [*Europe Moves towards Abyss*] (Poznań, 1977) and

his *Agonia pokoju i początek wojny* [*Agony of Peace and the Beginnings of War*]
(Poznań, 1969), and Henryk Jackiewicz, *Brytyjskie gwarancje dla Polski
w 1939 roku* [*British Guarantees to Poland in the Year 1939*] (Olsztyn,
1980). Also important are contributions by Henryk Bulhak, Jan
Cialowicz, Stefania Stanislawska and Marian Zgorniak.

2 Notably: *Diariusz i Teki Jana Szembeka* [*Diary and Papers of Jan Szembek*]
(eds) T. Komarnicki and Józef Zarański, Vol. 4 (London, 1964–72)
which is much superior to the French translation, Szembek, *Journal*;
the multivolume *Dokumenty i materiały do historii stosunków polsko-
radzieckich* [*Documents and Materials for the History of Soviet–Polish Rela-
tions*], jointly edited by the Polish Academy of Science and the
Academy of Science of the USSR and available in Polish and
Russian versions, Vols 4–6 cover the interwar period; *Diplomat in
Berlin 1933–1939: Papers and Memoirs of Józef Lipski, Ambassador of Poland*
(New York, 1968) and *Diplomat in Paris 1936–1939: Memoirs of Juliusz
Lukasiewicz, Ambassador of Poland* (New York, 1970), both edited by
Waclaw Jedrzejewicz; *Poland and the Coming of the Second World War:
The Diplomatic Papers of A. J. Drexel Biddle, Jr. United States Ambassador to
Poland 1937–1939* (Columbus, 1976) edited by Philip V. Cannis-
traro, Edward D. Wynot Jr., and Theodore P. Kovaleff. Separate
documents are scattered in various periodicals published in
Western and Polish languages.

3 Jules Laroche, *La Pologne de Pilsudski: Souvenirs d'une ambassade
1926–1935* (Paris, 1953); Hans Roos, *Polen und Europa: Studien zur
polnischen Aussenpolitik 1931–1939* (Tübingen, 1957).

4 See Tadeusz Jedruszczak, "A. J. P. Taylora – Geneza drugiej wojny
swiatowej" ["A. J. P. Taylor's the Origins of the Second World
War"], *Dzieje Najnowsze*, vol. 1, pt. 1 (1969), p. 129.

5 Hans-Adolf Jacobsen, *National-sozialistische Aussenpolitik 1933–1939*
(Frankfurt-am-Main, 1968), p. 445 ["is impossible to understand
without the role of ideology"].

6 General Gamelin, *Le prologue de drame* (Paris, 1946), p. 466.

7 If the thoughtful essay by T. Komarnicki, *Pilsudski a polityka wielkich
mocarstw zachodnich* [*Pilsudski and the Policy of the Great Western Powers*]
(London, 1952), was inaccessible to Taylor for linguistic reasons,
there were the memoirs of Laroche and Noël, Beck's *Dernier rapport*,
and several studies of Pilsudski and Beck, particularly Henry L.
Roberts, "The diplomacy of Colonel Beck" in Gordon A. Craig and
Felix Gilbert (eds), *The Diplomats* (Princeton, 1953) to provide some
clues.

8 Arnold Wolfers, *Britain and France between Two Wars: Conflicting Strategies of Peace from Versailles to World War II* (New York, 1940) and
works cited in note 1.

9 See Z. J. Gasiorowski, "The Russian overture to Germany of
December 1924", *Journal of Modern History*, vol. 30 (1958).

10 A summary of these plans – offensive until 1929, and defensive
thereafter – in General Paul-Emile Tournoux, *Haut Commandement,*

Gouvernement et défense des frontières du Nord et de l'Est 1919–1939 (Paris, 1960), pp. 333–41.

11   They are treated as a fact by, among others, Genevieve Tabouis, *They Called Me Cassandra* (New York, 1942), p. 166; V. A. Potiomkin, *Istoria diplomatii* (Moscow, 1945), Vol. 3, p. 471; Robert Dell, *The Geneva Racket 1920–1939* (London, 1943), pp. 200–204; Hans Roos, "Die 'Präventivkriegspläne' Pilsudskis von 1933", *Vierteljahrshefte für Zeitgeschichte* (October 1955), as well as by Flandin, Namier, and Vansittart.

12   Most recently this point of view was taken by Henry Rollet, "Deux mythes des relations franco-polonaises entre les deux guerres", *Revue d'Histoire Diplomatique*, vol. 96, nos 3/4 (1982). For a discussion of the literature see Waclaw Jedrzejewicz, "The Polish plan for a 'preventive war' against Germany in 1933", *Polish Review*, vol. 10 (Winter 1966), pp. 62–91. Compare also the note on the subject in Henry L. Roberts, op. cit., pp. 612–14.

13   Formulated as early as May 1926, see Piotr S. Wandycz, *August Zaleski, Minister Spraw zagranicznvch RP 1926–1932 w świetle wspomnień i dokumentów* [*August Zaleski, Minister of Foreign Affairs of Poland 1926–1932 in the Light of Memoirs and Documents*], (Paris, 1980), pp. 36–7. The best work on the Four Power Pact is Zbigniew Mazur, *Pakt Czterech* [*The Four Power Pact*], (Poznań, 1979).

14   Cited with extensive footnoting by Gerhard L. Weinberg, *The Foreign Policy of Hitler's Germany*: Vol. 1, *Diplomatic Revolution in Europe 1933–36* (Chicago, 1970), p. 72.

15   ibid., p. 193.

16   *Diariusz Szembeka*, Vol. 4, p. 380. Conversation with Grzybowski, 10 December 1938.

17   See "Wypowiedzi Marszalka Pilsudskiego na konferencji bylych premierów 7 marca 1934 roku" ["Utterances of Marshal Pilsudski at the conference of former premiers on 7 March 1934"], (ed.) Piotr S. Wandycz, *Niepodleglosc*, new series vol. 9, pp. 354–50.

18   General K. Fabrycy's account, *Diariusz Jana Szembeka*, Vol. 1, p. 155.

19   In May 1934, Pilsudski ordered the top military as well as Beck and Szembek to submit an opinion which of the two great neighbors was more dangerous to Poland. The majority of the army chiefs thought Germany represented the greater threat, but Pilsudski and a few top generals believed the contrary. Beck and Szembek regarded the Russian danger as greater in the short run, but opined that in three to four years they would have more to fear from Germany. See Henryk Bulhak, "W Sprawie oceny strategicznego zagrozenia Polski z maja 1934 r." ["Concerning the appraisal of the strategic threat to Poland in May 1934"], *Wojskowy Przeglad Historyczny*, vol. 15 (1970), pp. 370–2.

20   The recent literature on the eastern pact includes Lidia Radice, *Prelude to Appeasement: East Central European Diplomacy in the Early 1930s* (Boulder, Colo, 1981) which has had a good deal to say about

Poland. The most important Polish work on this period is Michal J. Zacharias, *Polska wobec zmian w ukladzie sil politycznych w Europie w latach 1932–1936* [*Poland and the Changes in the Political Balance of Forces in Europe 1932–1936*], (Wroclaw, 1981).

21 Among several studies on the subject, Henryk Bulhak, "Polska deklaracja sojusznicza w czasie remilitaryzacji Nadrenii, marzec 1936 r." ["Polish declaration of alliance during the remilitarization of the Rhineland, March 1936"], *Wojskowy Przeglad Historyczny*, vol. 19, no. 4 (1974), pp. 272–90 is the most detailed and perceptive. George Sakwa, "The 'renewal' of the Franco-Polish Alliance in 1936 and the Rambouillet Agreement", *Polish Review*, vol. 16 (Spring 1971), pp. 45–66, and Roman Debicki, "The remilitarization of the Rhineland and its impact on the French-Polish Alliance", in Thaddeus V. Gromada (ed.), *Essays on Poland's Foreign Policy 1918–1939* (New York, 1970), pp. 45–57 are useful.

22 See *Osteuropa-Handbuch: Polen* (ed.) Werner Markert (Cologne, 1959), pp. 150–1. According to calculations in this book the *total* number of Germans in Poland, who were scattered also through Eastern Galicia, Volhynia and Central Poland, amounted to more than a million. According to the Polish population census of 1931 the total was 741,000. Postwar Polish estimates, by the noted economic historians Z. Landau and J. Tomaszewski and others put the figure at 780,000.

23 See Alice-Catherine Carls-Maire, *La Ville libre de Dantzic en crise ouverte 24.10.1938–1.9.1939* (Wroclaw, 1982), pp. 202–3.

24 Cited in Jerzy Krasuski, "Stosunki polsko-niemieckie 1918–1939" ["Polish–German relations 1918–1939"], Janusz Zarnowski (ed.), *Przyjaznie i antagonizmy* [*Friendships and Antagonisms*] (Wroclaw, 1977), p. 209.

25 The Ukrainian angle is treated among others in Simon Newman, *March 1939: The British Guarantee to Poland – A Study in the Continuity of British Foreign Policy* (Oxford, 1976), p. 159. For Beck's stance see his directives of 14 February 1939, *Dokumenty i materialy do historii stosunków polsko-razieckich*, vol. 7, pp. 26–9.

26 See General Dyw. Waclaw Stachiewicz, *Pisma*, I: *Przygotowania wojenne w Polsce 1935–1939* [*Writings, Vol. 1: War Preparations in Poland 1935–1939*] (Paris, 1977), pp. 188–200. The author was Poland's chief of staff.

27 See Stefania Stanislawska, "Soviet policy toward Poland 1926–1939", in Alexander Korczynski and Tadeusz Swietochowski (eds), *Poland between Germany and Russia 1926–1939: The Theory of Two Enemies* (New York, 1975), p. 35.

28 For Grzybowski's views, 26 March 1939, *Diariusz Jana Szembeka*, Vol. 4, pp. 641–2.

29 Bullit to Secretary of State, 9 March 1939, *FRUS 1939*, Vol. 1, p. 30.

30 Cited in the Polish White Book, p. 69.

31 See the most detailed treatment based on British and Polish archival

material by Anna M. Cienciala, "The British guarantee to Poland of 31 March 1939: a retrospective view after 40 years". Unpublished paper presented at the session on East Europe in the Diplomacy of 1939 of the American Historical Association in New York, 29 December 1979.

32 L. B. Namier, *Diplomatic Prelude 1938–1939* (London, 1948), p. 107.

33 See Newman, *March 1939*, pp. 181–2.

34 This is confirmed among others by Beck's secretary. See Pawel Starzeński, *Trzy lata z Beckiem* [*Three Years with Beck*] (London, 1972), p. 182.

35 A good illustration of this is provided by Taylor's account of the following episode. He writes that Ambassador Henderson tried to convey warnings to Warsaw but Lipski apparently neglected to do so. When Henderson again summoned Lipski at 2 a.m. on 31 August to urge him to seek an interview with Ribbentrop, Lipski "took no notice, and went back to bed" (pp. 273–4). In fact, Lipski talked with Henderson until 4 a.m., slept for three hours, and dispatched counsellor Malhomme to the British embassy at 8 a.m. Two hours earlier he sent counsellor Lubomirski to Warsaw, since telephone communication with the Polish capital was no longer reliable. See documents in *Diplomat in Berlin*, pp. 568–71, and in *Diariusz Jana Szembeka*, Vol. 4, p. 704.

36 Newman, *March 1939*, pp. 196, 219.

37 Williamson Murray, *The Change in the European Balance of Power 1938–1939: The Path to Ruin* (Princeton, 1984), p. 290.

38 Newman, *March 1939*, p. 211.

39 Christopher Thorne, *The Approach of War 1938–1939* (London, 1967), p. 163. Thoughtful accounts of the April negotiations in London are found in Roy Douglas, *The Advent of War, 1939–40* (New York, 1978), pp. 9–11 and Newman, *March 1939*, pp. 209–11.

40 Cited in Sidney Aster, *1939: The Making of the Second World War* (London, 1973), pp. 197, 390.

41 Murray, *Change in the European Balance*, pp. 297, 366; E. H. Carr, *Britain. A Study of Foreign Policy from the Versailles Treaty to the Outbreak of War* (London, 1939), p. 186.

42 Adam B. Ulam, *Expansion and Coexistence: The History of Soviet Foreign Policy 1917–67* (New York, 1968), p. 267.

43 ibid., pp. 265–75.

44 John Erickson, *The Soviet High Command: A Military-Political History 1918–1941* (London, 1962), p. 572.

45 Robert C. Tucker, "The emergence of Stalin's foreign policy", *Slavic Review*, vol. 36 (December 1971), p. 558.

46 See M. J. Laloy, "Remarques sur les négociations anglo-franco-soviétiques de 1939", *Les Relations franco-britanniques de 1935 à 1939: Communications présentées aux colloques franco-britanniques à Londres et à Paris, 18–21 Octobre 1971, 25–29 Septembre, 1972* (Paris, 1975), p. 408.

47 See Murray, *Change in the European Balance*, p. 298; also pp. 126–7.

48 Erickson, *Soviet High Command*, p. 532.

49 This is not an isolated instance of Taylor's somewhat cavalier treatment of facts. In another place, he makes a big case of Danzig being "cut off from East Prussia" by the "unbridged Vistula" (p. 248). It so happens that Nogat and not the main flow of the Vistula constituted the border with East Prussia, and it was bridged near Marienburg (Malbork). Taylor's playing down of German–Soviet exchanges as "between subordinates" (p. 259) is highly arbitrary.

50 On this last point see Jean-Baptiste Duroselle, *La Décadence 1932–1939* (Paris, 1979), pp. 429–31.

51 For an overview see Henryk Batowski, "Le Dernier traité d'alliance franco-polonais", *Les Relations franco-allemandes 1933–1939: Colloques internationaux no. 563* (Paris, 1976).

52 That is how Duroselle characterizes it in *La Décadence*, p. 460.

53 For the minutes and the protocol see "Procès verbaux des conversations d'Etat Major Franco-Polonaises à Paris, May 1939", *Bellona*, Vol. 2 (1958).

54 Cited in Aster, *1939*, pp. 202–3.

55 This has been pointed out by T. W. Mason, "Some origins of the Second World War", *Past and Present* (December 1964), by H. R. Trevor-Roper and Alan Bullock in E. M. Robertson (ed.), *The Origins of the Second World War: Historical Interpretations* (London, 1971) and in many other writings by these and other British, German and French historians. Germany's deliberate war-like provocations, such as the faked "Polish" attack on the radio station in Gleiwitz are not mentioned by Taylor, although perhaps the evidence was not available to him. See G. L. Weinberg, *The Foreign Policy of Hitler's Germany: Starting World War II* (Chicago, 1980), p. 607.

56 See R. A. C. Parker, *Europe 1919–45* (New York, 1969), pp. 333–4.

57 Cited in Aster, *1939*, p. 204.

58 Newman, *March 1939*, p. 281.

9

Isolation and Appeasement: An American View of Taylor's *Origins*

LLOYD C. GARDNER

For students of American history, the appearance of A. J. P. Taylor's *The Origins of the Second World War* did not occasion anything like the debate it initiated among European and British historians. However unsettling the idea that Hitler's goals were little different from past German leaders, and however curious his interpretation of the inconsistencies of appeasement might be, the discussion of America's role did not raise the same issues. If his picture of Roosevelt as a confirmed isolationist seemed overdrawn, and surprisingly uncomplicated given Taylor's more subtle portraits of European statesmen, few were ready to dispute the general picture of the New Deal as wishing to be left alone to work out American salvation as best it could, free from any entangling alliances in Europe. That did not mean America played no role. It was like the famous episode, said Taylor, when Sherlock Holmes directed his friend's attention to the behavior of the dog in the night. "But the dog did nothing in the night," Dr Watson objected. "Exactly," Holmes replied. "That was the significant episode."

In the 1920s, however, and so Taylor's argument ran, American diplomats had indeed been involved in Europe. "The German problem, as it existed between the wars, was largely the creation of American policy." Here one is confronted with a Taylor specialty: the unanticipated outcome, that hidden nemesis that stalks all would-be doers of great deeds. By intervening in the war, the United States had made victory possible, and all its dreadful consequences. For a decade these consequences were postponed while Europe was propped up by American loans. Acting largely on its own initiative, the United States had overcome the reparations impasse, and, through economic coercion where necessary, instituted the Dawes Plan for achieving permanent stability on the foundations of a huge private loan to Germany. "American policy was never more active and never more effective in regard to Europe than in the nineteen-twenties . . . The recovery of Germany was America's doing . . . Every step towards treating Germany as an equal and towards dismantling the special securities which France obtained at the end of the First World War received American backing, tempered only by impatience that the steps were slow and halting."[1]

But then nemesis struck a second time. The depression brought disillusionment about economic remedies for Europe's ills, and installed governments in both Germany and the United States that were dedicated to economic nationalism. Hitler and Roosevelt came to power at approximately the same time, in both instances replacing governments that had valued international co-operation, however insincerely they behaved at crisis time. Roosevelt's election in 1932, therefore, not only continued the economic nationalism of the Republican Smoot–Hawley Tariff of 1930, it expanded that trend towards political isolation as well under the disillusioned Wilsonian Democrats. "President Roosevelt's first act in foreign affairs was to wreck the World Economic Conference, by means of which the British government had hoped to make Nazi autarchy unnecessary." From that point onwards, it appeared to Taylor, it was a downhill run into the deep valley of American isolationism. Whether Congress led the way, or Roosevelt himself, neither was inclined to turn back and face the uphill climb.[2]

Even those small gestures toward internationalism that other historians had regarded as indicating at least a lingering penchant for collective security, such as the diplomatic recognition of the Soviet Union in the fall of 1933, Taylor saw as additional evidence for isolationism triumphant. "Russia's exclusion from Europe now counted for righteousness in American eyes."[3] In other words, Roosevelt was saying that America cared so little for its former allies that it would elevate the Soviet state to an equal place among nations – not that it regarded any as worth the bones of a single American doughboy. Over and over again in the 1930s, Roosevelt proved his absolute sincerity in this regard.

Some British diplomats foolishly hoped to entice the United States into playing a positive role in Europe via the Far Eastern route where, it would have appeared, traditional American interests in China were threatened by Japanese aggressiveness. Roosevelt's famous "quarantine speech" in October 1937, which alarmed cautious policy-makers in the State Department if it accomplished nothing else, suggested to these men that the president had at last seen a way to lead the nation back towards its proper international responsibilities. But all Washington had to offer was moral disapproval. At the Brussels conference in 1937, moreover, it became clear that the United States, while it wished to have the powers join in a pious refusal to recognize any of Japan's ill-gotten gains, was not itself prepared to act in any other sphere. "There was no chance of American assistance if they resisted Japan. On the contrary, Japan would overcome them with American equipment."[4]

This last comment might have been uttered by Neville Chamberlain himself, for it certainly reflected his most acerbic pronouncements on the subject. Was there no single instance, then, no moment at all when Roosevelt stood ready to intervene to save Europe from the humiliation of appeasement? Taylor thought not. In so arguing, however, he crossed swords not with American historians, but with Winston Churchill. In the first volume of his Second World War memoirs, *The Gathering Storm*, Churchill declared that Chamberlain's refusal to respond warmly to Roosevelt's secret proposal in early 1938 for an international conference to consider a general settlement of European affairs amounted to a "veto," and thus forsook the "last frail chance to save the world from tyranny otherwise than by war".[5] As darkness was about to fall over Europe, the president had risked challenging the entrenched forces of isolation, but it would all go for naught. Roosevelt launched his initiative, as fate would have it, just as the British prime minister was about to embark, much to the consternation of Foreign Secretary Anthony Eden, on a foredoomed effort to enlist Mussolini's aid in coming to terms with Hitler's Germany.

"No event", lamented Churchill, "could have been more likely to stave off, or even prevent, war than the arrival of the United States in the circle of European hates and fears. To Britain it was a matter almost of life and death."[6] To Churchill, of course, his memoirs were also a matter of politics, future as well as past. For the past they were a reminder of party disputes among the Conservatives; for the future, a warning to Labour against a new appeasement of the Soviet Union; and for both past and future, a lesson about the need to maintain close relations with the United States. Taylor finds much less in the episode of Roosevelt's initiative than meets Churchill's eye, just as he discounts the traditional historical accounts of the appeasement policy in general.

Eden sincerely believed that such a meeting would draw the Americans in, Taylor concedes in a brief passage, and was genuinely angry over Chamberlain's aloofness; but the prime minister had "more justification" for his fears that Roosevelt's call for a "great international conference to discuss every imaginable grievance" would simply be a repetition of Brussels.[7] What would have happened had Chamberlain responded with enthusiasm no one can say. The argument that Roosevelt could not make – or would not wish to make – any political commitments in Europe is irrefutable given the American domestic climate. Chamberlain's initiative, on the other hand, was premised upon finding, and agreeing upon, just such a specific arrangement. Good fences make good neighbors. Yet that is not what Churchill contended. He most carefully did not say that Roosevelt would, or could, be expected to guarantee a new map of the continent. Instead, he wrote that the "arrival of the United States in the European circle of hates and fears" was the only chance to stave off war.

Churchill's indictment of the "guilty men" of Munich requires him to supply such alternatives for the accused, of course, and to find culpability in the behavior of those who ignored decent opportunities for a different policy. Granting that, an issue remains. If Chamberlain had confidence in his ability to manipulate the dictators, why was he so reluctant to add more players to the game? This is a question we shall want to consider somewhat later. In any event, both the president and the prime minister now found themselves unable to do very much except to respond to Hitler's initiatives, first in Austria and then in Czechoslovakia. As the latter crisis approached, notes Taylor, Roosevelt told a press conference that it was 100 per cent incorrect to associate the United States with France and Great Britain in a united front against Germany. When appeasement turned sour, of course, Americans "rejoiced that they had not been at Munich". And what a sorry spectacle they had made of themselves in the 1930s. "Lack of American support had helped towards making the 'democratic' powers give way. Yet Americans drew from Munich the moral that they should support these feeble powers still less. Roosevelt, entangled in troubles over domestic policy, had no intention of adding to his difficulties by provoking controversy over foreign affairs. Europe could go on its way without America."[8]

With these words, A. J. P. Taylor pronounces his final judgment on America's contribution to the *Origins of the Second World War*.

American historians have also pondered the question of "isolationism" and "appeasement" in the 1930s, arriving at divergent conclusions about America's role. Some support the essentials of Taylor's argument; others see a "positive" effort at appeasement, not isolationism, as the key to understanding what Roosevelt was about – something, in fact, not so very different from the policy pursued by London and Paris. Still others seek to get outside the Taylor framework, finding the explanation for American policy in the broader clash of interests and ideology that guided the perceptions of Roosevelt and his advisers in the 1930s. Far from being exhausted, moreover, the subject has recently attracted the attention of several new scholars in England and Germany, whose works have had a major impact on the writing of the diplomatic history of the prewar decade.

Soon after the appearance of *The Origins of the Second World War*, Professor Robert Divine published a study of congressional legislation entitled *The Illusion of Neutrality* (1962). Divine concluded that in general the American people strongly favored the cause of England and France, yet were unwilling to risk involvement in another "European" war. Here was one dilemma. Yet another loomed behind the equally strong desire to maintain the nation's export trade while avoiding a repetition of the tangled "submarine" issue that had brought Wilson to a fateful crossroads in the spring of 1917. Efforts to resolve these dilemmas produced the multiple neutrality laws Congress passed, as well as the "loopholes" Roosevelt used to maneuver as best he could. Foreign policy became a game of hide and seek with new rules being added as the players went along. If not the confirmed isolationist portrayed by Taylor, Roosevelt nevertheless emerges as an unequivocal, opportunistic politician rather than the far-seeing internationalist statesman of early postwar legend. Therein was the explanation for his otherwise strange behavior; and therein, also, lies the explanation for the way Congress went about attempting to legislate neutrality – and ultimately failed. In bare outlines, Divine's study thus supported Taylor's assertions about domestic constraints imposed on Roosevelt. On the other hand, Divine finds the president genuinely surprised and alarmed at the persistent strength of isolationist sentiment after Hitler's motives became clear, and ultimately moving away from the implications of the neutrality legislation that he himself had originally encouraged. The first indications of such a change are apparent, according to Divine, in the October 1937 "quarantine speech" and in the president's refusal to recognize that a "state of war" existed between Japan and China. Had he done that, he would have been forced to issue a proclamation of neutrality and institute the congressionally-mandated arms embargoes. Instead, he adopted the fiction that the Sino-Japanese "undeclared war" was nothing more than an "incident", allowing arms to continue to go to China.[9]

"Sometime in the late 1930s," concluded Divine, "Roosevelt had finally ended his own vacillations between isolation and a more active world policy."[10] But if that were so. it was also true that reforming Congress was a much more difficult task. Behind the scenes, the president was making new efforts at national "preparedness", yet he remained unwilling to attempt a frontal assault on the bastion of congressional pre-eminence by seeking a repeal of the arms embargo provisions of the neutrality laws until after the outbreak of war in Europe. He might have lost, opines Divine, but he could have had the satisfaction of knowing he had tried to reorient American foreign policy. "And he might have won."[11]

In important ways, therefore, Taylor and Divine are in agreement. Both men, to take a significant example, downgrade any real impact on the president or Congress of the behavior of Anglo-French "appeasers" in determining American policy. It was not disgust at the spineless behavior displayed before Hitler's strutting minions, or a contempt for Chamberlain's "City" dominated financial attitudes, that dissuaded American policy-makers from taking a more active role. Here was another legend furthered by Winston Churchill, among others, as well as American writers.

Two years after Divine's book appeared, this writer published *Economic Aspects of New Deal Diplomacy* (1964), which also concluded that Roosevelt did not yearn for an active role in European affairs in the mid-1930s. The New Deal's economic experimentation with intra-nationalism, sometimes blamed for dictating the stance of political isolation, was seen here as a temporary expedient, already on the wane in 1934 with the triumph of Secretary of State Cordell Hull over George N. Peek, the strongest advocate of a neo-mercantilist bilateral trade program that would complement state planning and, if carried out to its logical end, result in economic policies at least similar to those of the autarchic states. Peek had made his last stand with the negotiation of a trade "deal" with Germany.

In the short run Hull's victory changed little. He and his advisers persuaded Roosevelt that the Peek formula implied acceptance of ideas in both the political and economic spheres that were not compatible with American interests and institutions, and that by holding to "liberal" principles there was at least a chance that German policy could be modified, or even that the Nazi regime might be undone. German autarchy was not even dented by Washington's refusal to go through with the Peek deal, however, and the Secretary of State did not establish his personal control over the direction of policy within Roosevelt's inner circle. "We are not interested in the political element", Roosevelt instructed his delegate to the failing Geneva disarmament talks, "or in the purely European aspect of peace".[12]

On the world scene, as opposed to the "purely European aspect of peace", American policy-makers continued searching for the nation's proper role, convinced that the United States could not, however much some might desire it, shut out external influences or, and this was the rub, solve its domestic problems in isolation. They were unable to see very clearly how to go about finding that role. Hull's trade agreement plan, incorporating as it did about equal parts of Wilsonian idealism and nineteenth-century economic liberalism, won Roosevelt's approval in an early showdown against Peek's proposal for meeting the Germans on their own terms; and the passage of the Reciprocal Trade Agreements Act in 1934 pointed the nation away from extreme economic nationalism, but Roosevelt remained skeptical about the relevance of Hull's "theories" to the world of the 1930s.

Not the least of Roosevelt's concerns in this regard was the uncomfortable fact that Nazi Germany was only one of several autarchic or semi-autarchic "blocs" jostling for advantage. If world peace depended upon America's ability to lead *all* the powers back to economic sanity, a presumed precondition for dealing with Hitler's Germany and forcing it to moderate its political and military policies, then the outlook was grim indeed.

Perhaps it was absurd as well. The notion of attacking Nazism with an assault on the British imperial preference system, for example, or of persuading the Japanese to abandon their course in China with the promise of a better arrangement in world trade at some future date seemed almost utopian, and made Hull the object of some ridicule in New Deal Washington. The Secretary of State was dismissed as something of an anachronism by New Deal planners, a well-meaning voice from another era. His sermons on the universal benefits of freeing trade from the restraints imposed by rulers in Moscow, Tokyo, Berlin, London – and Washington – convinced few in the early New Deal years, as was the case concerning his quaint idea that world leaders, given half a chance, would forego arms for commerce. And the general notion that anyone could still believe in the primacy of economic causes behind international relations in a totalitarian era, or that there were "economic reasons" behind the political decisions leading to the outbreak of war in 1939 would also surprise Taylor in *Origins*.

Yet one of his conclusions on this point, ironically, runs counter to his observations about the dynamics of Nazi Germany's autarchic system, and opens the window a crack for re-assessing the determined isolationism of Roosevelt's America. In discussing the economic situation under Hitler, Taylor notes that, as Germany was not short of markets, the war was not a contest over "capitalist" spoils. Germany had practically a monopoly of trade in south-eastern Europe, and was developing finance wizard Hjalmar von Schacht's bilateralism into a weapon "for the economic conquest of South America" when the war's outbreak interrupted these plans.[13]

Throughout the 1930s, the United States was at "war" with Germany in Latin America, where the reciprocal trade agreements program was pitted against Schacht's ingenious schemes, Pan American Airways against Condor Lines, and the Export-Import Bank against the danger of German loans. But victory in this struggle could not be won by confrontation with Germany alone, not so long as other nations also closed off the channels of world trade, or diverted them into ever narrowing streams to serve political purposes. The determined effort, then, to negotiate a trade agreement with Britain was regarded as an anti-Hitler front, as was the Treasury Department's support for a 1936 tripartite currency stabilization arrangement between Britain, France, and the United States. Seen from this perspective, the State Department's obsession may have been unrealistic, but it was not quixotic.

The line of reasoning went this way: Germany was able to operate its schemes because other nations had few, if any, options, particularly the small countries in south-eastern Europe and the agricultural countries of Latin America. Only if genuine multilateralism prevailed once again could world trade be restored, options opened, and Nazism penned in a corner, where it would inevitably, if gradually, shrink out of existence. The level of trade between Germany and the United States, or between Germany and Britain, was irrelevant to this situation. What mattered was the damage done by German methods to a rational international economic system. Washington policy-makers were dismayed (if not really surprised) that their counterparts in London did not see things quite the same way. This cleavage would be remembered by American policy-makers all through the war, and it would inform much of Washington's postwar planning. Hull's apparent vindication pleased no one more, of course, than himself. "The camel is not too bright," he quipped to aides some months before Pearl Harbor, "is slow moving and ruminating, but after all – it carried a greater burden than a whole group of asses".[14]

It is of some significance, moreover, that policy-makers in both London and Washington blamed the other's economic ambitions for holding back a genuine Anglo-American *rapprochement* in this decade. On one occasion, indeed, Chamberlain himself seemed to agree with laments emanating from Washington concerning the political importance of the Anglo-American economic estrangement: "The conclusion of an Anglo-American commercial agreement when we have found ways of overcoming its obvious difficulties will undoubtedly be an important step in the right direction [in obtaining a] community of sentiment between our two countries as to the events in the Far East and the development in the European situation."[15]

Progress was painfully slow. Delays on the American side in initiating discussions were then matched by British reluctance to give any appearance of abandoning the 1932 Ottawa Agreements, a trade arrangement that provided special tariff benefits for inter-imperial commerce. It had not really afforded any lasting solutions to Britain's steady decline, despite the hopes of imperial thinkers. In theory, meanwhile, America preached economic liberalism as a cure-all; in practice it was as afraid of genuine "free trade" as any of the other powers. Agreement had not been reached even as the Czech crisis began, prompting Hull to challenge the British ambassador with memories of past glory: "If one – if only one – great British statesman would come out of the woods and proceed to make himself a crusader in the name of his government for the economic and peace program for which we are crusading in this country . . . there could be no more important step in the direction of stabilizing dangerous conditions on the continent of Europe."[16]

For all the effort that went into the 1938 Anglo-American trade agreement the initial impact was imperceptible. It only demonstrated that Washington would attach considerable importance to reforming the international economy, when the time came, as a preventative measure against the "next" war. Meanwhile, Hull's principal, President Roosevelt, had already concluded that not much was to be expected from the trade treaties in the immediate future. "Henry," he told Secretary of the Treasury Morgenthau in late 1938, "these trade treaties are just too goddamned slow. The world is marching too fast. They're just too slow."[17]

Roosevelt's January 1938 "appeasement" plan (for so it would be called) had been an attempt to cut across the gnarled landscape where Hull worked so futilely at trying to clear away the underbrush, while monster weapons of war stood by ready to lurch forward, smashing everything in their way. The Roosevelt initiative did indeed cut across Chamberlain's program, as the latter complained. That it was as well an ill-considered scheme, little more than a desperate plea, as the prime minister additionally complained, one that would actually encourage Hitler to ask for *more* than Chamberlain wanted to give, can be argued as well.[18]

But a different emphasis, both as to the origins of American appeasement and the reasons for its termination, was offered by Arnold Offner in *American Appeasement. United States Foreign Policy and Germany, 1933–1938* (1969). With the publication of this book the story reverts to Taylor's thesis. In Offner's view, the January 1938 "appeasement" plan as explained by Under Secretary of State Sumner Welles appears not as a desperate plea of any sort but as an aid to Britain in its search for an agreement with Germany over colonies and security, and an inducement to Hitler to accept arms limitations in return. Like Chamberlain, Offner saw a fatal weakness in Roosevelt's scheme: "One must conclude that he would not have been interested in a conference sponsored by a politically, and militarily, uninvolved United States."[19]

In contrast to Taylor, therefore, Offner suggests a positive American policy of appeasement, not isolationism, as the dominant motif of these years. But in Offner's view as well, American appeasement began where Taylor said it did: out of sympathy for Germany's rejection of the Treaty of Versailles. When that appeared to be only the first step for Hitler on the road to world domination, American policy changed, but even then all too slowly. Appeasement lasted, indeed, through the spring of 1940 when Roosevelt sent Sumner Welles on a mission to Europe to see if there was any chance at all for a mediated peace. "The economic argument has been exaggerated," asserts Offner. Whether one looks at American–German trade and investment, which rose throughout the 1930s, American willingness to hedge liberal trade principles to appease Germany in Central Europe, or at any index one chooses, the clash between America and Germany cannot be put down to economic causes. The "Nazi Masters", Roosevelt said at the end of 1940, intended "to enslave the whole of Europe and then . . . the rest of the world".[20]

No internal crisis in any shape or form determined American policy nor, as Robert Divine would stress, did congressional restraints. The shape of events was clear, concludes Offner. "From 1933 to 1940 the United States had done all it believed it could to appease Germany politically and economically, to take account of Germany's national political and economic aspirations and its relations to its European neighbors."[21] Offner thus reinforces the traditional view of American foreign policy as a reaction to external events, and a simple quest for national security. Appeasement was a tragically shortsighted policy, but the reasons for its adoption and for its abandonment are best understood one-on-one, Germany versus the world, first, and then Hitler's Nazi state against Roosevelt's liberal democracy – not in some roundabout discussion of a climate favorable to the expansion of trade and investment.

The most recent comprehensive account of New Deal foreign policy by Robert Dallek, *Franklin D. Roosevelt and American Foreign Policy, 1932–1945* (1979), finds its protagonist searching for ways to co-operate with other like-minded nations, even during the early days of "economic self-protection and political detachment".[22] Recognition of the Soviet Union, the inauguration of the "good neighbor" policy in Latin America, an active response to British suggestions for a combined policy in naval talks with the Japanese, all these indicated the president's willingness to go as far as he could in international affairs. But he needed encouragement. 'I too am downhearted," he wrote to Ambassador William E. Dodd in Germany in August 1934, "but I watch for any ray of hope or opening to give me an opportunity to lend a helping hand. There is nothing in sight at present."[23]

He got no encouragement from Europe – and none from domestic opinion. Dallek also finds the president stymied by the depression's resistance to New Deal recovery measures. Time and again the domestic crisis deflected the course of what he intended, or what he would have liked to accomplish, in foreign affairs. Back at the beginning, at the time of the 1933 London economic conference, Roosevelt felt compelled to choose between the domestic recovery program, then in its infancy, and the remedy "internationalists" said was needed, international currency stabilization. The choice was never in doubt. But, in a postscript to his "bombshell" message renouncing American participation in the plan his own delegates had devised, the president explained to Hull that he hoped recovery programs in other nations "would remove any necessity . . . for closing our borders to the goods of other nations and for most currency discrepancies and fluctuations".[24]

It was an illusory hope, at least in so far as it expressed confidence in early relief from emergency measures. Moreover, Roosevelt's skepticism about the London economic conference-had other sources in what might be called a general crisis of legitimacy in the 1930s. The origins of this vexed question reached back to the First World War era and the Bolshevik revolution. Liberal democracy had been on trial ever since. The depression and the rising voices of protest against the "old order" swept away all but the strongest democracies, and forced "radical" changes in those. The conference had been Herbert Hoover's idea, and was regarded with scorn by many New Dealers as merely a continuation of the sort of deformed "Republican" internationalism that had sprung up amidst the wreckage of Wilsonian dreams. Fed by speculative loans to Europe and Latin America, this lopsided growth then produced its hideous offspring: the Great Depression.

Roosevelt, accordingly, adopted expedients he hoped would not have long-term consequences, first, because he thought the New Deal would overcome the depression, but, secondly, because he felt unable to re-order priorities as a result of the ongoing crisis of legitimacy. As the decade wore on, and early hopes for recovery were shattered by the recession of 1937 – as the decade wore on, and fascism seemed to be growing steadily more powerful – as the decade wore on, and the New Deal coalition weakened at home, Roosevelt felt stranded as never before. Here was the real meaning of isolationism.

The president sought to gain the support of the American people in January 1938, Dallek notes, and to show the European dictators that the nation was not indifferent to their plans. Ironically, only if a world calamity seemed in the offing could an American president achieve such a breakthrough on both fronts. "Roosevelt took Chamberlain's rebuff as a sign that he placed no great stock in co-operation with the United States."[25] Despite this cool response (or perhaps because of it), Roosevelt tried to co-operate with Chamberlain's overtures to Italy. Dallek concludes: "However contradictory, this was Roosevelt's way of finding a path between rejecting appeasement and not standing in its way. The net effect, though, was to leave him largely immobilized in foreign affairs."[26]

Much that appears contradictory in these various accounts may not really be so. Divisions among historians are as natural as currents on the river; the water runs faster or slower depending upon a multitude of conditions, and upon where one stands. The recent writings of David Reynolds, C. A. MacDonald and Hans-Jürgen Schroder illuminate the internal debates in Washington and London, and offer the best overall explanations for Chamberlain's skepticism about the United States, Roosevelt's pursuit of his 1938 "economic appeasement" plan, and the ultimate outcome of that encounter. MacDonald puts British appeasement of Germany into the context of a need for an agreement that would not only stabilize Europe, but offer hope of a very urgently needed economic détente between "blocs".[27] Schroeder adds to this picture with a description of American fears that appeasement would end in just this way. "A German closed area and a British Empire closed area", read one example of a common observation by American policy-makers, "are different simply in degree, and the instruments used to effect the German and British purposes are of secondary importance".[28]

Roosevelt's proposal, it was feared in London, would call into question issues that Hitler had no intention of raising (if Chamberlain and his advisers were correct), and would force British policy-makers to appease the United States and Germany at the same time. Indeed, Britain might come away from such a conference at odds with the United States! In that case, Roosevelt's goals might be achieved on one level, with terrible results for the future. David Reynolds describes Anglo-American relations in the pre-Pearl Harbor days as those of "competitive co-operation". Discounting the Churchillian assertion, and that of historians after him, that Roosevelt was sorely disappointed by Chamberlain's coolness toward his proposal in January 1938, Reynolds nevertheless concludes that the episode was part of a "deeper" question at the heart of Anglo-American differences. "During the 1930s the British moved towards bilateral, controlled trade largely within a British-led bloc, while the Roosevelt Administration emerged as the new champion of economic liberalization and a multilateral world economy."[29]

It might be objected that such conclusions follow only because of a myopia concerning Anglo-American affairs; that so far as Chamberlain and his aides were concerned the real issues concerned Britain, France and Germany. What Paris would do, or would demand, was far more important than Roosevelt's spasmodic lurchings and gropings for an American "role". If there was an "outside" power to contend with in 1938, it was Russia, not the United States. It is significant, on the other hand, that those who pushed Chamberlain toward a stronger anti-German posture often urged both a "Russian" alternative and an "American" alternative. And while Reynolds cautions against exaggerating the economic factors, especially since neither Chamberlain nor Roosevelt were purists in defense of their foreign economic policies, these different outlooks provide insight into why Chamberlain thought the United States untrustworthy, and why he discouraged an "American" alternative to appeasement.[30]

A. J. P. Taylor's *Origins of the Second World War* forced historians to consider that the Second World War was not simply the result of a deranged man's design for world conquest. The argument remains controversial, but there is a greater measure of agreement today than when his book appeared that the war was the product of different forces, operating on several levels. What is unusual about the way the debate has developed, on the other hand, is that criticism of Taylor's work no longer focuses on Hitler and the "guilty men", but on the author's explicit assumption that international relations in the 1930s can be so narrowly defined. The Second World War almost becomes, as Taylor titles his final chapter, "The War for Danzig". A historian who delights in turning the tables, puncturing balloons and throwing monkey-wrenches into theoretical machines, Taylor wishes to de-mystify the 1930s. Perhaps because of this he must insist that the decade really was no different than those that witnessed earlier struggles for power among nations.

In one way, of course, that would suggest that the "guilty men" of Munich really *were* less courageous than their forebears, for whatever reason. However that may be, Taylor's effort to see "appeasement" as a rational response to the Anglo-French predicament requires him to portray the United States as a totally committed isolationist nation, asking only to be left alone. More dangerously, it also requires him to exclude "extraneous" matters, considerations of ideology not least, that other historians regard as essential to understanding the era. "Wars are much like road accidents," Taylor observes. They have general causes and specific causes; but the police and courts do not weigh profound causes. They must seek specifics. The analogy is an attractive one, having the great virtue of capturing in a few words what Taylor set out to do in *Origins*. Looking at the specifics suggests to Taylor that while Hitler "probably intended a great war of conquest against Soviet Russia [!] so far as he had any conscious design; it is unlikely that he intended the actual war against Great Britain and France which broke out in 1939".[31]

While Taylor assures his readers that he regards the profound causes and the specific causes as "complementary; they do not exclude each other", just such a division is on his mind most of the time. The road accident analogy lends itself to separation of profound and specific causes about as completely as is possible, and to dividing the "War for Danzig", the "actual war . . . which broke out in 1939", from the Second World War. In that case, however, *The Origins of the Second World War* would seem to be an inappropriate title. Colliding ironies and blunders are the theme Taylor has chosen. A study of American policy, while differences among historians remain, and while not finding Roosevelt anxious to become involved in strictly European affairs at any point in the decade, indicates that another analogy might be more useful to understanding those years: the dots and smears of an impressionist painting yield a shape and pattern barely discernible until the observer steps back. To see the image the artist intended requires perceptual analysis and understanding as well as ability to isolate details.

NOTES

1 A. J. P. Taylor, *The Origins of the Second World War*, "Preface for American Readers", p. vi. This preface appears in the edition published by Atheneum, New York, 1962.

2 ibid., p. vii.

3 ibid., p. 67.

4 ibid., p. 128.

5 Winston Churchill, *The Second World War*, Vol. 1, *The Gathering Storm* (Boston, 1948), pp. 254–5.

6 ibid.

7 *Origins*, pp. 144–5.

8 ibid., pp. 172, 191.

9 R. Divine, *The Illusion of Neutrality* (Chicago, 1962), pp. 216, 333.

10 ibid., p. 228.

11 ibid., p. 285.

12 Lloyd C. Gardner, *Economic Aspects of New Deal Diplomacy* (Madison, Wis., 1964), p. 91.

13 *Origins*, pp. 105–6.

14 Quoted in Lloyd C. Gardner, "The New Deal, new frontiers, and the Cold War", in David Horowitz (ed.), *Corporations and the Cold War* (New York, 1969), p. 119.

15 Gardner, *Economic Aspects*, p. 107.

16 Richard N. Kottman, *Reciprocity and the North Atlantic Triangle, 1932–1938* (Ithaca, NY, 1968), p. 256.

17 ibid., p. 257.

18 Interestingly, the Roosevelt initiative was also opposed by Secretary of State Hull, who found it too "appeasement"-minded to suit his tastes, or his economic policies. Chamberlain thought the plan erred on both sides. It could be seen by the dictators, on the one hand, as yet another attempt "on the part of the democratic bloc" to put them in the wrong. On the other hand, he felt that Roosevelt's open-ended references to past injustices opened the way for the "revisionist" powers to demand more than he had planned to offer. Officials at 10 Downing Street also took careful note of Roosevelt's statement that in the determination of "political frontiers U.S. Government can play no part".

19 Arnold Offner, *American Appeasement. United States Foreign Policy and Germany 1933–1938* (Cambridge, Mass., 1969), pp. 229–32; and see Arnold Offner, "The United States and National Socialist Germany", in Wolfgang J. Mommsen and Lothar Kettenacker (eds), *The Fascist Challenge and the Policy of Appeasement* (London, 1983), pp. 416, 423.

20 Offner, "United States and Germany", p. 419.

21 ibid., p. 424.

22 Robert Dallek, *Franklin D. Roosevelt and American Foreign Policy, 1932–1945* (New York, 1979), p. 78.

23 ibid., p. 91.

24   ibid., p. 56.
25   ibid., p. 156.
26   ibid., p. 158.
27   C. A. MacDonald, *The United States, Britain and Appeasement, 1936–1939* (New York, 1981). For the quotation see MacDonald, "The United States, appeasement and the open door", in Mommsen and Kettenacker, *The Fascist Challenge*, p. 403.
28   Hans-Jürgen Schroder, *Deutschland und die Vereinigten Staaten 1933–1939: Wirtschaft und Politik in der Entwicklung des deutsch-amerikanischen Gegensatzes* (Wiesbaden, 1970). For the quotation see H.-J. Schroder, "Britain, the United States and Germany", in Mommsen and Kettenacker, *The Fascist Challenge*, p. 397.
29   David Reynolds, *The Creation of the Anglo-American Alliance 1937–41* (Chapel Hill, NC, 1982).
30   ibid., p. 291.
31   *Origins*, pp. 102–3.

10

The Asian Factor

AKIRA IRIYE

The Second World War consisted of two wars, one in Europe and
the Atlantic, and the other in Asia and the Pacific. A. J. P.
Taylor's *The Origins of the Second World War* concerns the first of the
two, and stops in the first week of September 1939. At that time,
there was no Asian–Pacific war, except the one between China
and Japan which had been going on intermittently since 1931.
As Taylor himself writes, the war that broke out in September
1939 primarily involved three European countries (Britain,
France, and Germany), and was more a diplomatic crisis of the
traditional sort than the beginnings of what was to lead to
a long-drawn-out conflict. It could be argued, within such a
framework of analysis, that there would have been no Second
World War if the leaders of the three nations had been able to
manage their intra-European affairs as they had done, more or
less successfully, up to that point. The implication is that at least
until 1939 extra-European factors, in particular Asian issues,
had been of little relevance.

It is difficult to disagree with such an interpretation, at least at
one level of generalization. Certainly, the Chinese–Japanese war
had made little difference in the development of the Czechoslovakian or the Polish question. The system of European politics
defined by the Versailles peace treaty – the point of departure for
Taylor's analysis – had little or nothing to do with Asia and so, to
the extent that the crisis of 1939 could be said to have been
inherent in Versailles, it was purely a European story with little
input from the outside. For Asian countries, the functional
equivalent of Versailles was the Washington conference
treaties. The breakdown of the "Washington system" was anal-
ogous to that of the "Versailles system", but the two were not
intimately related, except in so far as both occurred at about the
same time and had the effect of pitting revisionist powers (Ger-

many, Italy, Japan) against status-quo powers. Even so, European and Asian politics would become closely linked only in September 1940, when the Tripartite Pact was signed. That belongs to the period after the outbreak of the European war, and is thus beyond the scope of the Taylor book.

The Asian factor, in other words, was essentially irrelevant to the British–French–German collision of 1939. The Chinese–Japanese conflict was carried on by these two countries, with some outside help to be sure, but without direct intervention by a third power. It was a local conflict much as, according to Taylor, the Polish crisis in 1939 was, or should have been.

There were, however, more subtle ways in which Asian and European affairs affected one another. To understand this it would be useful first to note that Taylor's is essentially a "rational actor" analysis in the context of the international system. It may be termed a "systemic" approach. Not that he sees governments drawing up and pursuing master-plans for system building – he rejects the notion that Hitler was a system-maker – but the book's key theme is to see foreign policy, including that of Nazi Germany. as comprehensible in traditional terms, as an interaction of geopolitical realities and national ambitions. Thus he would view a Hitler or a Stalin as no less "traditional" than a British or French policy-maker; their ambitions, successes, and mistakes should be attributed less to their diabolical personalities or fanatical ideologies than to the structural problems inherent in the post-1919 international system, and to the power realities that impelled them to determine their respective national responses. Such a framework is very useful, up to a point, and may be applied to Asia as well. A Taylorian analysis would emphasize the inherent instability of the Washington system and note, as he does with respect to the Versailles system, that because it did not explicitly limit Japanese prerogatives in China while, at the same time, encourage Chinese nationalism, sooner or later the clash between the two was inevitable. In that regard, it could be argued that what the Japanese militarists and their civilian supporters did after 1931 was to disregard the Washington system and to act unilaterally to retain and extend control over Manchuria. There was as much logic to such action as to Chinese resistance to it. Moreover, there were geopolitical considerations that went back to the nineteenth century: the strategic importance of preventing a third power, in particular Russia, from controlling the Korean peninsula, and the need to safeguard Japan's position there by establishing a sphere of influence in southern Manchuria. The situation had not changed by the 1930s, or so Japan's strategists believed. The army continued to view the Soviet Union as the primary hypothetical enemy, so that it would be of vital importance to maintain Japanese control over Manchuria. Here, too, Japan was behaving as a "rational actor".

To such geopolitical "realities" in the 1930s was added a new situation, derived from the world economic crisis. Taylor mentions how the crisis of world capitalism legitimized revisionism in Germany and elsewhere. Japan was no exception. The globe was becoming economically divided instead of linked as earlier, and under the circumstances there was a rush on the part of industrial nations to establish their respective regional systems in which they would retain economic control. Japanese leaders were quick to see this and justified the aggression in Manchuria and north China in the name of "autonomy", to lessen the nation's dependence on the vicissitudes of the world economy and to create a more stable arena for economic activities. The geopolitical and economic "realities" combined to produce Japan's program for building a "national defense state", a nation in a state of preparedness against the Soviet Union in which finance, production, and trade were all geared to enhancing military capabilities.

At such a level of analysis, it is not difficult to attribute logic and rationality to Japanese thinking. There was nothing radically new about it, any more than there was anything particularly Nazi about Hitler's foreign policy, in Taylor's account. Policy decisions in Japan or in Germany were made as responses to changing world conditions and reflected each country's traditional interests and ambitions. Just as Taylor maintains that even if the Nazis had not come to power, German foreign policy would have followed an essentially similar course, at least to a point, it could be argued that even if party politics had not come to an end in Japan, replaced by a type of military dictatorship, its policy in Asia would not have been drastically different, given such "realities" as rising Chinese nationalism, the Soviet Union's growing power, and the collapse of the world economic system. In other words, the foreign policy of Japanese "fascism" – a term historians have applied to Japan's politics in the 1930s – was as traditional as that of Nazi Germany.

All this is plausible, but then one should also note one striking contrast between German and Japanese policies as they developed through 1939. As Taylor argues, at least until 1 September 1939, German foreign policy could be seen as having been highly successful; Germany had freed itself from the humiliating encumbrances of the Versailles treaty, brought the Rhineland under its control, annexed Austria, and incorporated a large chunk of Czechoslovakian territory, all without incurring foreign intervention and in fact sometimes even with the blessings of the Western powers. Moreover, by signing a non-aggression pact with Russia, it managed to prevent the formation of a global coalition against itself. In contrast, Japan was in a much less enviable situation. Up until 1937, to be sure, it could conceivably be argued that Japan had gotten away with substantial gains without bringing about external sanctions. Just like Germany, Japan had taken advantage of the Western powers' disarray during the depression, when China had been unable to count on their help to stop aggression. Even so, one should recall that after 1933, Germany had been involved in Chinese military strengthening, providing the Nationalists with aircraft and aviation experts. The Soviet Union's call in 1935 for a global anti-fascist front was followed by small-scale shipments of arms to China. Britain, on its part, helped China stabilize its finances through drastic reform measures undertaken in 1935–6. The United States, in the meantime, remained passive, and it even damaged China economically when a silver purchase act (1934) had the effect of draining the metal out of the country. But after the Sian incident of December 1936, American opinion became increasingly impressed with the strength of Chinese nationalism.

All these developments were not sufficient to restrain Japan when it launched an all-out war against China in 1937. But the point is that in Asia there had been nothing comparable to the West's appeasement of Germany that preceded the outbreak of war in 1939. Whereas Britain, France, and the United States had made concerted attempts to stabilize Central Europe by co-opting Germany to rejoin a modified international system, no such efforts had been made with respect to accommodating Japanese ambitions in China. America's "non-recognition" doctrine, refusing to legitimize the puppet regime of Manchukuo, was adopted by other governments as well, so that no adjustment of their differences with Japan would work unless it entailed the latter's retreat to the situation existing before 1931. To put it another way, during 1931–7 Japan had not been able to count on the support of any of the major Western powers. It had decided to dismantle the Washington system, but unlike Germany, it found no serious interest on the part of its erstwhile partners in working together with Japan to redefine the structure of Asian international affairs. Japan, in other words, had become increasingly isolated in world politics, more so than Nazi Germany. (It is interesting to note that until the last moment the Western democracies remained hopeful of bringing Germany back into the League of Nations, but that they were not as eager to persuade Japan to rejoin the organization.)

The situation was confirmed after July 1937. The overwhelming sympathies of the major powers lay with China, as exemplified by the condemnation of Japan at the Brussels conference held in November, which was attended by the Soviet Union as well as the United States, in addition to the Western European powers. Germany did not, but initially Berlin assisted China's war efforts by increasing its shipment of aircraft and weapons. Despite its diplomatic isolation, Japanese forces kept on scoring battlefield victories, but they had the further effect of alienating the rest of the world, particularly when Japanese soldiers' atrocities committed against Chinese civilians became known.

The situation had to be faced by the Japanese leadership, and it responded to the nation's increasing isolation in two ways. One was to recognize the fact and decide further to separate Japan and the areas under its control from other parts of the globe. This was reflected in Tokyo's declaration of a new Asian order, enunciated in November 1938. It implied that Japan was establishing a regional system of international affairs that would be independent of the outside powers. This was the Japanese leaders' way of saying that since the West was not understanding of their intentions and interests, they would forget about obtaining their support and build a regional order that had its own rules irrespective of the strategies and precepts of outsiders. At the same time, Tokyo also sought to check Japanese diplomatic isolation by approaching Germany, to persuade it to stop aiding China and instead to accept the Japanese definition of Asian order. This effort was successful, as Hitler decided in January 1938 to reverse the policy that had hitherto been in effect and to recognize Manchukuo, thereby identifying with Japanese expansionism. Henceforth at least one Western power would be understanding to Japan, but it was not clear how the new German policy could help Japan in practice, at a time when the United States and the Soviet Union were growing more and more hostile. In 1939, the former undertook the first of a series of economic measures designed to sanction Japan, when Washington notified Tokyo of its intention to abrogate the treaty of commerce and also embargoed the export of certain grades of aviation fuel. Russian forces fought skirmishes with Japanese along the Manchurian–Mongolian border (Nomonhan) and scored significant victories. Even more serious was the signing in August of the Nazi–Soviet non-aggression pact, an event which so shocked the Japanese that the prime minister resigned, saying international affairs were truly "complicated and unfathomable". That statement was a fit epitaph to the bungling foreign policy of Japan.

A Taylorian analysis of the Asian war through September 1939 would proceed along some such lines. The framework is useful, and one learns much from the emphasis on traditional diplomatic and geopolitical factors. But the above summary also indicates that one should not stop here, for certain interesting questions suggest themselves that require further examination. Why was Japanese foreign policy less successful than German in that the latter had more support on the part of the Western democracies and the Soviet Union, whereas the former found itself increasingly isolated? Put another way, why were the United States, Britain, the Soviet Union and others more determined to assist China than Czechoslovakia and Poland? Was there anything special about Asia to have produced such a reaction?

Examination of such questions leads to a paradox. Asian affairs were, as Taylor suggests, quite distinct from European. Japan's unilateral expansionism, the bilateral war between China and Japan, and the latter's assertion of a new Asian order all pointed to the separation of the region from other parts of the world. Yet at the same time, Japan's growing isolation, which was creating enormous difficulties for it by 1939, could only be explained in terms of the Western powers' continued and even increasing involvement in Asia. The more the Japanese were determined to establish regional hegemony, the more frustrated they became, and the more elusive the goal of Asian autonomy. Asian affairs, in other words, were at once distinct from, and at the same time intertwined with, developments elsewhere.

At bottom was the question of definition, which was as much an ideological as a geopolitical one. When the Japanese talked of an Asian order, they were presenting one definition of Asia that was totally unacceptable to other countries. The United States, for instance, had long viewed itself as a Pacific as well as an

Atlantic nation, and next to the Caribbean it had always maintained a well-defined approach to east Asia. The acquisition of
the Philippines, Guam, and Hawaii had involved the need for a
Pacific strategy even more specific than an Atlantic strategy.
The Soviet Union, too, had inherited the Russian empire that
had embraced the vast reaches of Siberia, and it was physically
in Asia, bordering Manchuria, Mongolia, and Japan. As for
Britain, India had been the mainstay of its empire, and the lands
to the east – Burma, Malaya, Singapore, Hong Kong – were
integral parts of British strategy. Likewise, French Indochina
and the Dutch East Indies were as much part of Asia or Australia
and New Zealand. In other words, Asian international affairs
embraced all these territories and countries, so that any definition of Asian order would have to deal with their presence. As
of 1939, Japan's new Asian order primarily concerned East Asia
(Manchukuo, China, and Japan), but even here the United
States, the Soviet Union, and Britain would take exception to the
Japanese definition, for they were as deeply involved (politically
and economically, if not militarily) in China as Japan.

The Chinese, too, would want continued Western presence in
their midst. An isolated Asia would imply Japanese dominance,
so China's salvation lay, as many leaders pointed out again and
again, in retaining the West. That China was not alone was the
message Chiang Kai-shek sought to impart to his people to
encourage their continued resistance. A minority of Chinese, on
the other hand, despaired of such outside support and sought to
befriend Japan so as to moderate its pressure; they gambled on
the possibility that the West would give up China and leave it to
its own devices. They were wrong, for America, Russia, Britain
and others would never let Asia alone. For they were themselves
Asian powers.

Faced with such a reality, the Japanese responded by pro-
claiming the doctrine of pan-Asianism. At schools, in the press,
and in government publications, the theme of Asian unity was
emphasized. It was as if the Japanese believed they could bring
Asia into being if they talked about it long and loud enough.
Official propaganda and thought control aimed at spreading the
message that Japan was fighting for Asia's self-definition or
self-recovery. For too long, it was pointed out, Asia had been
under the control of Western powers, their political and
economic influence. The time had come to reassert Asia's
indigenous tradition so as to bring about the Asian people's
regeneration. That was why Japanese propaganda at that time

laid so much stress on the theme of culture. The war with China, it was noted by government spokesmen time and again, was as much a cultural as a military conflict. Japan was fighting the Chinese so that the latter would give up their reliance on Western culture and return to traditional purity. Japan and China were derived from common roots, it was asserted, and it was incumbent upon them to go back to them in a joint struggle for Asian civilization. Here Asia was said to value social harmony, community, and spirituality in contrast to the West's materialism, individualism, and inhumanity. Asians were opposed to excessive nationalism and to communism, instead cherishing the tradition of co-operation and mutual concern. All such ideas were designed to counter Chinese nationalism and to combat the influence of Western democratic thought, socialism, and liberalism.

The effort was a complete failure. It never convinced the Chinese, or for that matter the bulk of Japanese, not to mention Westerners, that there was something called Asia for the traditional purity of which Japan was fighting China. In a sense, the Japanese were becoming intellectually as well as politically isolated by indulging in such wishful thinking. Actually, its very existence may have reflected desperation that Asia, contrary to Japanese wishes, remained under Western influence and might even become more so. Japan's isolation meant the extension of Western influence. This was certainly the case in China. In fact, it could be said that Western influence remained strong in Japan despite official propaganda to assert Asianism. At one level, the nation continued to incorporate modern Western technology as it sought to accelerate the pace of industrialization. The "new bureaucrats", those who played prominent roles in the 1930s in various governmental agencies, were technocrats intent upon establishing the foundation of Japan's imperial growth. At another level, there was fascination with fascism and Nazi thought, as well as with Marxism. These ideologies had in common critical perspectives on Anglo-American liberalism and democracy, so that Japanese intellectuals and government spokesmen who turned against the West were actually making use of German, Italian, or Soviet ideology to attack British and American ideas and institutions. This was selective anti-Westernism, and not something that could fortify Japan's pan-Asianist pretensions.

Japanese policy, in other words, was geopolitically and intellectually senseless, even bankrupt. It did not succeed in isolating

Asia from the rest of the world. One could go farther and argue that Japanese behavior in China throughout the 1930s contributed to, and also reflected, the trends of the times toward selfishness and destructiveness. Igor Stravinsky called attention to what appeared to be the growing brutalization of mankind, and E. M. Forster predicted that "history will point to these years as the moment when man's inventiveness finally outbalanced his moral growth, and toppled him downhill". It was not just in Nazi Germany that race hatred was encouraged, cultural edifices brought down as incompatible with the national spirit, books burnt, or war glorified as ennobling the people. In the Soviet Union, a paranoid dictator was sending tens of thousands to purge trials and death camps, while in Spain countrymen were killing one another in merciless civil war. While these were extreme examples, elsewhere observers noted that the spirit of tolerance was being replaced by mass irrationality, and liberalism by anti-democratic movements. In fact, contemporary writers confidently spoke of the demise of liberalism. That was reflected in the weakening of internationalism and cosmopolitanism, and the preoccupation first and foremost with national interests. National selfishness is difficult to measure, but to the extent that one could judge from the abrogation of so many international agreements in the 1930s, or from the mushrooming of restrictive trade policies, one might safely conclude that the decade was not notable for concern with broader issues and interests.

Japanese behavior, both domestic and external, may or may not have been more selfish than other countries'. Certainly it did its share in leaving a sordid record of intolerance and brutality. The intellectually thin justification for the aggression in China in the name of pan-Asianism, the hypocrisy involved in calling the Chinese war a struggle for Asian culture, assassinations of political and business leaders with ties to Britain and America, suppression of academic freedom; all these were products of, and in turn confirmed, the mentality of the age. The vogue of Nazi ideology, in particular, provided the Japanese with a sense that they were sharing a worldwide trend and joining forces with other enemies of liberalism. Despite their interest in isolating Asia from the rest of the world, in other words, the Japanese were unwittingly maintaining their ties with it. Events and trends elsewhere continued to affect Japan and its position in Asia.

In some such fashion, European and Asian affairs affected one another throughout the 1930s. Still, Taylor seems essentially correct when he suggests that the Polish crisis of 1939 need not have developed into a world war. His book ends there, and it is left to the reader to supply the missing links, to work out a scheme through which a purely internal European crisis led to a global conflagration. As seen above, Japan was intent on localizing the war with China and preventing third-power interference, much as Hitler is depicted by Taylor as doing. Just as Hitler failed to prevent the enlargement of the conflict, so did Japan eventually find itself confronted with a hostile coalition of forces. How did the situation come about? Why did Japan, engaged in war with a single nation in 1939, end up fighting, besides China, the United States, Britain, the Netherlands, and the Soviet Union?

These are questions that lie outside the concerns of the Taylor book, but answers to them may further help assess some of the themes of the book. Put very simply, the thread that runs through 1939–41 in the Asian context was the emergence of what came to be called the ABCD coalition. The Japanese called it an ABCD encirclement, consisting of the United States, Britain, China, and the Dutch East Indies to try to check Japan. In December 1941, Japan went to war against all four, something it had managed to avoid for many years. The coalition/ encirclement was brought about as the United States, Britain, and the Dutch authorities in the Indies all felt the threat of Japanese expansion into Southeast Asia and perceived the need to fortify China's defenses so as to keep Japan tied down there. To that extent, America, Britain, and Holland were clearly intending to remain in Asia, and would frustrate Japan's interest in localizing the Chinese war. For the Chinese, of course, these were encouraging developments, and they would stiffen their resistance to Japan, knowing they would have the support of the Western powers.

Just as the Western powers were intent upon remaining in Asia, the Japanese were interested in expelling them from the region. They came to believe that they could never succeed in China unless they reduced, if not entirely eliminated, Western presence in Asia. The more isolated Japan became, the greater grew its desire to extend its sway over the wider Asian region. In this scheme, moreover, Japanese leaders believed they could turn to Germany, Italy, and the Soviet Union for support. During 1940–1, Japanese diplomacy aimed at establishing a global alliance of revisionist powers designed to repartition the world a scheme that would assign Asia to Japanese domination and

Europe to German. In other words, a separate, autonomous Asia under Japanese control would be brought about through the support of three outsiders, pitted against the ABCD combination.

That was the grand design. It backfired as soon as Germany went to war against the Soviet Union, in June 1941. Thereafter the ABCD alliance became a five-power coalition, although Russia outwardly maintained its neutrality. So, in December 1941, Japan was if anything more isolated than ever. Surrounded on all sides by hostile or near-hostile forces, and unable to count on substantial support of any outside power, Japan went to war against the world in the name of "national survival", as the imperial rescript declared on 8 December.

In this story the most important theme would seem to be Japanese isolation and the emerging coalition against it. This is a theme whose beginnings could be found in the years prior to 1939, as suggested above. If so, it would be of relevance to the whole question of the origins of the Second World War. To the extent that the war was a world conflict, it pitted the Axis powers against their opponents. But the latter group of nations was far more united and mutually co-operative than the first, so that Germany and Japan really fought two separate wars, one in Europe and the other in Asia, whereas the United States, Britain, the Soviet Union, and other Western allies were involved in both theaters. Only China remained entirely in Asia. This phenomenon leads to a related theme: the way in which these developments in Europe and Asia reinforced one another. More specifically, the gradual emergence of multi-power coalitions in Asia and in Europe may have reinforced one another. In this connection, the fact that the United States and the Soviet Union were both deeply involved in the Asia–Pacific region was of considerable significance. They were willing to come to China's assistance long before they involved themselves directly in European affairs, but their Asian involvement had the effect of experimenting with something similar in Europe as well. Thus ultimately both Japan and Germany would be confronted with a formidable combination of America, Russia, and other European powers.

This was what the German and Japanese leaders brought upon themselves and their nations by choosing to defy the existing world order. As A. J. P. Taylor suggests, however, they need not have done so, but could have gotten most of what they wanted through co-operation with, rather than defiance of, the treaty powers. The fact that soon after the Second World War both Germany – at least West Germany – and Japan rejoined the international system and resumed the policy of co-operation with the United States and Britain, may indicate that the aggressive policies the two nations pursued in the 1930s had been a temporary aberration. In the Japanese case, in particular, it is evident that the nation could have stayed within the Washington system and sought protection of its rights in that framework. Of course the increasingly strident Chinese nationalism, the world economic crisis, the growth of Soviet military power, and the European crisis would have combined to challenge the stability of the system even if Japan had not openly defied it, but at least there would have been no devastating and senseless war between Japan and the ABCD powers. In that sense, Japan made a conscious decision, however temporary, to forsake one definition of international relations for another. That aberration not only brought suffering to the Japanese people but victimized millions of Asians, who have not forgotten the war crimes.

When *The Origins of the Second World War* was published, much work on the origins of the Asian–Pacific war lay in the future. Since 1961 a great deal has been published, so that today one knows in minute detail every twist and turn in the deteriorating relationship between Japan and the ABCD powers. This does not mean that there are no unexplored questions or historiographical controversies; much still needs to be investigated in connection with the policies of China, the Soviet Union, and in particular other Asian countries. But historians have combed available archival data in Japan, the United States, Britain, the Netherlands, Germany, and other European countries and published numerous reliable studies. Here no attempt will be made to compile a full list of such studies. Rather, some of the important works will be cited to indicate the range of scholarly contributions that have been made to further our understanding of the origins of the Asian–Pacific war. (For more details on recent publications, consult the relevant chapters in two excellent bibliographic volumes: Ernest R. May and James C. Thomson (eds), *American-East Asian Relations*; and Warren Cohen (ed), *New Frontiers in American-East Asian Relations*.)

Shortly after the publication of Taylor's book, the Japan Association of International Relations issued an eight-volume study, *Taiheiyō sensō e no michi* [The road to the Pacific war].

These volumes contained monographs by some of Japan's leading historians, and were a major landmark. Many of the essays have been put together in English translation under the overall supervision of James W. Morley: *Deterrent Diplomacy, The China Quagmire,* and *The Fateful Choice.* More is on its way. The essays are notable for their use of archival documents that had been beyond the reach of earlier writers. While contributors to the volumes develop no consensual view of the road to the Pacific war, they succeed in tracing the often tortuous twists of that road, particularly when seen in the terms of Japan's decisionmaking. The authors have uncovered numerous committees and subcommittees within the army, the navy, the Foreign Ministry, and other organizations so that it is now possible to pinpoint with even greater accuracy where certain ideas originated, how they were filtered through bureaucratic channels, and what happened to them when they reached the top. The sum of the new findings amounts to stressing the theme of a fatal collision between Japan and the United States at least from 1939 onwards, given the latter's emergence as the major obstacle in the way of the former's designs for Asian empire.

Other studies supplement these volumes, but many of them are in Japanese and have not been translated. One exception is a highly subjective, but for that very reason insightful, book by historian Saburo Ienaga, *The Pacific War.* Contributions by Japanese historians to Dorothy Borg and Shumpei Okamoto (eds), *Pearl Harbor as History,* are also notable. They describe how various Japanese institutions dealt with foreign issues and paved the way for the American war. See also the essays in Ian Nish (ed.), *The Anglo-Japanese Alienation,* in which Japanese and British historians discuss the two countries' growing antagonism during the 1930s. Two recent publications illumine in great detail Japanese strategic thought on the eve of Pearl Harbor: Gordon W. Prange, *At Dawn We Slept*; and John Stephan, *Hawaii under the Rising Sun.*

Perhaps the study that comes closest to Taylor's in approach would be James B. Crowley's *Japan's Quest for Autonomy,* which argues that Japanese policy was quite rational and logical, given the perceived need to establish a region of economic self-sufficiency and military impregnability. Further insight into Japanese thinking is provided by Mark Peattie, *Ishihara Kanji.* The question of how far such autonomy could have been achieved is examined in a forthcoming book by Michael Barnhart. Concerning the nature of Japanese politics in the

1930s, there are three useful studies: Ben-Ami Shillony, *Revolt in Japan*; Gordon Berger, *Parties Out of Power in Japan*; and George Wilson, *Radical Nationalist in Japan*. See also Miles Fletcher, *The Search for a New Order*, a study of Japanese intellectuals' infatuation with fascism. While these authors deal with disparate subjects, what they describe reinforces the need to put the Japanese experience in a comparative perspective, and to examine Japanese foreign policy in the context of its domestic developments. Whether rational or not, the fact is that by 1940–1 Japanese politics and mentality were such as to make it extremely difficult to return to the framework of co-operation with the Anglo-American democracies. Still, as suggested above, neither nativism nor pan-Asianism had been sufficiently inculcated to replace liberalism as the ideological basis for foreign policy, and thus on the eve of the war the Japanese were intellectually far less prepared than the ABCD nations or, one could add, even the Germans and Italians. Whatever the relevance of ideological factors in foreign policy, in the Japanese case it may be said that compared with Nazi Germany there was much less intellectual cohesiveness and preparedness.

Toward nearby Asian lands, however, Japan attempted cultural imperialism, to transform Korean, Taiwanese, and Chinese thought to embrace Japanese influence. As documented in Mark Peattie and Ramon Myers (eds), *The Japanese Colonial Empire*, the 1930s saw the culmination of Japan's attempt to educate those under its jurisdiction and establish thought control. The inevitable irony, of course, was that the educated segments of the population in Korea, Taiwan, and China tended to become more nationalistic, and considerable portions of them turned to Marxism and Leninism for inspiration. The influence of foreign ideologies in China is well documented in such works as James C. Thomson, *While China Looked West*, and Lloyd Eastman's two books, *The Abortive Revolution* and *Seeds of Destruction*. The story of those few Chinese who remained committed to a vision of co-operation with Japan, rather than with Russia or the Western democracies, is chronicled in some of the essays in Akira Iriye (ed.), *The Chinese and the Japanese*, and by John Hunter Boyle in *China and Japan at War*.

Much has been written on American and British policies in Asia prior to the war. Among the notable works are Christopher Thorne, *The Limits of Foreign Policy*; Dorothy Borg, *The United States and the Far Eastern Crisis*; Stephen Pelz, *The Race to Pearl Harbor*; Waldo Heinrichs, *American Ambassador*; Bradford Lee, *Britain and the Sino-Japanese War*; Robert Dallek, *Franklin D. Roosevelt and American Foreign Policy*; Roger Louis, *British Strategy in the Far East*; Michael Schaller, *The US Crusade in China*; Peter Lowe, *Great Britain and the Origins of the Pacific War*; Aron Shai, *Origins of the War in the East*; and Jonathan Utley, *Going to War with Japan*. These authors present different themes, and are in fact divided between those who picture Japan and the United States as running on a collision course since the early 1930s and those who do not see the clash as inevitable until the very end. The British factor becomes rather crucial in this regard, for the formation of a *de facto* Anglo-American alliance, to match the Axis pact, made any compromise between Japan and America extremely difficult. Most suggestive in this regard are James R. Leutze, *Bargaining for Supremacy*, and David Reynolds, *The Creation of the Anglo-American Alliance*.

While most of these studies present formal, macroscopic pictures, analyzing the road to war in terms of governments, armed forces and embassies, others have filled gaps by tracing the activities of private individuals and groups caught in turmoil. For instance, Sandra Taylor's *Advocate of Understanding* shows how one American sought to struggle, vainly to be sure, to prevent a rupture in the relationship across the Pacific. Peace-making efforts by American Catholic priests is chronicled by Robert J. C. Butow, *The John Doe Associates*. On the other side of the coin, Warren Cohen's *The Chinese Connection* describes how several Americans mobilized national opinion against Japanese aggression. Concerning the business input into foreign policy, see Stephen L. Endicott, *Diplomacy and Enterprise*; Anne Trotter, *Britain and East Asia*; and Irvine H. Anderson, *The Standard-Vacuum Oil Company and United States East Asian Policy*.

Much less has been written on the roles of Germany, Russia, and other European countries in the origins of the Asian–Pacific war. The best treatment of Germany's Asian policy through 1938 is John P. Fox, *Germany and the Far Eastern Crisis*, and for the period after 1938 there are Gerhard Weinberg, *The Foreign Policy of Hitler's Germany*; Theo Sommer, *Deutschland und Japan zwischen den Machten*; and Saul Friedlander, *Prelude to Downfall*. On the Soviet Union, very few reliable accounts exist. Among the exceptions is Jonathan Haslam, "Soviet aid to China and Japan's place in Moscow's foreign policy", in Ian Nish (ed.), *Some Aspects of Soviet-Japanese Relations in the 1930s*. See also the "official" account in English: Nikolai Sivachev and Nikolai Yakovlev, *The United States and Russia*.

It is difficult to say how these monographs have modified Taylor's work, inasmuch as the latter has very little to say on the Asian–Pacific war. The work's importance, in any event, would seem to lie as much in its conceptual framework as in its interpretations, and in that sense it has inspired a generation of specialists in Asian international relations. While few have replicated Taylor's book for the Asian–Pacific war, his emphasis on systemic factors and on "rational" calculations has made an impact on historical writings on the origins of the 1941 war. At the same time, historians have been inspired to look more closely at domestic political and cultural factors, not so much in opposition to the Taylorian emphasis on system and power as in an effort to round out the picture.

That is all to be welcomed. One might note that the study of international history has been enriched by four approaches, which are not mutually exclusive but complementary. First, there is the traditional approach, focusing on decision-makers and their dealings with one another more or less as "rational actors" in pursuit of definable national interests. Second, the systemic approach examines the international system on the whole and traces its formation, development and breakdown over a period of time. Third, external affairs are analyzed in the context of domestic, political, economic and social affairs. Here foreign policy is seen as being produced by internal needs of society. Finally, the fourth approach stresses ideological, intellectual, emotional and psychological realities, viewing international affairs as intercultural affairs. All these approaches are important, particularly when one is dealing with countries as divergent as America, Britain, Russia, China and Japan. Taylor has given us a thought-provoking study of European foreign policy, presented in the framework of systemic and "rational actor" analyses. Others have added their insights into the foreign policies of several more countries in this and other frameworks. The result has been to enrich historical understanding and to contribute to international intellectual engagement among historians. That has been one of the most encouraging by-products of the war. Although some intellectuals seem unable or unwilling to transcend narrowly chauvinistic or dogmatic viewpoints, many more in different countries have been eager to share ideas and insights in a spirit of open-mindedness. It was the absence of this sort of intellectual tolerance and freedom that characterized the 1930s. Today, in contrast, at least it can be said that historians working on the Second World War are more cosmopolitan, committed to a co-operative search for a better understanding of the past, as can be seen in numerous scholarly symposia that have brought together historians from America, Britain, Japan, China and other countries to study jointly the origins of the war. In the long run, such endeavors across national boundaries may prove to have been the most important consequences of the war.

Epilogue:

A Patriot for Me

EDWARD INGRAM

The life and work of A. J. P. Taylor lie partly veiled by three disguises, all worn at the same time. The first disguise disguises the nature of his career. Taylor claims to have had three careers, as historian, journalist and television star. The three ought to be cut down to two: historian and personality posing as former historian. When, one wonders, did Taylor decide to give up being the first to acquire the trappings of the second? And why? Pique at missing the Regius and Stevenson chairs? Justified pique, of course; about the latter certainly. Anybody with a chance ought to try to escape from Oxford, where three years spent among such precious precocity is enough for one lifetime. But he ought not to flee to hagiography of Beaverbrook. Was that the first of the books one would rather not have read? Of the others, the autobiography without hesitation, and the embarrassing diary in the *London Review of Books*. One ended up with the sinking feeling one has when forced to listen to actors talking about their parts in plays; ended up wishing one had never *heard* Taylor at all, never watched the celebrated lectures on the television, never sat spellbound in the Schools. Ignore the personality and one would be left the pleasure of reading the remembered historian's earlier works. My favorite, by far, is *The Struggle for Mastery in Europe*. Not for many years have I read the book from beginning to end, nor should I recommend anybody else to do so. It is too old a friend, too good a book, to be treated as anything but a cook book, one written perhaps – what higher praise? – by Elizabeth David. Allow it to fall open, start to read, and one will be immediately engrossed; one's mind triggered into thought, speculation, silliness, it matters not, but active, conjuring up a feast. Beware, however, of bedtime. One will read too late, sleep too little, and curse Taylor for it in the morning.

If the personality poses as a former historian, the deeply conservative has posed throughout life as a radical. Taylor's so-called radicalism is the radicalism of the radical wing of mid-nineteenth-century liberalism: the radicalism of men who took it for granted that England had found the way, would show the way, and would expect others to follow the way. No Kiplingesque doubts about the "white man's burden" for them; no hesitation in assuming that when the light of Manchester shone in the darkness, the darkness would quickly comprehend. The way had been found, however, by England alone. Taylor has never shown much interest in Scotland and Wales, an odd oversight in a political historian of late nineteenth- and early twentieth-century Great Britain. Where did he imagine Rosebery, Balfour, Campbell-Bannerman, and Lloyd George had come from? Like Beaverbrook and Bonar Law – if they were lucky – from Canada? Very doubtful, because the colonial origins of Beaverbrook and Bonar Law are valued only for making them outsiders. Taylor has always portrayed himself as an outsider, supporting his claim by the refusal of the foreign office to let him look at its records ahead of their opening under the then fifty-year rule. But he remains an English outsider, a Little England patriot and heir to *The Troublemakers*, the subject of his favorite among his own books.

Alongside a conservative posing as a radical, a determinist poses as an idealist. During the famous debate between Taylor and Hugh Trevor-Roper over whether Hitler did or did not plan for war, both men worked from the idealist assumption that the proper task of the historian is to re-enact the thoughts and intentions of past actors. Not what men *did*, but what men *thought* must be explained. Such questions were considered as: how detailed must plans be to be called plans; how formal must the record of them be before any reliance may be placed upon the record; does it matter what type of war is shown to be planned; against whom; for what reasons? Taylor did not allow Hitler to have caused a war he did not intend, whereas Trevor-Roper will only allow Hitler to have been flexible in his approach to a goal – expansion in the east – set early on; a goal Alan Bullock claims that Hitler knew he could not reach without the risk of war. Taylor denies the existence of such a goal; more precisely, he denies that Hitler's series of speculations can be regarded as a plan to reach it. Such systems of plans, acted upon to reach predetermined goals, are rationalist fallacies, the creations of historians determined to find purpose in incident.

Hitler, according to Taylor, was an opportunist gambler with strong nerves who seized the chances that came his way, usually placed temptingly in front of him on a silver salver by Austrians, Czechs, Englishmen, but not Poles. Taylorian statesmen play chess, Hitler as well as Bismarck and Bülow. They look one move ahead, asking themselves whether a particular action will leave them stronger or weaker in relation to all the other states whose power and interests they must calculate as accurately as they can. Not only Hitler, but Taylor's other hero, Neville Chamberlain, appears in this book disguised as "second-hand Rose". Whereas Hitler is wearing hand-me-downs from Bismarck, Chamberlain is struggling to fit into the clothes worn by Palmerston on the day he tried to stop Prussia from annexing Schleswig–Holstein. Such a portrait of Hitler is rightly criticized, for even if Hitler made no plans and set himself no goals, Bismarck certainly did. The limit of Bismarck's ambition was clear from the start: Austria must not be destroyed as a great power. But if Hitler ought therefore to be made more dynamic, Chamberlain must not be made less so. He fits neatly among a group of dynamic British foreign secretaries, fond of posturing on the edge of the continent, who acted valiantly to little effect. Churchill would do it best, but in a worse cause. Whatever else may not be said of Neville Chamberlain, he worked hard to keep peace.

Hitler may not be denied all of his personal initiatives in order to reassign them to von Papen, Schuschnigg, or Benes. Taylor's Hitler sits like the ideal pukka sahib in the British Raj, unmoving, like a statue at Berchtesgaden, awaiting tribute. Perhaps this explains Taylor's belief that Englishmen drawn to the colonies would have been drawn, had they been German, to the Nazis. The Thousand Year Reich, like the British Raj, existed every day. It had a great, if legendary, past – but no future: not, anyway, one to be asked about or planned for. Sit still enough and the future would offer itself of its own accord. Hitler moved only when forced to respond to steps taken by others. Why forced? Why after the *Anschluss* did geography and politics automatically put Czechoslovakia on the agenda? And why was Hitler forced to occupy Prague to prevent the spread of chaos in what little of Czechoslovakia was left? The issue here is whether one may treat Hitler's talk and writing as the basis for his actions. Taylor says not. One is sympathetic: nobody believes any more that anything said by a politician is meant to enlighten rather than deceive. For the same reason, nobody may accept Hitler's claims that his actions were forced upon him by unreasonable threats to vital German interests. That is the corniest imperialist cover-up of all, one calling to mind Muriel Spark's Abbess of Crewe.

Taylor's Hitler as statue is designed to be a totem of evil (merely typical German, not particular, evil), a dark God whose powers must not be unleashed. The responsibility for correctly identifying the figure – recognizing for example that his is not the figure of Apollo or Demeter – is given by Taylor to others, English and French. Having correctly identified the figure, they must make sure that its evil powers are forever contained. Instead, having like Taylor himself seen Hitler as Bismarck, and having set both men into their own false history of modern Europe, they gave the first push towards war by offering Hitler opportunities they ought to have denied to him. Unfortunately for them, they were themselves denied the help of Taylor's yet unwritten books on German history. Chamberlain had to turn for help during the Munich crisis to H. W. V. Temperley's study of the foreign policy of George Canning. This book would encourage anybody to assume that Britain had traditionally taken the lead in making sure that peace settlements did not ossify; that the victors in war did not prohibit change, certainly not changes from which they themselves expected to benefit. In taking on Hitler, Chamberlain followed in the footsteps of Canning taking on the Holy Alliance. But his guide did not tell him the outcome. Had Chamberlain read C. W. Crawley on the Greek question, he would have learned that the treaty of Adrianople represented a dramatic defeat for Britain, one requiring a dramatic reappraisal of its interests and its place in the world. Canning saved his reputation by dying. Fate might have been kinder to wish a heart attack on Chamberlain after Munich.

In portraying Hitler as a statue, albeit an evil one, whose powers must not – and need not – be unleashed, Taylor seeks to absolve Hitler of responsibility for the war, transferring it to men like Schuschnigg and Chamberlain, foolishly, if not fatally, fond of action. Take away Hitler's responsibility for the war, he will still remain the cause of it. To find out why, one need only, as so often to find out how the world works, turn to Kipling. The stable life of the four white inhabitants in *A Wayside Comedy*, who cannot leave Kashima for they would have nowhere to go, is destroyed when one of them, Major Vansuythen, marries, bringing his wife to Kashima to join him. She is a beautiful virtuous woman, who follows strictly the accepted social and moral code of her day, having eyes only for her husband, whose happiness she is determined to preserve. Despite her virtue, the two other men of the station fall in love with her. The first, who has been having an affair with the second man's wife, hopes to break it off just at the moment when the cuckolded husband hopes to get rid of his wife and her lover by providing an opportunity for an affair, that has been kept secret, to become known. As none of them are able to go, and the former lover no longer wishes to go, all stay. They meet every day at sunset, when Major Vansuythen, who alone knows nothing of what has happened, plays the banjo to alleviate their pain. Mrs Vansuythen is not responsible for the destruction she has caused. She has done nothing. But she is unquestionably the cause of the destruction.

Is this an example of what Taylor means when he pretends to suppose that accident determines the lives of men? He himself became a diplomatic historian, he tells us, as the result of a visit to Vienna to work with A. F. Pribram. Taylor is fond of using his own life as an exemplar of historical truth, a bad habit borrowed from him by Marxist and feminist historians in Canada, who fondly imagine that the country has reached its apotheosis in themselves. Pribram, who was expected to be at work on Oliver Cromwell, was found switching to the origins of the First World War, the topic of the hour. Taylor followed him thence as far as the Italian question in 1848. This seeming accident was not, of course, accident at all. Taylor had loved reading history books since childhood. He may enjoy implying that a study of Cromwell would have better suited somebody of his radical political views: diplomatic history, however, offered an even better vehicle for one of his real rather than pretend characteristics: his Little Englander's abiding xenophobia. Taylor has never visited the United States, which plays as small a part in his work as he likes to pretend it has in his life. Nor, while working on the Italian question, did he deign to work in the Italian archives. How could he be expected to? Mussolini was in power.

Mussolini's Italy provides a litmus test for the xenophobia of the British. Italian fascism is disdained by Denis Mack Smith as well as Taylor in two complementary ways: for being nasty but for not being serious; it is not, therefore, to be treated seriously – as if not being serious, which ought to have redeemed it, compounded its offense. Should Mussolini have killed his Jews to make him worthy of respect? And if Hitler can wear Bismarck's clothes, why may not Mussolini wear Cavour's or Crispi's? Of course Italy postured; of course, like Poland, Italy claimed a status it could not support. Britain and France did likewise. Taylor explains at length and repeatedly that the victors of Versailles could not support the terms of their victory; rather that the terms of victory, in preserving a unified German state, were likely to undermine themselves. Italy's status as a great power arose out of the need for its help in maintaining the Versailles settlement. Which is it, one wonders, that galls Englishmen so much? Their need of Italy to help restrain Germany? Their sense that Italy's claims were no more inflated than their own? Or their unwilling recognition that in denigrating Mussolini as Hitler's lackey, they describe Churchill's relationship with Roosevelt. The Italians provided the only enemy the British could beat in the Second World War before they were forced to choose between subjugation by Germany or hiring themselves out as mercenaries for American imperialism.

In emphasizing the role of chance and accident, Taylor seems both to demand recognition for the heroic (what his critics call the dynamic) in history, while at the same time pre-echoing Paul W. Schroeder's insistence that results are more important than causes. Narrative of events is the best form of diplomatic history. Whereas an analytical form will lead to false analysis of motive, narrative will expose the gap between what men think they are doing, what they actually do, and the results they unexpectedly bring about. Need one make this choice? That Hitler was an opportunist need not preclude him from also being a fanatic with a dream of paradise for a sect. Hitler's opportunism may have been doubly effective precisely because it was matched with consistency of purpose; Mussolini's opportunism ineffective because he lacked any long-term goals. Naturally, men do not accomplish all they set out to accomplish, unless they live in dreams. Some, however, accomplish more than others and the reason why they are able to do so depends upon the extent to which their goals fit their moment. For all Taylor's emphasis on accident and opportunity, he is a determinist – of the Hegelian rather than Marxist type – in treating both Hitler and Chamberlain as the expression of Germany's and Britain's general historical will.

States, for Taylor, have roles to play in history: the task of their statesmen is to see that they play them. Hitler, as the apotheosis of the course of German history, plays the part, and borrows the clothes when necessary, of Barbarossa, Frederick the Great and

William II, as well as Bismarck. Similarly, Chamberlain as the apotheosis of Merrie Englande dresses up as Good Queen Bess, Marlborough, Wellington, even – regrettably perhaps – Haig, the line of Englishmen who marched into Europe at the beginning of each century. Ideally, they marched behind a shield held up by an unsuspecting ally, set everything to rights for a hundred years, then went about their business. If they could not go about their business after the peace of Versailles, something must be wrong with the peace; something they had only to put right. They failed, as they had always failed. Their novelty lay in having to admit it. The historically determined role of Germany lay in the domination of central and eastern Europe. Everybody can agree to that. Taylor differs from his critics only in insisting that this role did not require the domination of Belgium and France. If it did not, however, Hitler was a novelty, not an expression in different style of traditional goals. Germany's historical role had required the domination of France and Belgium for Bethmann-Hollweg.

Taylor's three disguises of historian posing as personality or personality posing as former historian, conservative posing as radical, and determinist posing as opportunist, must be stripped away before any of his work can be properly placed. This task is most necessary, because the effect of the disguises is most noticeable, in Taylor's treatment of what the boundaries of his book on English history would lead one to expect him to call the thirty years crisis.

The series of conceptual problems facing any reader of *The Origins of the Second World War* starts from the fact that, perhaps at the suggestion of the publisher, perhaps to increase sales, the book was given the obvious, but wrong because inaccurate, title. It should have been called *The Struggle for Mastery in Europe: Volume II*, not only as describing the subject of the book more accurately, but also for indicating more accurately Taylor's view of the world. The Second World War is of no interest to Taylor, beyond providing an opportunity for a mock-heroic British imperial suicide, of which as a pretend radical he must pretend to approve. For all other purposes, history, professional history that is, the subject he used to write about during his former incarnation as professional academic historian (words he would happily apply to others, if, like E. P. Thompson, not wishing them applied to himself), came to an end in 1940.

Readers must not be misled by Taylor's title in the way his

critics have been allowed to pretend that they were misled by it. Wars that are fought are not necessarily fought for the causes that caused them: the outbreak of war wipes the slate clean. Fritz Fischer's famous study of Germany's aims in the First World War, *Griff nach der Weltmacht*, fell rather flat in Britain, despite the best efforts of James Joll. Although most Englishmen already took it for granted that the First World War had been caused by the Germans, almost as many of them doubted whether war aims necessarily offered acceptable proof of prewar goals. Listening to Lord Curzon expounding his dream of a new middle eastern empire to the eastern committee of the War Cabinet in 1918 would have entirely misled a German about the use to which the British had expected to put the Anglo-Russian entente in 1907. Similarly, Hitler's responsibility for the outbreak of war in 1939, his willingness to threaten force confident he would not have to use it, his preparation for limited war to bring quick victory and equally limited political gain, whether true statements or false, may not be challenged by descriptions of the plans he made after he found himself at war with three of the other so-called Great Powers of Europe – wrapping up the first of them in weeks, while one of the other two, happy to be *at* war but dreading having to *make* war, stood breathlessly still in the hope that Hitler might not notice that the two of them were still there.

Taylor writes about the end of European history in the war that broke out in 1939 between Germany, Britain, and France, to be won in 1940 by Germany. The scene is touching, chosen to show Britain at its best; part of Europe, struggling for Europe, valiant, undefeated, the only hope for Europe. Britain must not succumb to Nazism, therefore it must tame the necessary but carnivorous allies from outside. By jettisoning its empire with barely a backward glance and a few self-righteous platitudes, it will save what matters to Europe most – the British Isles – home of freedom, home of freedom's most stalwart defenders, Lancashire, cotton, and Dissent. Should one look forward to the so-called "special relationship" with the United States, or to the bitter anti-Americanism that has permeated Britain since 1945, knowing that what was saved from the Nazis would be handed over to the Yanks? Taylor's war will be fought in the wrong place at the wrong time. It has to be. The United States and the USSR cannot be recognized as the new torch bearers for European civilization: one is not civilized, the other not European. In fact, their war against Germany and Japan, followed by the Cold War between the two of them, all take place within the Greater

European (now called Western) world. Taylor's work is therefore Anglocentric when he is looking at Europe and Eurocentric when looking at the wider world. Take note of Nirad Chaudhuri's warning that the real division in the world is the hatred felt by Asiatics for Westerners. Our challenge from outside is yet to come.

Taylor does for Britain before the Second World War a favor similar to that performed by Fritz Fischer for Germany before the First World War: gives it the star part. The Germans were not sure that they wanted to have played a second such part. Having already accepted the part played by Hitler in causing the Second World War, they preferred to think of the experience as exceptional. Taylor offers them a bargain: allow Fischer to play up the kaiser, and Taylor will play down Hitler. The bargain ought also to have suited the British. The star part taken away from Hitler was to be given to them. Better, surely, to have caused the war than have been merely caught up in it? If one is to fight for freedom against oppression, ought one not to have started the fight? Palmerston would have said so. The Hitler war was the most exciting moment of educated middle-class British life. Anybody fortunate enough to have played a part in it never forgets. My aunt broke away from a ghastly stepmother to drive huge trucks with a crowd of equally jolly girls, only to waste her one chance in life by marrying my uncle instead of a GI. Those too old or too young still feast on legends of imaginary victories, won by imaginary heroes, usually in an imaginary desert. Even if one can no longer claim – without the hint of a blush – to have won the war, though one is delighted to hear Danes and Norwegians say that one did, one need have no doubt that one had stood up to Hitler: the brightest and best offered him reasonable adjustments to the treaty of Versailles, but when he proved unreasonable drew a line. Never mind that the Italians disappointed, the French had to be browbeaten, the Czechs ratted on, the Poles and Norwegians left to their fate. By one's exertion and one's example one had shown the way, just like one had always done. Pitt the Younger had said so. Remember the Napoleonic Wars.

Taylor's favor to Britain depends on sleight of hand, on the pretence that Russia and the United States were not there – and would not be there in the future. The relationship between the present and the future provides the missing link sought for by critics between Taylor's general versus immediate, and impersonal versus personal, causes. Of course statesmen and soldiers blunder into war, but they do so only at moments of tension, when a shift in the balance of power or a shift in the perception of the balance of power demands a response. Taylor rightly emphasizes the fact that the terms of the treaty of Versailles predicted a powerful Germany; Britain's economy could not survive without it. One is promised this development at the beginning of the book; it has evidently taken place by the end of the book: in the middle of the book, it drops out of sight. The cause of the Second World War was similar to the cause of the First: a dramatic substantive shift in the balance of power, followed by an equally dramatic perceived shift in the goals of German foreign policy. Until the Munich crisis, both the power of Germany and the perceived aims of Germany could be harmonized with the Versailles settlement. As a result of the partition of Czechoslovakia, Germany became a much stronger state in relation to Britain and France. Simultaneously, it was perceived to be pursuing undefined, because unlimited, goals.

Both the increase in the power of Germany (and if German power was not increased, why make so much fuss about the partition of Czechoslovakia?) and the change in the perception of Germany's goals changed everyone's clocks. F. H. Hinsley suggests that if war had broken out before the Munich crisis, Hitler could not be held primarily responsible for it, but that for war any time after it, he can be. This formulation might be better turned around. Until Munich, British policy and the restraints placed by the British on the French can be interpreted as a desire to postpone, if not prevent, war; some would say at unreasonable cost. The latter is very doubtful. Why should Englishmen have died to save Czechs? Better to have not died in a pretence of saving Poles. After Munich what had been postponed was brought forward. The British still did not necessarily want war. However, whereas they had previously assumed that if war was to come, better it came later than sooner – after rearmament; a run on the banks now suggested that war would be preferable sooner rather than later, and short rather than long. How was a long war to be paid for when war itself would prevent the City from making the money needed to pay for it? Britain seemed so powerful a state for so long only because it suited other states – including Germany – to make use of the financial services offered in Britain and to hold large sterling balances to pay for them.

Just as the wars that are fought are not fought for the causes that caused them, they are usually not fought between the states that are actually fighting. Wars may be caused by present problems: they are fought over future ones. They are forcible answers to the question: what will happen twenty years from now – perhaps even ten – if it is not prevented by force in a year or so. Taylor's statesmen are not permitted to look beyond the end of next week. They resemble Manchester mill owners, loath to look for a new product. And they suffer the same fate: an unnecessarily early and hasty decline. When Germany after 1910 became more and more willing to use force to obtain political as well as economic dominance over central and western Europe, it was attempting to pre-empt the industrialization of Russia and turn itself into a world power ahead of the United States. Despite this, Fritz Fischer should not be allowed to say that Germany caused the war. His critics are equally right to blame Britain for its determination to hold onto positions it was not able – and had never been able – to defend by itself against a forcible challenge, but could only hope to persuade somebody else to defend on its behalf. Similarly in 1939, Hitler was taking up the task left to him by Hindenburg and Ludendorff. The invasion of Russia was not a blunder, for how else was Russia's future as an industrial state to be forestalled? Hitler's blunder was to declare war on the United States. War against Britain and France was war with the United States in disguise and, as the First World War had demonstrated, the longer the disguise could be kept up, the better for Germany.

Now that forty years have passed since the half century of Germany's moment of power came to an end, one may wonder whether Taylor's account of the origins of the Second World War is not a product of the dream world it portrays. The peace of Versailles was meant to take Europe back to the good old days of the mid-eighteenth century, when Britain and France, more often enemies than friends, nevertheless regulated the affairs of Europe. France monitored central and eastern Europe, denying Russia access to its affairs, through its clients Sweden, Poland, and the Turks, and by helping to sustain the rivalry between Austria and Prussia. Great Britain turned its empire into an unrivalled source of wealth, playing its part on the continent by purchasing the armies it chose not to maintain. The system was formally recreated in 1925 when the Locarno system reincarnated the Burgundian circle: it was formally destroyed in both the eighteenth and twentieth centuries by the conquest of Poland, an easier task the second time owing to the failure of Italy to play the part of necessary rival to Germany in south-eastern Europe. As long as the system lasted, however, shifts in the balance of power were registered and regulated in western Europe; in an area where navies might seem to challenge armies, where peripheral states like Britain could find necessary allies. Locarno was copied from the notebook of Captain Mahan.

Was the Locarno system sleight of hand by Austen Chamberlain or by A. J. P. Taylor? The shifts in the balance of power between the wars were all to take place in eastern Europe, as France, as it had in the mid-eighteenth century, lost control over its clients – matching its loss of ability to support them. The challenge of Versailles and the expenditure of the capital of Versailles loom large in Taylor's account, perhaps too large. Versailles' most grievous fault for Germans lay in denying them the fruits of their victory at Brest-Litovsk. The Allies had every right to make demands in the west, where the Germans knew that their armies had collapsed more than the sagging armies of Britain and France, already more frightened of their ostensible American ally than their ostensible German foe. The Allies had no right to demand political changes in eastern Europe (in particular the recreation of Poland) not warranted by the extent of their victory. *Mein Kampf* deserves more attention than Taylor will permit anyone to pay to it. Far from deviating from previous German plans for expansion and colonization in the east, it merely takes up a story broken up by the undoing of Brest-Litovsk. One is left wondering whether, whatever Hitler may have been made to do or not do by Taylor, he would have been willing to leave the west unconquered, and able, should it find the nerve, to try and overturn his bid for a second Brest-Litovsk by bidding for a second Versailles.

The thirty years crisis began in Bosnia and came to an end in Berlin. Taylor's book, written by an Englishman for Englishmen, leaves out the eastern European states whose economic histories played so important a part between the wars that Ernest Bevin was heard to lament the break-up of Austria–Hungary. Was the departure of the Habsburgs rather than the arrival of Hitler the cause of the Second German War? A foolish question except in the sense that the gradual reimposition of a variant of Brest-Litovsk might give a more accurate focus to the book than the gradual breakdown of Versailles. The conclusion of such an inquiry would be a war fought between Germany and Russia, won by Russia, whose leader was recently heard to remark, as Ronald Reagan and Margaret Thatcher strode along Omaha Beach, that they seemed to be making a great deal of fuss over a side show. Naturally Russia would play down the second front it had persistently demanded at the time. Naturally the British will play it up – one would think, reading British accounts, that Montgomery swept north through Germany unattended; that Patton, Bradley, and Devers had never even crossed the Atlantic. Hitler's invasion of Russia without first defeating Britain had left the latter only one important, in unenviable, strategic role to play in the war: well-watered offshore island base, peopled by friendly natives. What the British had sought at Trincomalee, Singapore, and Hong Kong, they themselves now provided for the Americans. Perhaps Locarno's faith in the power of peripheral states was justified. Deny the Russians the victory over Germany they claim, and the Second World War turns into a triumph of sea power.

Hurray for sea power, hurray for the triumph of *aussenpolitik*! Perhaps because social historians cherish the illusion – and have persuaded other people to believe – that they have made the running of late in the discipline, their diseases can be catching. The triumph of *innenpolitik* is one of them: the assumption that the foreign policies of states are determined by what goes on inside them, rather than by events in the outside world. Most unlikely, however comforting the pretence. Although states may select their own goals in an attempt to satisfy the aspirations of their inhabitants, their success in reaching the goals will partly depend on other people. Not that Taylor would wish states to stop trying to reach their goals or, necessarily, to give way to others. Having selected their goals, however unrealistic they may seem, they ought to try to reach them. What else are states for? Or their ambassadors? Shirley Temple Black was not sent to Accra to benefit Ghanaians nor Nevile Henderson to Berlin to benefit Germany, although from the conduct of both of them one might begin to have doubts.

Supporters of *innenpolitik* are always likely to triumph over supporters of *aussenpolitik* because the former is much the easier to carry off. Pick your language, pick your state; set out its social structure, its political and economic systems, its demands; there you have it – the foreign policy of Britannia or Ruritania between the wars. Taylor knows better. Ruritania's foreign policy is not defined until tried out; it awaits the response of other states with whom it has to deal. Taylor therefore takes up a position above the European world – dream world though it may be – and sets out the important connections between all of the European states as he sees them. He slips easily and often misleadingly between what men expected to happen and what did happen, pinning both within a Cartesian framework set up before the book begins. How may one fault such an argument? On what does it rest? On the documentary evidence cited in the worthy books selected by the worthy authors of the worthy chapters of this book? Of course not. Pull out a brick and the wall will stand. Pull out all the bricks? The wall still stands. It is an imaginary wall. It is supported by the spaces between the evidence, not on the evidence itself. How else could it be supported? Evidence of the past is not found in documents, only in what historians decide that documents mean. Historical truth is never self-evident. It is revealed most clearly to the enlightened ignorant. A. J. P. Taylor has read widely in the history of the Europe he has created. He is careful not to know too much about anything. What he does know about must be what matters.

How odd that *The Origins of the Second World War* should have appeared in the same year as *Griff nach der Weltmacht*, lauded in the United States for having provoked more controversy than any other book for a generation. One can see why Fischer's work should be so popular in the United States and Taylor's disparaged. Fischer's work is manifestly serious, announcing its own importance on every page; Taylor's work apparently frivolous by comparison. Perhaps this difference in tone explains David Hackett Fischer's dismissal of Taylor in *Historians' Fallacies* for his Herodotean interest in wonders and marvels; for writing essays in which irresistible forces meet immovable objects and both have their way. David Fischer's own interests represent an American preference for the bludgeon rather than the rapier, for books that inform rather than books that illumine. E. H. Carr is chastised as severely as Taylor, for having remarked that accuracy in a historian is merely a duty, not a virtue. But how could it be anything else? If much of the criticism of Taylor's work arises out of doubts about its accuracy, much of the criticism of its inaccuracy is beside the point. A tale was told of the rival who chortled that *The Struggle for Mastery* contained two errors on every page (Henry Pelling tried hard but could not quite compile such a list when reviewing *English History*), and of American graduate seminars where students spend snowbound winters sweating to devil them out. Hurray for error! Why value truth when error prove so fertile?

How could anybody who grew up in England or the dominions (despite Taylor's taste for sniffing at colonials) not feast on Taylor's books? What Churchill did for himself – hog all the glory – Taylor has done for all of us. He is the quintessential patriotic historian, pining for nineteenth-century triumphs when England, safe behind her wooden walls, armored in the righteousness of Methodism, and offering everyone security for property and the just rewards of labour, stood beside Everyman in the fight against Apollyon. Find a coin commemorating patriotic history and you will find Taylor's head struck on one side, Arthur Bryant's on the other. Read *The Origins of the Second World War* after *The Years of Victory* and before Chester Wilmot's *Struggle for Europe*. Better still, read *Origins* before *The Years of Endurance*, for Bryant's Napoleonic wars and Taylor's 1930s are closer to one another than to anything else. How can Britain's most patriotic of prime ministers have missed her cue? Surely the KCMG is in the mail.

Bibliography

The literature of on the origins of the Second World War is now immense, and it would require several volumes to list all of the sources available. The bibliography offered here is not meant to be comprehensive, but the books listed have been carefully selected to include all of the most important work done by historians since *The Origins of the Second World War* appeared. Collections of documents, diaries, memoirs and autobiographies have not been included. A list of the journals in which articles on the subject of the war's origins regularly appear will be found at the end of the bibliography.

Abendroth, Hans-Henning, *Hitler in der spanischen Arena: Die deutsche spanischen Beziehungen im Spannungsfeld der europäischen Interessenpolitik vom Ausbruch des Bürgerkrieges bis zum Ausbruch des Weltkrieges 1936–1939* (Paderborn, 1973).

Adamthwaite, Anthony P., *France and the Coming of the Second World War* (London, 1977).

Adler, Selig, *The Isolationist Impulse. Its Twentieth Century Reaction* (New York, 1966).

Aldcroft, Derek H., *From Versailles to Wall Street 1919–1929* (Berkeley, 1977).

Allard, Sven, *Stalin und Hitler: Die sowjetrussische Aussenpolitik 1930–1941* (Munich, 1974).

Amoja, Fulvio d', *Declino e prima crisi dell'Europa di Versailles 1931–1933* (Milan, 1967).

Angress, Werner T., *Stillborn Revolution* (Princeton, 1963).

Artaud, Denise, *La Question des dettes interalliées et la reconstruction de l'Europe 1917–1929*, 2 vols (Lille, 1978).

Aster, Sidney, *1939: The Making of the Second World War* (London, 1973).

Baer, George W., *The Coming of the Italian-Ethiopian War* (Cambridge, Mass., 1967).

Bariéty, Jacques, *Les Relations franco-allemandes après la première guerre mondiale* (Paris, 1977).

Barnett, Corelli, *The Collapse of British Power* (London and New York, 1972).

Bennett, Edward W., *Germany and the Diplomacy of the Financial Crisis 1931* (Cambridge, Mass., 1962).

Bennett, Edward W., *German Rearmament and the West 1932–1933* (Princeton, 1979).

Benz, Wolfgang, and Graml, Hermann (eds), *Sommer 1939. Die Grossmächte und der Europäische Krieg* (Stuttgart, 1979).

Bialer, Uri, *The Shadow of the Bomber: The Fear of Air Attack and British Politics 1932–1939* (London, 1980).

Birn, David S., *The League of Nations Union 1918–1945* (London, 1981).

Bischof, Erwin, *Rheinischer Separatismus 1918–1924* (Bern, 1969).

Bloch, Charles, *Hitler und die europäischen Mächte 1933–1934: Kontinuität oder Bruch?* (Frankfurt-am-Main, 1966).

Bolech, Cecchi D., *L'accordo di due imperi: L'accordo italo-inglese del 16 aprile 1938* (Milan, 1977).

Bond, Brian, *British Military Policy between the Two World Wars* (Oxford, 1980).

Borg, Dorothy, *The United States and the Far Eastern Crisis of 1933–1938* (Cambridge, Mass., 1964).

Braunthal, Julius, *History of the International*, Vol. 2, *1914–1943* (New York, 1967).

Brundu, Olla P., *L'equilibrio difficile: Gran Bretagna, Italia e Francia nel Mediterraneo 1930–1937* (Milan, 1980).

Budorowycz, Bohdan B., *Polish-Soviet Relations 1932–1939* (New York, 1963).

Bullock, Alan, *Hitler and the Origins of the Second World War* (London, 1967).

Burgwyn, H. J., *Il revisionismo fascista: La sfida di Mussolini alle grande potenze nei Balcani e sul Danubio 1925–1933* (Milan, 1979).

Campbell, F. Gregory, *Confrontation in Central Europe: Weimar Germany and Czechoslovakia* (Chicago, 1975).

Carls-Maire, Alice-Catherine, *La Ville libre de Dantzic en crise ouverte* (Wroclaw, 1982).

Carlton, David, *MacDonald versus Henderson: The Foreign Policy of the Second Labour Government* (London, 1970).

Carlton, David, *Anthony Eden* (London, 1981).

Carocci, Giampiero, *La politica estera dell'Italia fascista 1925–1928* (Bari, 1969).

Carr, William, *Arms, Autarky and Aggression: A Study in German Foreign Policy 1933–1939* (London, 1972).

Carroll, Berenice A., *Design for Total War: Arms and Economics in the Third Reich* (The Hague, 1968).

Cassels, Alan, *Mussolini's Early Diplomacy* (Princeton, 1970).

Cienciala, Anna M., *Poland and the Western Powers 1938–1939: A Study in the Interdependence of Eastern and Western Europe* (Toronto, 1968).

Cienciala, Anna M. and Komarnicki, Titus, *From Versailles to Locarno: Keys to Polish Foreign Policy 1919–1925* (Lawrence, Kans., 1984).

Colvin, Ian, *Vansittart in Office* (London, 1965).

Colvin, Ian, *The Chamberlain Cabinet* (London, 1971).

Compton, James V., *The Swastika and the Eagle. Hitler, the United States and the Origins of the Second World War* (London, 1968).

Costigliola, F., *Awkward Dominion* (Ithaca, NY, 1985).

Coverdale, John F., *Italian Intervention in the Spanish Civil War* (Princeton, 1976).

Cowling, Maurice, *The Impact of Hitler* (Cambridge, 1975).

Crowley, James B., *Japan's Quest for Autonomy: National Security and Foreign Policy 1930–1938* (Princeton, 1966).

Dallek, Robert, *Democrat and Diplomat: The Life of William E. Dodd* (New York, 1968).

Davies, Norman, *White Eagle, Red Star: The Polish-Soviet War 1919–1920* (New York, 1972).

Debicki, Roman, *The Foreign Policy of Poland 1919–1939* (New York, 1962).

Deist, W. *et al.*, *Das Deutsche Reich und der Zweite Weltkrieg*, Vol. 1, *Ursachen und Voraussetzungen der deutschen Kriegspolitik* (Stuttgart, 1979).

Dilks, David (ed.), *Retreat from Power*, 2 vols (London, 1981).

Dingman, Roger, *Power in the Pacific* (Chicago, 1976).

Divine, Robert, *The Illusion of Neutrality* (Chicago, 1962).

Drechsler, Karl, *Deutschland-China-Japan 1933–1939: Das Dilemma der deutschen Fernostpolitik* (Berlin, 1964).

Duroselle, Jean-Baptiste, *From Wilson to Roosevelt. Foreign Policy of the United States 1913–1945* (London, 1964).

Duroselle, Jean-Baptiste, *La Décadence, 1932–1939* (Paris, 1979).

Dyck, Harvey L., *Weimar Germany and Soviet Russia 1926–1933: A Study in Diplomatic Instability* (London, 1966).

Elissar, Eliahu Ben, *La Diplomatie du IIIe Reich et les Juifs 1933–1939* (Paris, 1969).

Emmerson, James T., *The Rhineland Crisis 7 March 1936: A Study in Multilateral Diplomacy* (London, 1977).

Enssle, Manfred J., *Stresemann's Territorial Revisionism* (Wiesbaden, 1980).

Erickson, John, *The Soviet High Command: A Military-Political History 1918–1941* (London, 1962).

Eubank, Keith, *Munich* (Norman, Okla, 1963).

Fabry, Philipp W., *Die Sowjetunion und das Dritte Reich: eine dokumentierte Geschichte der deutsch-sowjetischen Beziehungen von 1933 bis 1941* (Stuttgart, 1971).

Favez, Jean-Claude, *Le Reich devant l'occupation franco-belge de la Ruhr en 1923* (Geneva, 1969).

Felice, R. de, *Mussolini il Duce*, 2 vols. Vol. 1, *Gli anni del consenso 1929–1936*; Vol. 2, *Lo Stato totalitario 1936–1940* (Turin, 1974, 1981).

Felix, David, *Walther Rathenau and the Weimar Republic* (Baltimore, 1971).

Fink, Carole, *The Genoa Conference: European Diplomacy 1921–1922* (Chapel Hill, NC, 1984).

Frankenstein, Robert, *Le prix du réarmement français 1935–1939* (Paris, 1982).

Friedländer, Saul, *Prelude to Downfall: Hitler and the United States 1939–1941* (London, 1967).

Fry, Michael G., *Illusion of Security* (Toronto, 1972).

Fuchser, Larry W., *Neville Chamberlain and Appeasement: A Study in the Politics of History* (New York, 1982).

Funke, Manfred, *Sanktionen und Kanonen: Hitler, Mussolini und der Abessinienkonflikt 1934–1936* (Düsseldorf, 1970).

Gannon, Franklin R., *The British Press and Germany 1936–1939* (Oxford, 1971).

Gardner, Lloyd C., *Economic Aspects of New Deal Diplomacy* (Madison, Wis., 1974).

Gardner, Richard N., *Sterling-Dollar Diplomacy* (New York, 1969).

Gates, Eleanor M., *End of the Affair: The Collapse of the Anglo-French Alliance 1939–1940* (Berkeley, 1980).

Gatzke, Hans W. (ed.), *European Diplomacy between Two Wars 1919–1939* (Chicago, 1972).

Gehl, Jürgen, *Austria, Germany and the Anschluss 1931–1938* (London, 1963).

George, Margaret, *The Hollow Men* (London, 1965).

Geyer, Michael, *Aufrüstung oder Sicherheit: Die Reichswehr in der Krise der Machtpolitik 1924–1936* (Wiesbaden, 1980).

Gilbert, Martin and Gott, Richard, *The Appeasers* (London, 1963).

Gilbert, Martin, *The Roots of Appeasement* (London and New York, 1966).

Giordano, G., *Il Patto a Quattro nella politica estera di Mussolini* (Bologna, 1976).

Gromada, Thaddeus V. (ed.), *Essays on Poland's Foreign Policy 1918–1939* (New York, 1970).

Gruchmann, Lothar, *Nationalsozialistische Grossraumordnung: die Konstruktion einer deutschen Monroe-Doktrin* (Munich, 1965).

Grundmann, Karl-Heinz, *Deutschtumpolitik zur Zeit der Weimarer Republik* (Hanover, 1977).

Guerri, Giordano B., *Galeazzo Ciano, una vita 1903–1944* (Milan, 1979).

Haggie, Paul, *Britannia at Bay: The Defence of the British Empire against Japan* (Oxford, 1981).

Haraszti, Eva H., *Treaty-Breakers or Realpolitiker? The Anglo-German Naval Agreement of June 1935*, trans. by S. Simon (Boppard, 1973).

Hardie, Frank M., *The Abyssinian Crisis* (London, 1974).

Haslam, Jonathan, *Soviet Foreign Policy 1930–1933: The Impact of the Depression* (New York, 1983).

Haslam, Jonathan, *The Soviet Union and the Struggle for Collective Security in Europe 1933–1939* (New York, 1984).

Heineman, John Louis, *Hitler's First Foreign Minister: Constantin von Neurath* (Berkeley, 1980).

Henke, Josef, *England in Hitlers politischen Kalkül 1935–1939* (Boppard-am-Rhein, 1973).

Herwig, Holger H., *Politics of Frustration: The United States in German Naval Planning 1889–1941* (Boston, 1976).

Hildebrand, Klaus, *Vom Reich zum Weltreich: Hitler, NSDAP, und koloniale Frage 1919–1945* (Munich, 1969).

Hildebrand, Klaus, *The Foreign Policy of the Third Reich* (London, 1973).

Hildebrand, Klaus, *The Third Reich* (London, 1984).

Hochman, Jiri, *The Soviet Union and the Failure of Collective Security 1934–1938* (Ithaca, NY, 1984).

Hoepke, Klaus-Peter, *Die deutsche Rechte und der italienische Faschismmus* (Düsseldorf, 1968).

Höltje, Christian, *Die Weimarer Republik und das Ostlocarno-Problem*

1919–1934: Revision oder Garantie der deutschen Ostgrenze von 1919 (Würzburg, 1958).

Hölzle, Erwin (ed.), *Die deutschen Ostgebiete zur Zeit der Weimarer Republik* (Cologne, 1966).

Howard, Michael, *The Continental Commitment: The Dilemma of British Defence Policy in the Era of the Two World Wars* (London, 1972).

Hughes, Judith M., *To the Maginot Line* (Cambridge, Mass., 1971).

Hyde, H. Montgomery *British Air Policy between the Wars* (London, 1976).

Iriye, Akira, *After Imperialism: The Search for a New Order in the Far East 1921–1931* (Cambridge, Mass., 1965).

Irving, David, *The War Path: Hitler's Germany 1935–1939* (London, 1978).

Issraeljan, V. and Kutakov, L., *Diplomacy of Aggression: Berlin–Rome–Tokio Axis* (Moscow, 1970).

Jäckel, Eberhard, *Hitler's World View* (Cambridge, Mass., 1981).

Jacobsen, Hans-Adolf, *National-sozialistische Aussenpolitik 1933–1939* (Frankfurt-am-Main, 1968).

Jacobson, Jon, *Locarno Diplomacy: Germany and the West 1925–1929* (Princeton, 1972).

Jarausch, Konrad, *The Four Power Pact 1933* (Madison, Wis., 1965).

Kennedy, Malcolm D., *The Estrangement of Great Britain and Japan 1917–1935* (Manchester, 1969).

Kennedy, Paul, *Strategy and Diplomacy 1870–1945* (London, 1983).

Kimmich, Christoph M., *The Free City: Danzig and German Foreign Policy 1919–1934* (New Haven, Conn., 1968).

Kimmich, Christoph M., *Germany and the League of Nations* (Chicago, 1976).

Knox, Macgregor, *Mussolini Unleashed 1939–1941* (New York, 1982).

Koblyakov, I. K., *USSR: For Peace, Against Aggression 1933–1941* (Moscow, 1976).

Köhler, Henning, *Novemberrevolution und Frankreich* (Düsseldorf, 1980).

Korbel, Josef, *Poland between East and West: Soviet and German Diplomacy toward Poland 1919–1933* (Princeton, 1963).

Korczynski, Alexander and Swietochowski, Tadeusz (eds), *Poland between Germany and Russia 1926–1939: The Theory of Two Enemies* (New York, 1975).

Krekeler, Norbert, *Revisionsanspruch und geheime Ostpolitik der Weimarer Republik* (Stuttgart, 1973).

Lammers, Donald N., *Explaining Munich: The Search for Motive in British Policy* (Stanford, 1966).

Latour, Conrad F., *Südtirol und die Achse Berlin–Rom 1938–1945* (Stuttgart, 1962).

Ledeen, Michael A., *Universal Fascism: Theory and Practice of the Fascist International 1928–1936* (New York, 1972).

Lee, Bradford A., *Britain and the Sino-Japanese War 1937–1939* (Stanford, 1973).

Leffler, Melvyn P., *The Elusive Quest* (Chapel Hill, NC, 1979).

Leutze, James R., *Bargaining for Supremacy: Anglo-American Naval Collaboration 1937–1941* (Chapel Hill, NC, 1977).

Link, Werner, *Die amerikanische Stabilisierungspolitik in Deutschland 1921–1932* (Düsseldorf, 1970).

Louis, W. Roger, *British Strategy in the Far East 1919–1929* (Oxford, 1971).

Louis, W. Roger (ed.), *The Origins of the Second World War: A. J. P. Taylor and His Critics* (New York, 1972).

Low, Alfred D., *The Anschluss Movement 1918–1919 and the Paris Peace Conference* (Philadelphia, 1974).

Lowe, Peter, *Great Britain and the Origins of the Pacific War 1937–1941* (Oxford, 1977).

Lundgreen-Nielsen, Kay, *The Polish Problem at the Paris Peace Conference: A Study of the Policies of the Great Powers and the Poles 1918–1919* (Odense, 1979).

MacDonald, Callum A., *The United States, Britain and Appeasement 1936–1939* (New York and London, 1981).

Mack Smith, Denis, *Mussolini's Roman Empire* (London, 1976).

Mack Smith, Denis, *Mussolini* (London, 1981).

Maier, Charles S., *Recasting Bourgeois Europe* (Princeton, 1975).

Maksimychev, I. F., *Diplomatii mira protiv diplomatii voiny* (Moscow, 1981).

Marder, Arthur J., *Old Friends, New Enemies: The Royal Navy and the Imperial Japanese Navy* (Oxford, 1981).

Marks, Sally, *The Illusion of Peace: International Relations in Europe 1918–1933* (London, 1976).

Marks, Sally, *Innocent Abroad: Belgium at the Paris Peace Conference of 1919* (Chapel Hill, NC, 1981).

Mayer, Arno J., *Politics and Diplomacy of Peacemaking: Containment and Counter-revolution at Versailles* (New York, 1967).

McSherry, James E., *Stalin, Hitler, and Europe* (Cleveland, Ohio, 1968).

McDougall, Walter A., *France's Rhineland Diplomacy* (Princeton, 1978).

Merkes, Manfred, *Die deutsche Politik gegenüber dem spanischen Bürgerkrieg 1936–1939* (Bonn, 1961).

Meskill, Johanna M., *Hitler and Japan: The Hollow Alliance* (New York, 1966).

Meyers, Reinhard Peter F. W., *Britische Sicherheitspolitik 1934–1938* (Bonn, 1976).

Michaelis, Meir, *Mussolini and the Jews: German-Italian Relations and the Jewish Question in Italy 1922–1945* (Oxford, 1978).

Michalka, Wolfgang (ed.), *Nationalsozialistische Aussenpolitik* (Darmstadt, 1978).

Michalka, W. and Lee, M. M. (eds), *Gustav Stresemann* (Darmstadt, 1982).

Middlemas, Keith, *Diplomacy of Illusion: The British Government and Germany 1937–1939 (London, 1972)*.

Mommsen, Wolfgang J. and Kettenacker, Lothar (eds), *The Fascist Challenge and the Policy of Appeasement* (London, 1983).

Mori, Renato, *Mussolini e la conquista dell 'Etiopia* (Florence, 1978).

Morley, James W. (ed.), *Deterrent Diplomacy: Japan, Germany, and the USSR 1935–1940* (New York, 1976).

Murray, Williamson, *The Change in the European Balance of Power 1938–1939: The Path to Ruin* (Princeton, 1984).

Murray, Williamson, *Luftwaffe: A History 1933–44* (London, 1985).

Narochitskii, A. L. (ed.), *SSSR v bor'be protiv fashistskoi agressi 1933–1941* (Moscow, 1976).

Neidpath, James, *The Singapore Naval Base and the Defence of Britain's Eastern Empire 1919–1941* (Oxford, 1981).

Nelson, Harold I., *Land and Power: British and Allied Policy on Germany's Frontiers 1916–1919* (Toronto, 1963).

Nelson, Keith L., *Victors Divided* (Berkeley, 1975).

Newman, Simon, *March 1939: The British Guarantee to Poland – A Study in the Continuity of British Foreign Policy* (Oxford, 1976).

Niclauss, Karlheinz, *Die Sowjetunion und Hitlers Machtergreifung: Eine Studie über die deutsch-russischen Beziehungen der Jahre 1929 bis 1935* (Bonn, 1966).

Niedhart, Gottfried, *Grossbritannien und die Sowjetunion 1934–1939* (Munich, 1972).

Nish, Ian H., *Alliance in Decline: A Study in Anglo-Japanese Relations 1908–1923* (London, 1972).

Noel, Léon, *Les illusions de Stresa* (Paris, 1975).

Noel-Baker, P., *The First World Disarmament Conference 1932–1933, and Why It Failed* (New York, 1979).

Offner, Arnold, *American Appeasement. United States Foreign Policy and Germany 1933–1938* (Cambridge, Mass., 1969).

Ogata, Sadako N., *Defiance in Manchuria. The Making of Japanese Foreign Policy 1931–1932* (Berkeley, 1964).

Orde, Anne, *Britain and International Security 1920–1926* (London, 1978).

Ovendale, Ritchie, *Appeasement and the English-Speaking World* (Cardiff, 1975).

Peden, G. C., *British Rearmament and the Treasury 1932–1939* (Edinburgh, 1979).

Petersen, J., *Hitler-Mussolini: Der Entstehung der Achse Berlin-Rom 1933–1936* (Tübingen, 1973).

Petzina, Dieter, *Autarkiepolitik im Dritten Reich: Der nationalsozialistische Vierjahresplan* (Stuttgart, 1968).

Pohl, Karl-Heinrich, *Weimars Wirtschaft und die Aussenpolitik der Republik 1924–1926* (Düsseldorf, 1979).

Ponomaryov, B., Gromyko, A. and Khvostov, V. (eds), *History of Soviet Foreign Policy, 1917–1945* (Moscow, 1969).

Post, Gaines, Jr., *The Civil-Military Fabric of Weimar Foreign Policy* (Princeton, 1983).

Pratt, Lawrence R., *East of Malta, West of Suez: Britain's Mediterranean Crisis 1936–1939* (Cambridge, 1975).

Preradovich, Nicholas von, *Die Wilhelmstrasse und der Anschluss Österreichs 1918–1933* (Bern, 1971).

Preston, Adrian (ed.), *General Staffs and Diplomacy before the Second World War* (London, 1974).

Quartararo, Rosario, *Roma tra Londra e Berlino: Politica estera fascista dal 1930 al 1940* (Rome, 1980).

Radice, Lidia, *Prelude to Appeasement: East European Central Diplomacy in the Early 1930s* (Boulder, Colo., 1981).

Reynolds, David, *The Creation of the Anglo-American Alliance 1937–1941* (London, 1981).

Rich, Norman, *Hitler's War Aims*, 2 vols (New York, 1973 and 1974).

Riekhoff, Harald von, *German-Polish Relations 1918–1933* (Baltimore, Md, 1971).

Robertson, Esmonde M., *Hitler's Pre-War Policy and Military Plans 1933–1939* (London, 1963).

Robertson, Esmonde M., (ed.), *The Origins of the Second World War: Historical Interpretations* (London, 1971).

Robertson, Esmonde M., *Mussolini as Empire-Builder: Europe and Africa 1932–1936* (London, 1977).

Rönnefarth, Helmuth K. G., *Die Sudetenkrise in der Internationalen Politik: Entstehung, Verlauf, Auswirkung*, 2 vols (Wiesbaden, 1961).

Roskill, Stephen, *Naval Policy between the Wars*, 2 vols (London, 1968 and 1976).

Ross, Dieter, *Hitler und Dollfuss: die deutsche Österreich-Politik 1933–1934* (Hamburg, 1966).

Rupieper, Hermann J., *The Cuno Government and Reparations 1922–1923* (The Hague, 1979).

Rusinow, Dennison I., *Italy's Austrian Heritage 1919–1946* (New York, 1969).

Russett, Bruce M., *No Clear and Present Danger. A Skeptical View of the US Entry into World War II* (New York, 1972).

Schmidt, Royal J., *Versailles and the Ruhr* (The Hague, 1968).

Schmokel, Wolfe W., *Dream of Empire: German Colonialism 1919–1945* (New Haven, 1964).

Schroder, Hans-Jürgen, *Deutschland und die Vereinigten Staaten 1933–1939: Wirtschaft und Politik in der Entwicklung des deutsch-amerikanischen Gegensatzes* (Wiesbaden, 1970).

Schubert, Günter, *Anfänge nationalsozialistischer Aussenpolitik* (Cologne, 1963).

Schuker, Stephen A., *The End of French Predominance in Europe* (Chapel Hill, NC, 1976).

Schwabe, Klaus, *Woodrow Wilson, Revolutionary Germany, and Peacemaking 1918–1919* (Chapel Hill, NC, 1985).

Scott, William Evans, *Alliance Against Hitler: The Origins of the Franco-Soviet Pact* (Durham, NC, 1962).

Shai, Aron, *Origin of the War in the East: Britain, China and Japan 1937–1941* (London, 1976).

Shay, Robert P., Jr., *British Rearmament in the Thirties: Politics and Profits* (Princeton, 1977).

Silverman, Dan P., *Reconstructing Europe after the Great War* (Cambridge, Mass., 1982).

Smith, Malcolm S., *British Air Strategy between the Wars* (Oxford, 1984).

Sommer, Theo, *Deutschland und Japan zwischen den Machten 1935–1940* (Tübingen, 1962).

Steinmeyer, Gitta, *Die Grundlagen der französischen Rheinlandpolitik, 1917–1919* (Stuttgart, 1979).

Suval, Stanley, *The Anschluss Question in the Weimar Era* (Baltimore, Md, 1974).

Tai, Tsien, *China and the Nine-Power Conference at Brussels in 1937* (New York, 1964).

Taylor, Telford, *Munich: The Price of Peace* (London, 1979).

Thompson, John M., *Russia, Bolshevism and the Versailles Peace* (Princeton, 1966).

Thompson, Neville, *The Anti-Appeasers. Conservative Opposition to Appeasement in the 1930s* (Oxford, 1971).

Thorne, Christopher, *The Approach of War 1938–1939* (London, 1967).

Thorne, Christopher, *The Limits of Foreign Policy: The West, the League and the Far Eastern Crisis of 1931–1933* (London, 1972).

Tillman, Seth P., *Anglo-American Relations at the Paris Peace Conference of 1919* (Princeton, 1961).

Toscano, Mario, *The Origins of the Pact of Steel* (Baltimore, Md, 1967).

Toscano, Mario, *Designs in Diplomacy* (Baltimore, Md, 1970).

Trachtenberg, Marc, *Reparation in World Politics* (New York, 1980).

Trotter, Anne, *Britain and East Asia 1933–1937* (Cambridge, 1975).

Turner, Henry Ashby, *Stresemann and the Politics of the Weimar Republic* (Princeton, 1963).

Ulam, Adam B., *Expansion and Coexistence: The History of Soviet Foreign Policy 1917–1967* (New York, 1968).

Vaïsse, Maurice, *Sécurité d'Abord. La politique française en matière de désarmament, 9 décembre 1930–17 avril 1934* (Paris, 1981).

Vietsch, Eberhard von, *Wilhelm Solf: Botschafter zwischen den Zeiten* (Tübingen, 1961).

Vivarelli, Roberto, *Il dopoguerra in Italia e l'avvento del fascismo 1918–1922*, Vol. 1, *Dalla fine della guerra all'impresa di Fiume* (Naples, 1967).

Waley, Daniel P., *British Public Opinion and the Abyssinian War 1935–1936* (London, 1975).

Wandel, Eckhard, *Die Bedeutung der Vereinigten Staaten von Amerika für das deutsche Reparationsproblem 1924–1929* (Tübingen, 1971).

Wandycz, Piotr S., *France and Her Eastern Allies: French-Czechoslovak-Polish Relations from the Paris Peace Conference to Locarno* (Minneapolis, Minn., 1962).

Wandycz, Piotr S., *Soviet-Polish Relations 1917–1921* (Cambridge, Mass., 1969).

Watkins, Kenneth W., *Britain Divided: The Effect of the Spanish Civil War on British Public Opinion* (London, 1963).

Weinberg, Gerhard L., *The Foreign Policy of Hitler's Germany*, Vol. 1, *Diplomatic Revolution in Europe 1933–1936*; Vol. 2, *Starting World War II 1937–1939* (Chicago, Ill., 1970 and 1980).

Weinberg, Gerhard L., *World in the Balance* (Hanover, 1981).

Wendt, Berndt Jürgen, *Appeasement 1938: Wirtschaftliche Rezession und Mitteleuropa* (Hamburg, 1968).

Wendt, Berndt Jürgen, *Economic Appeasement: Handel und Finanz in der Britischen Deutschland Politik 1933–1939* (Düsseldorf, 1971).

Wojciechowski, Marian, *Die polnisch-deutsche Beziehungen 1933–1938* (Leiden, 1971).

Wurm, Clemens A., *Die französische Sicherheitspolitik in der Phase der Umorientierung 1924–1926* (Frankfurt, 1979).

Young, Robert J., *In Command of France: French Foreign Policy and Military Planning 1933–1940* (Cambridge, Mass., 1978).

JOURNALS

American Historical Review
Australian Journal of Politics and History
British Journal of International Studies
Central European History
China Quarterly
Die Welt als Geschichte
Diplomatic History
East European Quarterly
English Historical Review
European Studies Review
Francia
Historical Journal
Il Politico
International Affairs
International History Review
International Relations
Journal of Central European Affairs
Journal of Contemporary History
Journal of Modern History
Militärgeschichtliche Mitteilungen
Orbis
Pacific Historical Review
Past and Present
Polish Review
Political Quarterly
Political Science Quarterly
Relations Internationales
Revue d'Histoire Diplomatique
Russian Review
Slavic Review
Storia e Politica
Transactions of the Royal Historical Society
Vierteljahrshefte für Zeitgeschichte
World Affairs Quarterly
World Politics

Notes on Contributors

Alan Cassels is Professor of History at McMaster University. He is the author of *Fascist Italy*, *Mussolini's Early Diplomacy*, *Fascism*, and *Italian Foreign Policy 1918–45: A Guide to Research and Research Materials*.

Lloyd Gardner is Professor of History at Rutgers University. Among his many books on US foreign policy are: *Economic Aspects of New Deal Diplomacy*, *Imperial America*, *American Foreign Policy Since 1898*, and most recently, *Safe for Democracy: The Anglo American Response to Revolution, 1913–23*.

Edward Ingram is Professor of Imperial History at Simon Fraser University. He is Senior Editor of *The International History Review* and author of *The Beginning of the Great Game in Asia*, *Commitment to Empire*, and *In Defence of British India*.

Akira Iriye is Distinguished Service Professor at the University of Chicago. His books include *After Imperialism: The Search for a New Order in the Far East, 1921–31*, *Across the Pacific: An Inner History of American–East Asian relations* and *Power and Culture: The Japanese–American War, 1941–45*.

Paul Kennedy is J. Richardson Dilworth Professor of History at Yale University. He is the author of *The Rise and Fall of British Naval Mastery*, *The Rise of the Anglo–German Antagonism, 1860–1914*, *The Realities Behind Diplomacy* and *Strategy and Diplomacy 1870–1945*.

Gordon Martel is Associate Professor of History at Royal Roads Military College. He is editor of *The International History Review* and author of *Imperial Diplomacy: Rosebery and the Failure of Foreign Policy*, and *The Origins of the First World War*.

Sally Marks is Professor of History at Rhode Island College. She is the author of *The Illusion of Peace: International Relations in Europe 1918–33*, and *Innocent Abroad: Belgium at the Paris Peace Conference of 1919*.

Norman Rich is Professor of History at Brown University. His books include *The Age of Nationalism and Reform*, *Ideology, the Nazi State and the Course of Expansion*, and *Friedrich von Holstein: Politics and Diplomacy in the Era of Bismarck and Kaiser Wilhelm II*.

Stephen Schuker is Professor of History at Brandeis University. He is the author of *The End of French Predominance in Europe: The Financial Crisis of 1924 and the Adoption of the Dawes Plan.*

Teddy Uldricks is Associate Professor of History at the University of North Carolina, Asheville. He is the author of *Diplomacy and Ideology: The Origins of Soviet Foreign Relations, 1917–30.*

Piotr Wandycz is Professor of History at Yale University. His books include *Czech–Polish Confederation and the Great Powers, 1940–43, France and Her Eastern Allies, 1919–24, Soviet-Polish Relations, 1917–21,* and *The United States and Poland.*

Robert Young is Professor of History at the University of Winnipeg. He is the author of *In Command of France: French Foreign Policy and Military Planning, 1933–40* and *French Foreign Policy 1918–45: A Guide to Research and Research Materials.*

Index